AMERICA'S NATURAL PLACES

Regional Volumes in *America's Natural Places*

East and Northeast, Donelle Nicole Dreese

Pacific and West, Methea Kathleen Sapp

Rocky Mountains and Great Plains, Kelly Enright

South and Southeast, Stacy Kowtko

The Midwest, Jason Ney and Terri Nichols

AMERICA'S NATURAL PLACES

PACIFIC AND WEST

Methea Kathleen Sapp

Stacy Kowtko, General Editor

GREENWOOD PRESS
An Imprint of ABC-CLIO, LLC

A B C 💮 C L I O

Santa Barbara, California • Denver, Colorado • Oxford, England

Library of Congress Cataloging-in-Publication Data

Sapp, Methea Kathleen.
    America's natural places. Pacific and West / Methea Kathleen Sapp.
       p. cm. — (Regional volumes in America's natural places)
    Includes bibliographical references and index.
    ISBN 978-0-313-35088-7 (set hardcover : alk. paper) — ISBN 978-0-313-35089-4 (set ebook) —
ISBN 978-0-313-35318-5 (hardcover : alk. paper) — ISBN 978-0-313-35319-2 (ebook)
    1. Protected areas—Pacific States.   2. Protected areas—Southwest, New.   3. Protected areas—
Alaska.   4. Protected areas—Hawaii.   5. Endangered ecosystems—Pacific States.   6. Endangered
ecosystems—Southwest, New.   7. Endangered ecosystems—Alaska.   8. Endangered ecosystems—
Hawaii.   I. Title.
    S932.P33S27   2010
    333.780979—dc22   2009032365

14   13   12   11   10   1   2   3   4   5

This book is also available on the World Wide Web as an eBook.
Visit www.abc-clio.com for details.

ABC-CLIO, LLC
130 Cremona Drive, P.O. Box 1911
Santa Barbara, California 93116-1911

This book is printed on acid-free paper ∞
Manufactured in the United States of America

CONTENTS

Series Foreword

The United States possesses within its borders some of the most diverse and beautiful natural wonders and resources of any country on earth. Many of these valuable natural places exist under a constant threat of damage from environmental pollution, climatic change, and encroaching civilization, just to name a few of the more destructive forces. Some natural areas enjoy the care and protection of neighboring human societies, but some have fallen to the wayside of concern. This series of reference volumes represents a collection of distinct areas of preservation concern in the following five geographical divisions of the United States: the East and Northeast, the Pacific and West, the Rocky Mountains and Great Plains, the South and Southeast, and the Midwest. The goal is to present representative challenges faced across the country, providing information on historical and ongoing preservation efforts through the process of identifying specific sites that representatively define the United States as an environmental entity. Individual entries were chosen based on the following criteria: biodiversity, ecology, rare or endangered species habitats, or unique environmental character. Many of the entries are nature preserves, state or national parks, wildlife habitats, or scenic vistas. Each selection focuses on a particular area and describes the site's importance, resident flora and fauna, and threats to the area's survival, along with historical and current information on preservation efforts. For sites that are physically accessible, there is information on location, access methods, and visiting tips. Although each volume is organized by state, many natural places cross state borders, and so the larger focus is on environmental ecosystem representation rather than state definition. The goals are to inform readers about the wide variety of natural places across the country as well as portray these natural places as more than just an exercise in academic study. The reality of natural preservation in the United States has an immediate impact on everyone.

Each volume contains a short introduction to the geographical region, including specific information on the states' natural environments and regionally specific concerns of restoration and preservation. Content entries represent one or more of the following criteria: ecological uniqueness; biodiversity; rare or endangered species habitat; exceptional natural beauty; or aging, fragile, or disappearing natural environs. By reading the various entries in each volume, readers will gain understanding concerning environmental issues of consequence as demonstrated by the representative entry choices. The audiences especially suited to benefit from this series are high school and undergraduate students as well as hobbyists and nature enthusiasts. Readers with an interest in local, regional, and environmental health will find easily accessible, useable information throughout the series. The following paragraphs offer short excerpts from the introductions of the regional volumes in *America's Natural Places*.

The East and Northeast United States is a corridor, a doorway to America that has facilitated movement and migration into the continent. The subject of corridors is revisited frequently in the East and Northeast volume as it covers natural areas beginning as far west as Kentucky, as far south as Virginia, and voyages up the coast to Maine. Smaller corridors are described here as well, because many of the places featured in this book have their own respective passageways, some more wild than others. This volume is also about larger corridors—those that connect the past to the present and the present to the future. These natural areas are storytellers chronicling the narratives of cultural and ecological histories that not only have much to tell about the region's past, but also are microcosmic indicators of the earth's current global health. They are corridors into our future as they tell us where our planet is going—toward the loss of countless native species, archeological treasures, and ecosystems that are vital for a sustainable planet. These natural areas are themselves guided paths, passageways into a healthier future as they teach us what is happening within their fragile ecological significance before their lessons are lost forever.

The American Pacific and West is a place of legendary proportions; its natural resources have beckoned to entrepreneurs, prospectors, immigrants, adventurers, naturalists, writers, and photographers, thereby deeply embedding the region into U.S. history, culture, commerce, and art. J. S. Holliday wrote. "I think that the West is the most powerful reality in the history of this country. It's always had a power, a presence, an attraction that differentiated it from the rest of the United States. Whether the West was a place to be conquered, or the West as it is today, a place to be protected and nurtured. It is the regenerative force of America." Over the course of its history, the ecosystems of the Pacific and West have been subject to a variety of forces, both restorative and destructive. Individual entries in the Pacific and West volume seek to not only detail the effects of these forces but to describe the flora, fauna, and topography that make each entry unique. As a cumulative effect, the volume offers an inclusive depiction of the region as a whole while echoing the famous call to "Go West."

"The western landscape is of the wildest variety," Wallace Stegner wrote of his homeland. "There is nothing in the East," he continued, "like the granite horns of Grand Teton or Teewinot, nothing like the volcanic neck of Devil's Tower, nothing like the travertine terraces of Mammoth Hot Springs." Consisting of deserts, grasslands, alpine mountains, plateaus, canyons, cliffs, and geyser basins, the Rocky Mountains and Great Plains is a region of great biodiversity and natural beauty. From the 100th meridian over the peaks of the Rocky Mountains, this landscape has been the source of frontier legends, central to the nation's geography as well as its identity. Home to the world's first national park and some of the most extractive industries in the nation, this landscape displays the best and worst of human interactions with the natural world. Fossils in Colorado are evidence of ancient inland seas. Tall-grass prairies reveal pre-Anglo American ecology. This volume teaches students to read natural landscapes as products of interacting dynamics between culture and nature. People of many backgrounds, ethnicities, and cultures have contributed to the current state of the environment, giving readers a strong, provocative look at the dynamics of this ever-changing landscape.

"The American South is a geographical entity, a historical fact, a place in the imagination, and the homeland for an array of Americans who consider themselves southerners. The region is often shrouded in romance and myth, but its realities are as intriguing, as intricate as its legends." So states Bill Ferris. This volume explores the variable, dynamic South and Southeast through the details of its ecoregions and distinct areas of preservation. Individual entries provide the elements necessary for examining and understanding the threats, challenges, and promises inherent to this region. State partitions serve as geographical divisions for regional treatment, but the overall goal of this work is to present representative examples of the varying ecosystems across the area rather than focusing on the environmental character of individual states. When combined, the sections present a total picture of the South and Southeast through careful selections that portray not only the coastal wetlands and piedmont areas characteristic of the region but also the plateaus, mountains, highlands, plains, and woodlands that define the inland South and Southeast. The goal is to produce a comprehensive picture of the South and Southeast natural environs as they combine to present a unique character and quality that shapes Southern reality today.

The Midwest stands historically as the crossroads of America, the gateway to the West. The region is incredibly diverse, long shaped by geological forces such as the advance and retreat of glaciers. It is a transitional region, where the eastern temperate forests meet the Great Plains of the West and where the southern extent of the northern forests transitions from the mixed-wood plains to the Ozark forests and southeastern plains of the South. Human presence and interaction, however, have greatly reduced and currently threaten this diversity. The Midwest's rich soils and forests, along with its abundant lakes and streams, make this region's natural resources some of the county's most desirable for farming, logging, and development. As a result, little of the once-vast prairies, forests, and wetlands remains. Nonetheless, many efforts, both public and private, are underway to restore and protect the diversity of the Midwest. By taking a holistic approach, individual entries in this volume exemplify the varied ecosystems of the region with the volume as a whole covering all the major Midwest ecoregions. As readers explore the various entries, a comprehensive understanding of the natural systems of the Midwest will emerge, grounded in the region's natural and cultural history and shaped by its current and future challenges.

PREFACE

The American Pacific and West is a vast and restless landscape of heaving volcanoes, tectonic grinding, coursing rivers, shifting ice fields, and pounding surf. These elemental forces have created a region that is as ecologically rich as it is sensitive; a region where polar bears, coral reefs, California condors, and Gila monsters garner wonderment for the biodiversity of all life on earth.

Collectively, the eight states of Alaska, Arizona, California, Hawaii, Nevada, New Mexico, Oregon, and Washington encompass some of the most extreme environments in the United States: the highest mountain peaks, driest desert, deepest lake, and oldest forests in addition to well over 35,000 miles of coastline. However, for the most part, the natural places selected for this volume have yet to be discovered by the public. Their anonymity is only occasionally due to remoteness, as many of these natural places are in close proximity to urban development and others are embedded within some of the West's largest metropolises. Regardless of locale, each of the entries calls attention to the area's flora and fauna, with particular consideration paid to those places that support endemic or threatened and endangered species. A great deal of effort has also been made to elucidate the food webs that not only interconnect an area's flora and fauna but contribute to a greater understanding of the whole ecological unit.

Without exception, each entry represents a natural place that is currently threatened or is undergoing significant preservation or restoration. While endangerment and protection run conversely, the source of both is ultimately human, and, as such, human exchanges within these natural places are of great consequence throughout the book. The sources of degradation are as complex and varied as each locale is biologically diverse; the introduction of invasive species, urban sprawl, water depletion, climate change, and the harvest of natural resources are just a few of the activities that threaten many of the region's natural places. In response to these challenges, each of the natural places described in this volume sets a unique precedence regarding its protection and restoration, and special care has been taken to underline the human partnerships—be they legislative, cultural, social, or economic—that have been the propagators of environmental protection. Readers will also be able to compare and contrast the successes and failures of government directives and nongovernmental organizations that are represented by a number of local, regional, and national associations. Finally, a complete depiction of the American Pacific and West would not be complete without a discussion of private landowners and their singular efforts to conserve the region's natural resources.

The information herein is intended to aid both advanced high school and undergraduate students with their academic endeavors. The book has been careful to identify key statutes, dates, names, and places along with suggestions for further reading, all in an effort to foster and support students' additional research and writing projects. A mass of pertinent information also awaits travelers, naturalists, and educators, as well as those interested in the environmental history of the Pacific and West. Ultimately, this volume has been crafted with the intent to not only educate but to ignite and encourage an interest in the natural world while deepening the understanding of one's own role in the health of our country's ecosystems.

PACIFIC AND WEST

INTRODUCTION

The American Pacific and West is a place of legendary proportions; its natural resources have beckoned to entrepreneurs, prospectors, immigrants, adventurers, naturalists, writers, and photographers, thereby deeply embedding the region into U.S. history, culture, commerce, and art. J. S. Holliday wrote, "I think that the West is the most powerful reality in the history of this country. It's always had a power, a presence, an attraction that differentiated it from the rest of the United States. Whether the West was a place to be conquered, or the West as it is today, a place to be protected and nurtured. It is the regenerative force of America." Over the course of its history, the ecosystems of the Pacific and West have been subject to a variety of forces, both restorative and destructive. Individual entries in the Pacific and West volume seek to not only detail the effects of these forces but to describe the flora, fauna, and topography that make each natural place unequaled. And while each entry is unique, the ecological significance of the Pacific and West is best understood via a holistic measure of the region as a whole.

In biological terms, the concept of emergent properties is used to explain that the whole is greater than the sum of its parts; in respect to the ecology of the Pacific and West, this means that, while individual entries illuminate the nature of a specific setting, the true scope and significance of the region is best appreciated when viewed as a continuous undivided entity. Similarly, it is important to recognize that the flora and fauna of the Pacific and West utilize the region as a whole and not according to county, state, or international boundary lines. The ability to migrate freely via land, water, or air not only ensures that animals are able to reach breeding, spawning, and feeding grounds but that plants as well are able to cast their seeds and disperse their pollen into viable terrain. More importantly, the natural dispersal of plants and animals allows for species interaction and the inevitable mixing of genes, which in turn yields an increase in genetic diversity and a more robust population for any given species.

Much of the biological diversity for which the Pacific and West are well known is a function of its geography. Alaska, for example, at its northernmost latitude of 71° N, lays well within the Arctic circle, while Hawaii, at its southernmost reach, sits at a latitude of 18° N and is bisected by the Tropic of Cancer. The remaining six states, while contiguous with the rest of the United States, maintain the north-south spans of latitudes. This geographical spread is especially significant, because latitude is a major determinant of terrestrial climate. Climate in combination with dominant vegetation, elevation, and precipitation patterns are used to define the major ecological communities or biomes of the world. The classification of the world's biomes varies according to several models that may depict anywhere from 12 to 14 biomes. Within the Pacific and West, no fewer than 9 of these biomes are represented: tundra, taiga, Great Basin desert, Mediterranean scrub, temperate rainforest, montane forest, desert, grassland, and rainforest. Each of these biomes supports a unique array of plants and animals that are linked via intricate food webs. Humans, too, are inextricably connected to these biomes, depending on them for various natural resources, from the basics of food, shelter, and water to minerals, fuel, and pharmaceuticals.

Tundra and taiga are the biomes of northern climates. While both are infamously harsh environments due to long, dark winters and brief summers, the tundra is the most severe with an average annual temperature of −18° F (−28° C) and a precipitation rate of 6 to 10 inches per year. As harsh as these conditions may seem, the tundra is home to well over 1,000 species of plants, which in turn support a variety of herbivores and predators. In comparison to other biomes, the tundra exhibits relativity low diversity, but the organisms that occupy this land are highly adapted to subfreezing temperatures, blasting Arctic winds, and a brief growing season. The tundra is characterized by a layer of permanently frozen soil called permafrost. This soil layer softens during the summer growing season, which typically spans just 50 to 60 days. During this time, low-laying lichens, mosses, grasses, shrubs, and some dwarfed species of willow will sprout, grow, reproduce, and then die with the onset of winter.

During the growing season, these plant communities carry out the processes of photosynthesis by which the plant takes in carbon dioxide and releases oxygen. In most circumstances, the plant eventually dies and decomposes and in doing so releases its carbon dioxide back into the atmosphere. Within the tundra, however, the quick onset of winter immediately freezes the dead or dying plants, thereby preventing decomposition and locking the carbon dioxide within the plant tissues. In fact, thousands of years' worth of seasonal plant growth and carbon dioxide are locked away within the permafrost. Historically, the ability of the tundra to sequester carbon dioxide had earned it the title of a carbon sink. Excessive melting and overall warming in the Arctic region have altered the tundra and permafrost in ways that scientists do not yet fully understand. Many biologists think that the rates and duration of permafrost thawing are such that the tundra is now contributing to our planet's ever-increasing levels of atmospheric carbon dioxide. The effects of invisible greenhouse gases inevitably translate into more tangible changes for the region's polar bears, caribou, musk oxen, wolves, and snowshoe hares, each of which is finely evolved for life on the tundra. The details of this biome and its inhabitants are chronicled within the various entries in the chapter on Alaska, because Alaska is the only place in the United States where tundra may be found.

Lying at a latitude just south of the tundra is the taiga—the largest biome in the world, covering sizeable regions of Eurasia and North America. In the continental United States, the taiga is sparsely represented in a few northern states. In contrast, however, much of Alaska is covered by this biome and thus is one of the few locations in North America where this biome may be protected in large, undisturbed tracts. Like the tundra, the soils of the taiga are shallow, nutrient poor, and frozen for much of the year. Yet the southerly drop in latitude extends the growing season and allows summer temperatures to reach upward of 70° F. Numerous species of trees, including larch, spruce, fir, pine, oak, and maple, form dense forests that are sometimes referred to as boreal forests. True to the fate of many of the nation's forests, the boreal forests are in rapid decline due to logging in the form of clear-cutting. The timber harvested from this region is utilized to make everything from toilet paper to yachts. While the necessity of using these resources to produce such products could be debated, these forests also absorb massive amounts of atmospheric carbon dioxide while releasing oxygen, stabilizing topsoils, and providing habitat for the region's resident herbivores and carnivores as well as hundreds of species migratory birds. The boreal forests of Alaska are protected only so far as they have been incorporated into state and federal forest systems.

Despite plentiful snow and ice, the tundra and taiga are relatively dry because the region's water is locked away in the form of ice for much of the year. Similarly arid biomes also occur at more southerly latitudes and occupy large portions of the West. In fact, every state in this volume contains at least one ecoregion that receives less then 10 inches of rain per year and thus meets the classic definition of a desert. Desert biomes along with the Great Basin biome support a variety plants and animals that are highly adapted to drought and heat. Plants such as cacti abound and thrive due largely to their modification of leaves into spines and alterations to the photosynthetic process. Other dominating plants such as sagebrush and creosote bush secrete volatile chemicals into the soil in an effort to keep competing vegetation at bay. Animals of the desert tend to be nocturnal and therefore possess remarkable sensory adaptations and unusual be-haviors. All of these adaptations result from incredible competition for relatively scarce resources, be it water, soil, nutrients, or simply shade.

Given the sparseness of resources, it would seem unwise for humans to settle within these ecosystems, yet the many of the West's largest and most rapidly growing cities are situated within or near these desert biomes. Just as water is central to all life, it is also a pivotal and controversial issue for much of the West. The West is home to a large number of rivers that funnel melting snowpack from its numerous mountain ranges into fertile agricultural valleys and sprawling cities before finally draining into the Pacific Ocean or, in some cases, the Gulf of Mexico. Along the way, numerous dams create vast reservoirs of water, generate energy, and provide recreational activities while simultane-ously preventing fish migrations, altering water temperatures, and diverting water from people living downstream. Such activities have embroiled much of the West in a constant deluge of legal actions that call into question the issues of water rights for private citizens, industry, and the states at large.

Covering approximately 5 percent of the earth's surface, Mediterranean scrub is one of the smallest biomes on the planet. Despite its meager size, it supports a phenomenal amount of biodiversity. Biologists estimate that 20 percent of the world's 48,250 known vascular plant species can be found in this habitat. Mediterranean scrub occupies very specific regions within the latitudes of 30° to 40° N. The extent of the scrublands is further confined to the western, ocean-facing slopes of the continents upon which it occurs. There are only five locations worldwide that support Mediterranean scrub communities. In the United States, only one location fulfills such prerequisites: the coastal mountains and valleys of southern California. California's Mediterranean scrub ecosystems are commonly referred to as chaparral and are characterized by a specialized forest community made up of a variety of broad-leafed evergreens, including several species of live oak, along with Pacific madrone, golden chinkapin, tan oak, and Pacific bayberry. The leaves of these trees are distinctive in many respects. First, they are evergreens and thus retain their leaves year around. They do not, however, have needles like most other evergreen trees. Instead, the leaves are small and paddle shaped, leathery in texture, and coated with a hard wax—all of which prevent the leaves from drying out during the region's long, hot summers.

In addition to the forest community, there are a number of other distinctive plant communities including scrublands, woodlands, grasslands, and shrublands, all of which are equally well adapted to heat and drought. In fact, many of the plants within these five plant communities are classified as pyrophytes, meaning "fire-loving plants." In the case of pyrophytes, fire is needed for reproduction and germination, new vegetative growth, nutrient inputs, and the elimination of old growth so that room can be made for young seedlings. Just as water is the pivotal issue in the desert and Great Basin regions, so is fire in the Mediterranean scrub. Fire suppression combined with human encroachment have cumulative effects on the region. As humans continue to settle the region, they bring with them a profound but understandable intolerance for fire. Meanwhile, the old, dry plant material from several seasons of growth piles up and becomes a tinder reserve. When ignited, these fires burn with an intensity that makes them both difficult to fight and nearly impossible for even the pyrophytes to survive. The soils left behind are often sterile due to the extreme temperatures with which the fire burns and are practically devoid of viable seed. The onset of winter then brings between 6 and 20 inches of rain. An especially wet winter can induce massive amounts of erosion and devastating landslides, the sediments of which quickly run off into the neighboring coastal ecosystems, thus fouling water resources and habitat.

The Pacific and West are also home to two very different types of rainforest, one tropical and the other temperate. Both receive astonishing levels of rainfall each year: 50 to 260 inches in the tropical rainforest and 79 to 118 inches in the temperate rainforest. Within the Pacific and West, there exists a massive swath of temperate rainforest that begins on western coast of Alaska and runs southward through Washington, Oregon, and northern California. This region represents the largest area of temperate rainforest in the world and is dominated by of a variety of conifers and broad-leaved evergreens. Evergreens like the Sitka spruce, coast Douglas fir, and coast redwood not only dominate the upper canopy but are famous for their record-setting height, girth, and age. The coast redwood, for example, holds the record for the world's tallest tree at 379 feet and can live for more than 2,000 years. Very little old growth timber still stands, as most of it has been clear-cut to supply world markets with lumber products for making everything from pianos to plywood. Management of these temperate rainforests is a constant topic of concern as the world's appetite for lumber products seems insatiable and the immediate economic rewards are undeniable.

In addition to meeting human necessity, the temperate rainforests of the West support a vast number of insects, many of which have only recently been discovered. While the insects rarely make the evening news, the plight of the spotted owl, wolf, bald eagle, marbled murrelet, and various salmon species are often part of the daily headlines. Each of these species relies heavily on the temperate forest habitat during some phase of their life cycle, and many use some aspect of the forest's resources to breed and reproduce.

In contrast to the sizable temperate rainforests of the American West, the tropical rainforest biome is represented in only one state in the United States and occupies a relatively small speck of land on the Hawaiian Islands. Although comparatively slight in overall acreage, the rainforests of Hawaii support more life forms than a parcel of temperate rainforest of equal size. Hawaii's rainforests are a mix of diverse habitats often dominated by koa and ohia lehua trees, large ferns, bromeliads, vines, orchids, and mosses along with patches of swamplike boglands. The diversity of this vegetation in turn supports a wide array of insects, snails, and birds, many of which are endemic to Hawaii and therefore found nowhere else on earth. Regions such as Hawaii that experience high rates of endemism are also subject to high rates of extinction since endemic species are not widespread but are instead limited to a localized area or habitat. Alteration of this habitat generally leads to population declines and extinction. Case in point: Scientists estimate that one-half of Hawaii's native bird populations are now extinct, largely due to habitat loss and the introduction of disease. Introduced species—whether they are disease-causing microbes or larger species such as pigs, rats, and feral cats and dogs—typically outcompete native species and have been blamed for much of Hawaii's ecological losses. Urban development, agriculture, and uncontrolled tourist activity have also contributed to reductions in wildlife and the loss of approximately two-thirds of Hawaii's native rainforests.

Hawaii's rainforests also play a critical role in the region's numerous watersheds. Although a few areas of the state are arid deserts and grasslands, most of Hawaii's landscape receives copious amounts of rainfall. Mount Waialeale, for example, receives 450 inches of rainfall on an annual basis. To prevent such a deluge from eroding the landscape and washing its precious topsoil out to sea, the rainforest, with its dynamic multitiered canopy, serves as a living sponge. Much of the falling rain does not hit the ground directly but instead hits the tree canopy, dribbles across its leaves, drips into the understory, and then trickles down to ground level. Thirsty roots draw up much of this moisture, and some of the rainfall will eventually find its way into streams and creeks and then to the sea. This natural catchment system also ensures that people have a clean and adequate fresh water supply, which is all the more critical considering that this tiny island chain is set amid the vast, open Pacific Ocean.

Perhaps no other biome is as prominent as the montane biome, for in its company are the eastern Cascades, Sierra Nevada, Blue Mountains, Selkirks, and Wallowa Mountains, among many others. Although concentrated in Alaska and the Pacific Northwest as well as northern California, the montane biome also exists in small remnant patches throughout the American Southwest. The vegetation of these montane forests is dominated by stands of conifers including fir, spruce, pine, and cedar, which may be punctuated with aspen or cottonwood or other hardwoods, especially in areas where water is prevalent. Compared to the saturated biomes of the temperate and tropical rainforest, the montane biome is characterized by a much drier climate. Precipitation can still be plentiful, especially in the form of winter snowpack, but these ecosystems sit atop inland mountain ranges and thus receive much less rain than their coastal counterparts. The snowpack is therefore an essential source of water for both the people and wildlife of the West, because its seasonal melt recharges the region's rivers and wetland areas. Conservation in the montane biome is centered on safeguarding mountain stream beds on behalf of cold-water fisheries including trout and salmon and managing timber harvests on both public and privately owned land. The West is, however, experiencing dramatic changes in its mountain habitats; climate change is altering snowpack levels, infestations of bark beetles are killing large tracts of timber, forest fire is becoming harder to manage as dead and dying tree debris accumulates; and there is ongoing debate regarding the protection of designated wilderness areas and grazing permits. This biome continues to be a central topic discussed by policymakers and conservationists alike, given that so much of the West's economy relies on the health of its forests and fisheries.

Each of the eight states making up the Pacific and West contains areas that are representative of the grassland biome. Some of these grasslands occupy the mesas of New Mexico, while others dot the central valley of California and coastal prairies of western Washington. Although climate varies drastically among the grasslands ecosystems of the West, the biome is universally characterized by the presence of native bunch grasses, which grow in tufts or clumps, along with season wildflowers and other herblike perennials. Herbivores typically dominate this landscape and may include pronghorn, deer, rabbit, and a number of burrowing rodents as well. Historically, the grasslands of the Pacific and West, with their flat terrain, generally good soil, and broad vistas, have been prime locales for development. Agriculture, grazing, and urban sprawl have fragmented nearly all of the West's major grassland habitats with comparatively little relief coming by the way of conservation. As a result, grassland birds including sage grouse, chucker, curlew, and meadowlarks are becoming increasingly rare as their habitat disappears. In many cases, the grassland habitat is being lost not to strip malls and condos but to grazing livestock and intensified agricultural production. The planting of monoculture crops, dispersion of nonnative grass seed, erosion, and pesticide application are just a few of the agricultural practices that both degrade and alter native grasslands and thus eliminate suitable habitat for native wildlife.

Remarkably, however, some of the greatest strides toward grassland conservation have been taken by farmers, ranchers, and property owners who are reexamining their daily operations in order to simultaneously protect their land and their business. This is, in fact, a familiar story among the natural places of the West: common people organizing themselves into private land trust groups, forming alliances to protect their water rights, donating property so that school children and song birds can occupy the same green space, volunteering to restore a wetland, or voting for a more sustainable future. The culmination of their efforts is evident on every page of this volume, which not only offers an intimate depiction of the region's most spectacular natural places but at the same time echoes the famous call to "Go West."

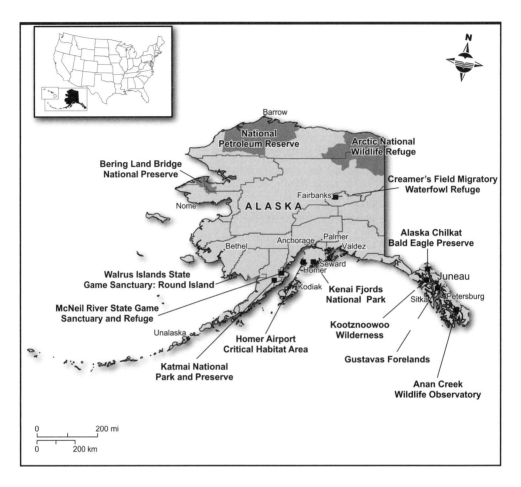

Alaska Chilkat Bald Eagle Preserve, 2

Anan Creek Wildlife Observatory, 4

Arctic National Wildlife Refuge, 6

Bering Land Bridge National Preserve, 7

Creamer's Field Migratory Waterfowl Refuge, 8

Gustavas Forelands, 10

Homer Airport Critical Habitat Area, 11

Katmai National Park and Preserve, 12

Kenai Fjords National Park, 13

Kootznoowoo Wilderness, 15

McNeil River State Game Sanctuary and Refuge, 17

National Petroleum Reserve, 18

Walrus Islands State Game Sanctuary: Round Island, 20

ALASKA

Often referred to as America's last frontier, Alaska is a state of phenomenal magnitude. If superimposed over the continental United States, Alaska's landmass would stretch from California all the way to Florida. The topography of Alaska is not only sprawling but texturally diverse; it is etched by more than 3,000 rivers and pocked with some 3 million lakes. Fire and ice coexist amid the state's 70 active volcanoes and 100,000 glaciers. Alaska is also home to the nation's highest peak (Mount McKinley), sprawling ice fields, temperate rainforest, and Arctic tundra. This terrestrial diversity is met with more than 33,900 miles of shoreline, some of which is cut into deep fjords, while other coastlines are forested in dark conifers or encrusted in ice.

The diversity of Alaska's landscape gives rise to an equally diverse set of flora and fauna that are uniquely adapted to life in the northern latitudes. While still famous for its long, cold winters, Alaska is experiencing the impacts of climate change. For example, scientists estimate that, over the past 50 years, the state's average annual temperatures have increased 3 to 5° F. This seemingly trivial increment has not only led to reduced snowpacks and receding ice fields but has altered entire ecosystems, shifting animal hibernation patterns, feeding strategies, migrations, and insect hatches.

The polar bear, which has been the iconic image of both Alaska and climate change, has also been at the forefront of U.S. policy, politics, and conservation. Since the polar bear's highly contested and controversial listing in May 2008 as an endangered species, Alaska has not been able to retreat from the spotlight. Closely tied to the plight of the polar bear are Alaska's famous oil fields. Located in the northernmost reaches of the state, both the Arctic National Wildlife Refuge and National Petroleum Reserve hold significant oil and natural gas reserves. However, these same landscapes embody some of the nation's most pristine wilderness and, as such, serve as a final stronghold for species struggling amid an already rapidly changing environment.

Future conservation efforts will undoubtedly try to focus on the flora and fauna most jeopardized by climate change and petroleum exploration, yet the dialogue promises to be both lengthy and tumultuous as the entire nation looks for its next source of energy. Alaska is, however, seasoned when it comes to readjusting the manner in which is utilizes its natural resources. Following the collapse of Alaska's salmon fishery in the late 1950s, Alaska reexamined and redefined the policies governing its entire salmon fishing industry and now runs one of the world's most sustainable fisheries.

Alaska, in fact, boasts a long history of conservation dating back to the mid-1800s, with the establishment of the Pribilof Islands as a national reservation for fur seals. Since then, conservation efforts (both public and private) have steadily and decisively preserved a diverse assemblage of habitats. Groups including Trout Unlimited, the Audubon Society, Rocky Mountain Elk Foundation, Tongass Conservation Society, and Alaska Marine Conservation Council serve to protect their obvious interests. The Nature Conservancy, while a relative newcomer to Alaska (the Alaska office opened in 1988), has focused much of its work on preserving wild salmon systems, along with Arctic coastal lands and polar marine systems. Several public land trust groups also work to preserve the Alaskan landscape and ensure that these lands stay open for the pubic to enjoy. The working partnerships forged in the name of conservation are numerous and diverse, many times consisting of private organizations similar to those mentioned above as well as government entities. Also notable are the numerous occasions when conservation was initiated not by any one organization but by local communities consisting of business leaders, government officials, teachers, school kids, and native tribes.

ALASKA CHILKAT BALD EAGLE PRESERVE

Perhaps no other natural entity is as embedded into the American psyche as the bald eagle; long before it was inaugurated as the national bird, the eagle was central to Native American culture and religious ceremony and in more recent times has come to symbolize the success of a species brought back from the brink of extinction. Estimates suggest that in 1782 (the year that Congress established the bald eagle as the national symbol), there were at least 100,000 nesting pairs in the lower 48 states; by 1963, that number had been reduced to an estimated 487 nesting pairs. This drastic decline was attributed to the combined effects of habitat loss, agriculture, hunting, and the use of an insecticide called DDT.

During this time, Alaska served as a final stronghold for the bald eagle, since the state's wilderness areas had, for the most part, been devoid of human encroachment and disturbance. The establishment of the Alaska Chilkat Bald Eagle Preserve in 1982 sought to preserve prime bald eagle habitat and serve as a national model for conservation and species protection. The exact boundaries of the 48,000-acre preserve were based solely on the needs of the bald eagle; thus, every habitat within this preserve is utilized by the eagles at some point in their life cycle.

While the rest of Alaska settles in for a long and bitter winter, the Chilkat Preserve hosts the world's largest known gathering of bald eagles. Between the months of

October and February, 3,000 to 4,000 birds assume their perches along a specific portion of the Chilkat River to await the final run of late chum salmon. Like many of Alaska's rivers, the Chilkat is cemented over with ice during the winter months, except for a five-mile stretch of river, which may be easily observed by anyone traveling along the Haines Highway between mile markers 18 and 21. Long before the highway, glacial activity created an underground reservoir of water while depositing a large layer of alluvial sediment, both of which now lay under this unique segment of the river. The reservoir's water percolates up through the sediment and, as it does so, creates friction between the water molecules and the fine sediment particles. This friction generates enough heat to increase the water temperature and thus maintains an open field of water in which the bald eagles pursue their prey. These extraordinary natural features make the Chilkat region a critical feeding habitat for the area's resident eagles as well as the large migratory population of bald eagles that dissipate across the rest of Alaska, Canada, and the Pacific Northwest when the feeding frenzy is done.

The preserve is fantastically eagle-centric; in early November, the American Bald Eagle Foundation sponsors the Alaska Bald Eagle Festival and hosts a variety of workshops and lectures centered on the bald eagle theme. The preserve also serves as a release location for wild rehabilitated eagles. Photographic safaris, viewing stations, and roadside pullouts are all geared toward viewing the majestic bird. With so much of the focus on the bald eagle, many of the preserve's other inhabitants go largely unnoticed. A vast number of mammals further diversify the region; both brown and black bears, red fox, wolves, lynx, wolverine, mink, bats, snowshoe hare, and Sitka black-tailed deer are just a few of the animals that are integrated into the food web. Water birds such as kingfishers, mergansers, pintails, mallards, and trumpeter swans find ample habitat along the banks of the preserve's three rivers. The Chilkat, the Kleheni, and the Tsirku rivers also serve as natal spawning grounds for several species of salmon, including chum, pink, king, and sockeye. Protection of such spawning grounds offers vital support to salmon populations, which are heavily influenced by the combined effects commercial and sport fishing, subsistence fishing, predation, and stream degradation.

The Alaska Chilkat Bald Eagle Preserve along with other such preserves and with protection under the Endangered Species Act and the banning of DDT have helped to foster the comeback of the national bird. Population estimates now suggest that there are approximately 9,789 breeding pairs of bald eagles in the lower 48 states. In 2007, the U.S. Fish and Wildlife Service deemed the population stable enough to federally de-list the bird. (The bald eagle remains listed as threatened by some states in the American Southwest.) In addition to being a national symbol, the bald eagle is now a symbol of conservation, representing the combined efforts of both public and private entities and a deep-seated human desire to preserve the natural world.

Further Reading
Breining, Greg. *Return of the Eagle: How America Saved Its National Symbol*. Guilford, CT: Globe Pequote Press, 1994.

ANAN CREEK WILDLIFE OBSERVATORY

The Anan Creek Wildlife Observatory garners protection by virtue of the observatory's location within the Tongass National Forest. Located in southeast Alaska and encompassing the famous Inside Passage, the Tongass encompasses 26,250 square miles and is the nation's largest national forest. The Tongass is also one of the largest swaths of temperate rainforest in the world. While much of the Tongass is accessible to hikers, kayakers, campers, other outdoor adventurers, the Anan Creek Observatory is reachable only by privately chartered boat or floatplane. Located about 30 miles southeast of the town of Wrangell, Anan Creek is devoid of modern amenities but does have a sheltered wildlife viewing platform and a few simple cabins that may be rented for an overnight stay.

The Anan Creek Wildlife Observatory is biologically unique in that it not only exemplifies the temperate rainforest biome but its isolation leaves this habitat largely untouched by humans. This isolation has been especially critical for the area's black and brown bear populations. Bears by nature are opportunistic omnivores, meaning that they will eat almost anything. This feeding behavior brings success to the bear when living in an undisturbed natural environment, as it will readily feed on fish, grubs, nuts, berries, carrion, and small rodents. When faced with human encroachment, bears find easy meals in trash cans, garbage dumps, and campsites; over time, they also lose their fear of people. In many cases, these human-tolerant bears have been slated for hunting, because they pose a foreseeable threat to human safety. This scenario is becoming especially problematic within our nation's more popular and easily accessible parks and reserves, which are visited by thousands of people every year.

Anan Creek, however, receives relatively few people over the course of Alaska's brief summer, thereby preserving a more sustainable bear-human relationship. Visitors to Anan observe the bears from a tall wooden viewing platform that overlooks the creek below and gives the observer a virtually unobstructed view of both the upstream and downstream landscapes. Platform viewers may watch the bears foraging the creek banks for berries and other succulent vegetation; yet, more often than not, the bears have come to feed on pink salmon that run up the creek during the summer. The Anan Creek run of pink (also known as humpback) salmon is the largest run of this species in southeast Alaska. Not surprisingly, this species of salmon is a mainstay of the bear's diet and also of the Alaskan salmon fisheries. Thanks to diligent monitoring and sustainable fishing practices, both bears and the people of Alaska have enough pink salmon to go around. This, however, has not been the case for pink salmon populations in parts of Washington and California, which have been on the decline for a number of years—a fact that underscores the importance of preserves such as Anan Creek.

In addition to viewing black and brown bears, onlookers may also use the platform to spot river otters, bald eagles, mergansers, and a variety of songbirds. Also present but notoriously elusive are wolves, mink, and owls. The flora of the Anan Creek Wildlife Observatory provides these animals with a lush, dense habitat of coniferous trees such

Anan Creek Wildlife Observatory viewing platform. (Courtesy of Robert Broussard)

as western hemlock, Sitka spruce, and cedar as well as a variety of lichens, mosses, ferns, and deciduous trees.

The Anan Creek Wildlife Observatory is relatively safe from many of the threats that commonly plague America's natural places. The most immediate concern, however, surrounds a set of legalities that preside over areas of the Tongass that are referred to as roadless areas. A 2001 initiative prevented construction of new roads in currently road-less areas, thus preserving large tracts of timber land by leaving them inaccessible to excavating and logging equipment. A series of court decisions failed to uphold the road-less initiative, but a 2006 court decision reinstated the 2001 initiative yet exempted the Tongass. Despite being exempt from the roadless rules, the U.S. Forest Service has found road building (and subsequent road maintenance) through the Tongass to be financially unrealistic. Setting logging issues aside, building roads through the Tongass would inevi-tably offer easy access to people and allow places such as Anan Creek to be a common stopping point. These same roadways bring invasive species of another sort as well. The seeds and viable fragments of invasive plants are easily spread when they are caught in the underside of motor vehicles and are then dislodged in a new location. Several recent studies have documented and mapped outbreaks of invasive weeds in some of Alaska's most remote settings, including the Tongass.

Further Reading

Durbin, Kathie. *Tongass: Pulp Politics and the Fight for the Alaska Rain Forest*. Corvallis: Oregon State University Press, 2005.

ARCTIC NATIONAL WILDLIFE REFUGE

The Arctic National Wildlife Refuge encompasses 18 million acres of land and lies completely within the northern latitudes of the Arctic Circle. Such extreme remoteness does not, however, offer this refuge much in the way of protection; climate change and oil drilling are set to alter this terrain in ways that scientists, conservationists, lobbyists, executives, and politicians do not fully understand.

The ecosystem of the Arctic National Wildlife Refuge consists of more than a handful of animal species that are highly adapted to life in the Arctic. Barren ice fields, tundra, highlands, lowlands, uplands, marine coastal systems and water ways, along with the eastern portions of the Brooks Mountain range make for a landscape that is as diverse as its inhabitants. Near the bottom of the food chain sit about 26 species of small rodent-like mammals including (but not limited to) lemmings, shrews, voles, beavers, muskrats, squirrels, porcupines, and hares. Large herbivores such as caribou, moose, musk ox, and Dall sheep provide significant amounts of food and clothing (in the form of animal hide) to the area's native Eskimo and Gwich'in populations and also fulfill the diet of large predators like the grizzly bear, black bear, and wolf. Other meat eaters occupy specialized niches in the food chain. Polar bears, for example, occupy the winter ice fields in the northernmost reaches of the refuge. These ice fields form when the Beaufort Sea freezes and is then used by the polar bears in their hunt for seals. This predator-prey relationship is critical to the bears' survival and is being jeopardized by climate change. Milder and shorter winters have prompted a reduction hunting territory for the bear, and scientists project that the warming trend will continue. A U.S. Geological Survey study has predicted that polar bears in Alaska could be wiped out by 2050. Despite an overwhelming sense of urgency, the U.S. Fish and Wildlife Service let pass a January 2008 deadline for a decision to list the polar bear on the endangered species list.

Listing the species would have widespread implications: Hunting of the polar bear would be deemed illegal and thereby eliminate the revenue upon which native hunting guides and their families rely. Listing of the bear also extends protection to the bears' habitat, thus prohibiting resource extractions such as mining, timber harvests, and oil drilling. The area has already been explored for oil reserves, and the U.S. Department of the Interior estimates that the refuge holds between 5.7 billion and 16 billion barrels of oil. The financial and economic implications of such oil reserves are tremendous, both for the state of Alaska and the U.S. government. The decision to officially list the polar bear as an endangered species was made in May 2008 amid a storm of public and political debate. To list or not to list—either way, the outcome of such decisions will document America's preference for and attitude toward the environment and the economy.

Further Reading

Borneman, Walter R. *Alaska: Saga of a Bold Land*. New York: HarperCollins, 2003.
Kaye, Roger. *Last Great Wilderness: The Campaign to Establish the Arctic National Wildlife Refuge*. Fairbanks: University of Alaska Press, 2006.
U.S. Fish and Wildlife Service. "Arctic National Wildlife Refuge." http://arctic.fws.gov/.

BERING LAND BRIDGE NATIONAL PRESERVE

The Bering Land Bridge National Preserve is located on the Seward Peninsula, which can best be described as a fingertip of land that projects from the central coast of Alaska and points directly westward to Russia. In fact, it is here on the Seward Peninsula that the two continents are at their closest, being separated by a mere 52 miles. This geographical proximity has profoundly shaped the Americas; in fact, the prehistoric narrative of the Bering Land Bridge is very likely one of the most famous and well-known sagas that any natural area can lay claim to.

The relevance of the prehistoric Bering Land Bridge to the future preserve started somewhere during the last ice age. This span of time, known as the Pleistocene, began 1.6 million years ago and ended 10,000 years ago. During this epoch, it is estimated that as much as 30 percent of the earth's surface was covered in massive sheets of ice. These glaciers locked much of the earth's water away in the form of ice and, in doing so, lowered global sea levels by about 300 feet. As sea levels dropped, the land between northern Asia and North America became exposed and eventually formed a wide swath of land that connected the two continents. The Bering Land Bridge was, in all actuality, much more than a bridge of land. In some locations, the exposed landmass was 1,000 miles wide and teeming with plant and animal life. Among some of the most noteworthy animals to graze their way across the Bering Land Bridge were musk ox, bison, camel, and mammoth. Humans naturally followed their food source, and most archeologists agree that it was the northern Asiatic peoples who were the first to cross the Bering Land Bridge and populate North America.

Of the large mammals that also made the crossing, the ancient bison, camel, and mammoth would become extinct shortly after the last ice age. The musk ox, however, survived well into modern times only to suffer steep declines in population during the early 19th century. Records indicate that the last known wild Alaskan musk ox was shot by a hunter in 1895. In the fall of 1930, a herd of musk ox consisting of 15 males and 19 females were captured in Greenland and loaded on ships bound for the United States. After crossing under the Statue of Liberty, the herd arrived in New Jersey, where they sat in quarantine for 33 days. They were then loaded on trains bound for Seattle. Once in Seattle, the musk ox endured yet another steamboat ride to Seward, Alaska, and then a final train ride to Fairbanks, where the herd was maintained within a monitored enclosure. The herd stayed in captivity for several years in Fairbanks but was eventually relocated and released on the island of Nunivak. Between 1936 and 1968, the musk ox population grew from 31 to an estimated 750. Breeding populations were then taken from Nunivak Island and released in various areas across Alaska. In the early 1970s, the Bering Land Bridge National Preserve received its own population of musk ox, which have since flourished.

The success of the musk ox has as much to do with habitat preservation as it does with human ingenuity. Thanks in part to the remoteness of the Bering Land Bridge National Preserve, the habitat here remains largely undisturbed. This is critical especially for the Bering Preserve, because it is classified as a tundra biome and is home to more than 400 species delicate plants, sedges, lichen, and mosses, which abound in the relatively poor soil. In fact, the subsoils of this region consist of a unique combination of lava, frozen ash, and permafrost, which is a permanently frozen layer of soil that can be found at various depths underground. Nonetheless, the treeless tundra of the Bering Land Bridge supports a dense mat of lush low-laying vegetation upon which numerous herbivores including musk ox, caribou, and moose feed. Grizzly bears, wolverines, wolves, and fox are among the preserve's top predators.

The flora and fauna of the region have traditionally coexisted alongside the indigenous peoples of Alaska. Even in modern times, the Bering Preserve has been spared mass human intrusions largely because it exists in such a remote location. Access to the preserve is very limited, reachable during the summer months by bush plane or boat and by sled dog or snowmobile in the winter. Safeguarding the remote nature of the preserve is one of the most critical issues for the preserve. A February 2003 ruling reinstated a 130-year-old rule designed to promote road building during the Civil War era. Congress repealed the rule in 1976, thereby preventing road construction, but the 2003 ruling allows for an unprecedented number of roads to be built in many national preserves, including the Bering Land Bridge National Preserve.

Further Reading

O'Neil, Dan. *Last Giant of Beringia: The Mystery of the Bering Land Bridge.* Cambridge, MA: Basic Books, 2005.

Creamer's Field Migratory Waterfowl Refuge

From about 1910 to 1966, the Creamer's Dairy was dotted with dairy cows and hay fields and laid claim to the title of North America's northernmost dairy. What began as a large and successful agricultural endeavor eventually evolved into a refuge for dozens of species of birds. Year by year, as the dairy expanded, its sprawling pastures and fields served as a resting ground for migratory birds. Over the years, the congregation of birds grew as did public recognition of its significance as prime bird habitat. When, in 1966, the dairy went up for sale, community members raised money to ensure that the fields and pasturelands would be conserved as bird habitat. Today, the state of Alaska manages the 1,800-acre parcel, which includes the old pasture lands and fields as well as the original farmhouse and outbuildings, which were listed on the National Register of Historic Places in 1977. Forested areas and wetlands further diversify the habitat not only for the refuge's birds but also for a variety of other mammals including ermine, voles, lynx, wolves, bats, porcupines, moose, and caribou.

The farmhouse now serves as a nature and visitor center, while the pastures and the rest of the property serve as breeding, nesting, and feeding grounds for approximately 144 species of birds. Many of the birds that visit Creamer's Field are in the midst of migration via the Mississippi, Central, and Pacific flyways. These flyways mark the various north-south migration routes used by birds that spend the summer in Alaska but winter as far south as Patagonia. The miles traveled can total in the thousands, making protected refuges essential for rest and refueling during the long journey. The golden eagle, long-billed dowitcher, Arctic tern, and rosy finch are just a few of the passers-through, but a number of species utilize the refuge for nesting purposes. Pocket-sized songbirds like the orange-crowned warbler and dark-eyed junco are among the many birds that find prime nest-building materials and habitat within the fields and shrubbery of the preserve. Similarly, numerous waterfowl, cranes, grebes, and other shorebirds lay their eggs and care for their fledglings while preparing for their southern migration as fall sets in on Alaska.

Meeting the diverse habitat and feeding needs of so many different species does not occur here without human intervention. Soil improvement, controlled burns, grain spreading, crop rotations, and pond building are all overseen by the state and supported by numerous volunteers. Their efforts are extremely important as climate change, suburban sprawl, industrial development, and corporate farming threaten both the quantity and quality of avian habitat.

The importance of Creamer's Field Migratory Waterfowl Refuge was recently underscored when the Audubon Society compiled 40 years of bird-counting data into its 2007 publication of the *Top 20 Common Birds in Decline*. Creamer's Field is utilized by 7 of these 20 species, including the northern pintail duck, which experienced a decline of 77 percent over the course of the study. Populations of the greater scaup have decreased an estimated 75 percent and, like the pintail, rely on Creamer's Field for breeding and nesting habitat. Other refuge inhabitants, also experiencing staggering declines of between 54 and 73 percent are boreal chickadee, snow bunting, rufous hummingbird, horned lark, and ruffed grouse.

Visitors frequent the refuge year round, walking its trails in summer and cross-country skiing them in winter. Viewing platforms and observation towers ensure a good look at a number of species within each of the three main habitats, and tours may be self-guided or conducted as a group with a knowledgeable volunteer. The refuge also hosts a variety of events aimed at educating and exposing the public as to the natural wonders of Creamer's Field. These and other educational opportunities and community outreach programs are supported and sponsored by the Friends of Creamer's Field and the Alaska Department of Fish and Game.

Further Reading

National Audubon Society. "State of the Birds." http://stateofthebirds.audubon.org/.

Wells, Jeffery V. *Birder's Conservation Handbook: 100 North American Birds at Risk.* Princeton, NJ: Princeton University Press, 2007.

GUSTAVUS FORELANDS

Two hundred years ago, travelers to the Gustavus Forelands would have found themselves staring up at the walls of a massive glacier. The glacier has since receded some 80 miles, and the land that was once covered with ice is now literally springing to life. With the weight of the glacier gone, the land in and around Gustavus is rising at a rate of 1.5 inches every year. The forelands are also undergoing a unique ecological process called primary succession. This type of succession occurs when new land is exposed or formed (as is the case with lava flows) and is thereby open to settlement by various plant communities along with the inevitable insects and animals that follow suite. The process is gradual, with the first pioneer plants such as lichen, mosses, and algae taking hold directly onto the rocky surfaces. The life and death cycles of these first species, combined with the erosional forces of wind and water, eventually give rise to thin layers of topsoil. Grasses and low shrubs then settle in sparse earth but will also contribute to and deepen the topsoil until one day it will anchor and nourish the tallest of trees.

The plant communities here are still undergoing rapid changes partly due to the natural flow of succession and partly due to human disturbance. Herbaceous wet meadows of buckbean, horsetail, and cottongrass transition to short thicket, which is dominated by sweet gale only to eventually become tall thicket as willow takes over. Tall thicket then changes into pine or spruce parkland but will eventually come to be dominated by spruce forest. In time, and if left to natural devices, the spruce woodlands will change to hemlock forest. The pathway of succession, however, is anything but linear, and any one plant community may revert back to what it once was.

Regardless of sequence, the variety of plant communities in the Gustavus Forelands supports a highly diverse population of animals. The animal populations are also subject to the forces of primary succession, moving into and out of habitats as plant assemblages morph from one vegetative form to another. For example, moose had not been documented in the forelands area until 1958; by the mid-1980s, they were commonplace; and today some biologists estimate that the wintering populations of moose outnumber the town's people two to one. Originally drawn to prime uncrowded feeding grounds, the moose's heavy grazing habits now contribute to the region's soil and microbial dynamics as well as vegetative growth patterns.

Conservation of the Gustavus Forelands has been a community effort, uniting private landowners; state, local, and federal agencies; and conservation groups in a common cause. These partnerships enabled the Nature Conservancy to purchase about 4,000 acres in the forelands area in November 2004. The acquisition protects several habitats, including a swath of coastal forest along with meadowlands and beachfront and thus allows the natural pace of primary succession to proceed with limited human interference.

Further Reading

Walker, Lawrence R., and Roger del Moral. *Primary Succession and Ecosystem Rehabilitation*. New York: Cambridge University Press, 2003.

HOMER AIRPORT CRITICAL HABITAT AREA

The Homer Airport Critical Habitat Area is unique in several respects; not only does it lay within Homer's city limits but the habitat is situated directly adjacent to the town's busy municipal airport. Established in 1996 and managed by the Alaska Department of Fish and Game, this critical habitat encompasses roughly 280 acres of wetlands that are an extension of the Beluga Wetlands Complex and part of the Kachemak Bay watershed. Wetlands in general are important for naturally managing floodwaters, nutrient flow, and for filtering groundwater. Likewise, the Homer Airport wetlands improve water quality and moderate water flow in addition to supporting a seasonal flux of shorebirds and songbirds in spring and summer and moose in the winter.

It is estimated that more than 200 species of birds use the Homer Airport Critical Habitat Area either as a rest stop during migration or as breeding and nesting grounds. The area is particularly important to the Aleutian tern, which migrates from Indonesia and Malaysia to breed and raise their young off the coast of Alaska. While the wetlands host a variety of raptors, songbirds, swans, and ducks, it is particularly dense with shorebirds including the greater and lesser yellow legs, western sandpiper, short-billed dowitcher, and semipalmated plover. In all, some 25 species of shorebirds numbering in the hundreds of thousands of individuals congregate in the Homer Airport Critical Habitat Area. Humans also flock to the area to attend the Kachemak Bay Shorebird festival, which offers bird enthusiasts the opportunity to attend workshops and lectures and partake in world-class bird-watching.

Most of the birds that rely on the Homer Airport Critical Habitat Area will migrate south as fall settles in. As snow accumulates, the area around the Homer Airport becomes increasingly important to the region's moose populations. Biologists estimate that Homer's moose herd numbers a steady 500 individuals. Moose, along with a number of other large mammals including black bears and coyotes find shelter from deep snow and harsh winter winds within the low-laying wetlands.

Continued protection of the Homer Airport Critical Habitat Area is dependent on a variety of factors, many of which are tied to the growth and development of the airport itself, as well as fostering partnerships with the organizations that oversee the conservation of properties neighboring the airport. Airport expansion and subsequent noise levels have been a primary concern as the demand for infrastructure leading into and out of the airport increases. Continued cooperation with the Federal Aviation Administration (FAA) is also crucial, since flocks of large migratory birds such as sandhill cranes pose a threat to aircraft and passengers. Due to the proximity of the airport and the critical habitat area, the FAA required the airport to develop and adhere to a wildlife hazard management plan to minimize the risk of aircraft strikes with birds and land mammals. Also of concern is the need to maintain a series of migration corridors around the airport and those properties that have already been developed for housing. The natural beauty of the wetlands and adjacent Beluga Lake has deemed the property prime real estate; therefore, it is increasingly difficult for organizations like the Kachemak Moose Habitat Inc. to purchase land for conservation purposes.

The Homer Airport Critical Habitat Area is open to the public and is heavily utilized by residents and visitors alike: Berry picking, cross-country skiing, bird-watching, and hiking are among the most popular activities in the area. Wildlife viewing platforms are located across from the main terminal of the Homer Airport. The adjacent protected areas, including the Beluga Wetlands Complex and lands held by Kachemak Moose Habitat Inc., are privately held yet open to the public.

Further Reading

Weller, Milton W. *Wetland Birds: Habitat Resources and Conservation Implications.* New York: Cambridge University Press, 1999.

KATMAI NATIONAL PARK AND PRESERVE

Located at the base of the Alaskan Peninsula in southwestern Alaska, the Katmai National Park and Preserve is a dynamic landscape, rich in both human archeological and geological history. For the past 9,000 years, people have inhabited the area in and around the Brooks River, which flows through Katmai. Evidence of their dwellings, stone and flint tools, ceramics, and other cultural artifacts make the area an important link with the past. Archeological evidence also suggests that humans and volcanoes have coexisted in the Katmai region for thousands of years.

Permanent human occupation of the region ceased in 1912 when Mount Novarupta erupted with such force that it buried 40 square miles of the valley below in ash that was 700 feet deep in some places. Although the occupants of the valley's villages escaped, the abundant wildlife, pristine waterways, and lush vegetation were instantly destroyed. What remained was a Mars-like landscape of ash, earthen fissures, and jagged mountain peaks. Several years after the eruption, explorers entered the valley and discovered thousands of smoking fumaroles and hence coined the name Valley of Ten Thousand Smokes. To preserve the smoking valley, Congress established the Katmai National Monument in 1918. In 1980, the monument was upgraded to the status of a national park and preserve and now encompasses 4.7 million acres, most of which is classified as wilderness area.

Although five of Katmai's volcanoes are still classified as active, the landscape appears to have cooled and settled; even the Valley of Ten Thousand Smokes has ceased its smoldering. In the areas previously smothered by volcanic lava and ash, the process of secondary succession has led to the reemergence of new plant and animal communities. The park's unique blend of mature and recently established habitats sustains a variety of mammals, fish, and birds. Katmai protects large populations of brown bear in addition to mink, porcupine, moose, fox, wolves, beaver, and caribou. Both migratory and residential bird populations find refuge along the banks and shorelines of the park's numerous rivers, ponds, and lakes. Most notably, these freshwater sources are among the few on earth that do not bear evidence of contamination via manmade substances. In contrast, the park's rugged coastline was heavily impacted by the 1989 *Exxon Valdez* oil spill. Although the spill site was located some 250 miles away, the oil drifted and soon washed ashore. Clean-up efforts at Katmai lasted upward of five months and yielded more than 1,055 tons of oil-soiled waste.

Human impacts on Katmai National Park and Preserve are concentrated in areas that are easily reachable to visitors, namely Brooks Camp. While most of the park is accessible to only the most determined adventurers, Brooks Camp is easily reached via float plane or boat. Furthermore, a variety of activities such as sport fishing, hiking, wildlife viewing, and photography attract numerous visitors. Preventing the development of human-tolerant bears, controlling the spread of invasive species, restoring habitat, and securing alternative energy sources by which to operate the National Park Service housing have all been cited as areas of concern in the *First Annual Centennial Strategy Report for Katmai National Park*.

Further Reading
Alaska Volcano Observatory. http://www.avo.alaska.edu/.
Exxon Valdez Oil Spill Trustee Council. http://www.evostc.state.ak.us/.

Kenai Fjords National Park

Kenai Fjords National Park spans 1,760 square miles of south central Alaska. The biological diversity of the park is due in part to its dramatic topography. Carved by eons' of glacial advancement and retreat, the land here is a series of deep valleys, sheer cliffs, and jagged peaks. The landmark feature for which the park is named was also a result of glacial action: Fjords are formed when a glacier cuts a deep V-shaped valley which fills with melted glacial water. The resulting inlet is enclosed on three sides by nearly vertical landmass, while the mouth of the inlet is open to the sea.

The Kenai Fjords teem with life: humpback, minke, orca, and blue and gray whales cruise the deep fjords, as do sea otters, Dall's porpoise, and Stellar sea lions. A variety of birds make use of the abruptly steep and craggy shoreline cliffs, including puffins, bald eagles, common murres, and cormorants, which all feast on the abundant fish life. The landscape hosts an equally rich assortment of land animals but does so on a narrow swath of terrain that is sandwiched between the Pacific Ocean and the not-so-distant Harding Icefield. Again topography plays a pivotal role in determining the habitats found within this narrow life zone. In some locations, elevation rises by as much as 1,000 feet per mile, thus resulting in abrupt transitions between costal habitats, coniferous forest, alpine meadows, and snowy peaks. Collectively, these diverse environments support wolves, moose, mountain goats, bears, hoary marmots, and freshwater fish, in addition to a large variety of plants and trees.

Not far from this fertile landscape sits a sprawling field of ice, known as the Harding Icefield. Arguably the main attraction for many of the park's visitors, the Harding Icefield and its associated glaciers cover 1,100 square miles of the park in glacial ice. Exit Glacier is one of several glaciers that continue to actively shape their surroundings as they advance and retreat. This mass movement of ice scours rocks off the floor and walls

Aialik Glacier is a tidewater glacier in Kenai Fjords National Park, Alaska. (imnowl)

of the valley. These boulders are consequently pulverized by the force of the glacier and eventually deposited as coarse pebblelike substrate when the glacier retreats.

Worldwide climate change has drastically accelerated the rate of glacial retreat; the Harding Icefield and its glaciers are no exception. Their melting waters flow into the Pacific, contributing to rising sea levels and altering salinity levels. However, as the ice melts, it exposes new terrain that has not seen the light of day in recent times. Kenai Fjords is one of the most accessible places on earth where visitors may not only witness glacial retreat but also view the various stages of primary succession. Primary succession is a rare ecological event during which a series of plant and animal communities will colonize the barren substrate. The initial phases of primary succession in Kenai Fjords are characterized by the growth of hardy lichens and low-profile plants such as woodrush, lingonberry, and pincushion plant. These pioneer plants eventually die and decay, thus increasing both the quantity and quality of the topsoil. Willow and other shrubs will be the next to settle the habitat, followed by alder and cottonwood. Succession will be complete when spruce and hemlock come to dominate.

In addition to climate change, Kenai Fjords National Park faces a variety of challenges that stem from its accessibility. Established in 1980, the park has experienced a 150 percent increase in tourism within the past 15 years, and the National Park Service now estimates that 140,000 tourists visit each year. During this same time frame, the park observed an 80 percent decrease in two of its marine mammal species. Invasive species, waste management, and carbon emissions are just a few of the issues that the National Park Service is attempting to resolve while simultaneously continuing to inventory and monitor the flora and fauna that rely on the park for continued preservation.

Further Reading

Collier, Michael. *Sculpted by Ice: Glaciers and the Alaskan Landscape*. Anchorage: Alaska Natural History Association, 2004.

Olthuis, Diane. *It Happened in Alaska*. Guilford, CT: Globe Pequote Press, 2006.

Spies, Robert B. *Long-term Ecological Change in the Northern Gulf of Alaska*. Oxford, UK: Elsevier, 2007.

KOOTZNOOWOO WILDERNESS

Meaning "fortress of the bears," the Kootznoowoo Wilderness is an island-bound landscape that encompasses roughly 937,400 acres and is located on Admiralty Island in southeastern Alaska. This wilderness area provides protection to the world's largest intact swath of temperate rainforest, while also sustaining its infamous population of bears.

The temperate rainforest is characterized by plentiful rainfall, moderate temperature, and infrequent disturbance due to wildfire. As a result, these forests contain more biomass (living and decaying plant material) than any other biome on the planet. The forests of the Kootznoowoo Wilderness are populated by ancient conifers, mainly Sitka spruce, shore pine, western red cedar, and both western and mountain hemlock, all of which have life spans of 500 or more years. Also notable is the yellow cedar, which may live for up to 1,000 years. The longevity of these trees creates a uniquely structured old-growth forest that is strikingly different than a young forest. The trees of an old-growth forest are very tall and wide in girth with equally impressive branching patterns. These branches often form a closed canopy which then limits penetration by the sun and consequently reduces the density of the understory. The canopy is, however, not without gaps; occasionally, weather, age, or disease will take down a tree, thus providing an opening through which new vegetation will arise. Old-growth forests are also distinguished by eons' worth of vegetative material that lays on the forest floor in various stages of decay. Decomposers like microbes, grubs, and other insects will eventually reduce giant fallen trees to mounds of nutrient-rich soil, which will in turn support new timber growth.

The verdant old-growth rainforest of the Kootznoowoo does not run continuously but is punctuated by areas of boggy muskeg and an abundant collection of lichens, mosses, and ferns. Wildflowers, including river beauty, mountain monkshood, northern rice root, jewelweed, and western buttercup, dot the land with color. The wilderness also protects a variety of animals, both large and small; among them are brown bears, American bald eagles, salmon, marten, beaver, and Sitka black-tailed deer. The Kootznoowoo's categorization as a wilderness is critical to the protection and preservation of the region's flora and fauna because it severely limits direct human disturbances that result from activities such as timber harvest, mining, hunting, and recreational vehicles. The most immediate threats to the Kootznoowoo are a result of its location inside the borders of the Tongass National Forest. The Tongass has long been the center of debate among conservation groups, the timber industry, indigenous tribes, taxpayer watch groups, and policymakers. Millions of board feet have been clear-cut from the Tongass since the 1950s, but an updated Tongass Land Management Plan published by the U.S. Forest Service in January 2008 aims to both protect the forestland while also serving the economic needs of the people of Southwestern Alaska. The new plan, however, left the "Allowable Sale Quantity" (ASQ)—the amount of timber that the Forest Service was able to lawfully sell—unchanged from previous decades, thereby permitting the Forest Service to sell 2.67 billion board feet per decade, a number which equates to an average of 267 million board feet per year. This is enough timber to build 21,894, three-bedroom homes on an annual basis.

The turmoil of the Tongass underscores the importance of the Kootznoowoo Wilderness. As a designated wilderness area, the Kootznoowoo and its inhabitants are protected via more stringent conservation regulations and thus become a source of ecological stability within a region that stands to undergo extreme ecological disruption.

Further Reading

Haycox, Stephen W. *Frigid Embrace: Politics, Economics, and Environment in Alaska.* Corvallis: Oregon State University Press, 2002.

Scott, Doug. *The Enduring Wilderness: Protecting Our Natural Heritage through the Wilderness Act.* Golden, CO: Fulcrum, 2004.

U.S. Forest Service. "Tongass National Forest." http://www.fs.fed.us/r10/tongass/.

McNeil River State Game Sanctuary and Refuge

McNeil River State Game Sanctuary and Refuge runs parallel to both the eastern and western banks of the McNeil River as it flows through southern Alaska and empties into Kamishak Bay. On paper, the McNeil River Sanctuary, which was established in 1967, is separate from and managed under different regulations than the adjacent McNeil River Refuge, which was founded in 1991. The distinctions between sanctuary and refuge are of little consequence to the region's star attraction, the brown bear.

The bears congregate around the McNeil River and several other nearby streams to fish for salmon. All five species of Pacific salmon run through the region, thus supplying the bears with plentiful food. As many as 72 bears have been recorded feeding in the reserve at one time, and it is believed that the McNeil River Sanctuary protects the world's largest concentration of brown bears. People have traveled the globe to view these brown bears up close. While the sanctuary is open to the public, it is operated via a permit lottery system. The 185 permits that are available on an annual basis must be applied for. Permit winners are then drawn at random from the application pool, which regularly numbers nearly 1,000 applications; 1993 brought a record of 2,150 applications for the 185 permits, and in 2006, 783 people entered the lottery for a chance to view the bears along the McNeil River.

The bears, and the people who come to view and photograph them have developed a rather intimate, nearly symbiotic, if not ultratolerant, relationship (a few meters of river and a steep embankment are all that separate bear from viewer). The McNeil River bears carry out their daily activities of foraging, grooming, napping, and nursing young all in very close proximity to people and, in doing so, offer humans a unique opportunity to witness the life of an animal whose icon is deeply embedded in human culture. As is true of all symbiotic relationships, both partners must benefit; in recent years, the bears have relied on their devoted human advocates for protection.

In 2005, the Board of Game, which regulates hunting and trapping in Alaska, reopened the McNeil River Refuge to brown bear hunting beginning in the summer of 2007. The interim two years were filled with passionate debate on behalf of both the prohunting advocates and those who felt that protection of McNeil River bears should extend beyond the sanctuary. In the end, a widespread media campaign and public petition in combination with well over 10,000 letters from the public led the Alaska Board of Game to rescind the hunt.

Despite these extra protective measures, the bear population along the McNeil River has exhibited an overall decline since 1998. The specific reason or reasons have yet to be determined, but a general consensus points to a reduction in chum salmon (the bears' favorite food) runs in the McNeil River in combination with an increase in bear hunting and harvesting in Katmai National Preserve, which is located near the McNeil River Sanctuary and Refuge. Bears may also be moving from the McNeil River area to feed in other nearby streams that are home to more productive runs of chum salmon.

Conservation groups anticipate future obstacles to be centered on oil exploration, drilling, and spills as the lower portions of the Cook Inlet (into which the McNeil River flows) hold valuable deposits of oil. Such a scenario might call for further protective measures not only for the McNeil River bears but also for the waterfowl, harbor seals, sea otters, seabirds, salmon, and herring that migrate, feed, and reproduce along the coastal borders of the McNeil River State Game Sanctuary and Refuge.

Further Reading

Alaska Department of Fish and Game. "Status of Brown Bears and Other Natural Resources in the McNeil River State Game Sanctuary and Refuge in 2006." http://www.wc.adfg.state.ak.us/refuge/pdfs/mcneil_legis_rpt.pdf.

Troyer, Willard A. *Into Brown Bear Country.* Anchorage: University of Alaska Press, 2005.

NATIONAL PETROLEUM RESERVE

In order to secure oil for the U.S. Navy, President Warren G. Harding set aside 23.5 million acres on the north slope of Alaska and called it the National Petroleum Reserve. The reserve is sandwiched between the northern foothills of the Brook Range, which lay to the south, and the Arctic Ocean, which defines its northern border. To the west lays the smaller (19 million acres) but better known Arctic National Wildlife Refuge.

Since the reserve's inception in 1923 and continuing into the late 1990s, the land was left largely untouched and undeveloped. Caribou, wolves, grizzly bears, polar bears, whales, migratory waterfowl, and indigenous people found sustenance and shelter among the region's tundra, wetlands, alpine meadows, lakes, and marine environments. Of particular importance are the Arctic wetlands and plains that surround the 22-mile-long Teshekpuk Lake. This freshwater habitat provides protection to a myriad of migratory birds, including the threatened spectacled eider, about 33 percent of the world's population of Pacific black brants, and an estimated 60,000 molting geese. (Molting is a particularly fragile part of a goose's life cycle during which it sheds its feathers and thus cannot rely on flight to escape predation.) Teshekpuk Lake also has a long history of use by the native Inupiat, who have hunted and fished along its banks for thousands of years.

In 1980, the Bureau of Land Management (BLM) became the governing authority of the National Petroleum Reserve and began planning for the sale of oil and gas leases. Such leases are purchased by oil companies who then explore, drill, and extract the area's petroleum and natural gas deposits. The BLM first divided the land into three main regions: northeast, northwest, and south. One and a half million acres of the northeast region were the first set of leases to be sold off, followed by the 2004 lease sale of 2,300,000 acres in the northwest. Acreage in the south region was also slotted for sale, but those efforts were abandoned due to concerns that disruption of the region would be detrimental to the western Arctic caribou herd, which calves in the southern part of the National Petroleum Reserve.

Of the three regions, it is the development of the northeast section that has caused the most turmoil. The original plan for development of the northeast set aside some 800,000 acres of ecologically sensitive habitat in and round Teshekpuk Lake. A 2005 ruling by the Bush administration overruled the BLM and revoked protection of the lake and adjoining wetlands. This executive action was challenged in district court and resulted in a 2006 ruling that blocked the sale of 600,000 acres of leases around the lake. The BLM countered the court decision in May 2008 by placing 219,000 acres of Teshekpuk Lake under protection, insofar as this acreage could not be leased for oil and gas development.

The jostle of compromise will undoubtedly continue as conservation groups like the Nature Conservancy team up with the Inupiat in an effort to preserve their native hunting grounds. Nonetheless, February 2008 was marked by $2.7 billion in lease sales that secure drilling off the northern coast of the National Petroleum Reserve. Meanwhile, other grassroots initiatives are calling for the conversion of the National Petroleum Refuge into the National Pleistocene Refuge. And all the while, climate change is leaving its mark. Ice sheets thawing around the Teshekpuk Lake region have contributed to the rapid erosion of the narrow strip of land that separates the freshwater lake from the neighboring Beaufort Sea. Biologists anticipate that the flux of seawater into the lake system will further contribute to the profoundly changing landscape of the National Petroleum Reserve.

Further Reading

Johnson, Stephen R., and Joe Clyde Truett. *The Natural History of an Arctic Oil Field: Development and the Biota.* San Diego, CA: Academic Press, 2000.

U.S. Department of the Interior, Bureau of Land Management. "National Petroleum Reserve—Alaska." http://www.blm.gov/ak/st/en/prog/energy/oil_gas/npra.html.

WALRUS ISLANDS STATE GAME
SANCTUARY: ROUND ISLAND

Collectively known as the Walrus Islands State Game Sanctuary, this small chain of seven islands are located in the northern reaches of Bristol Bay. The islands and their surrounding waters offer protection to countless numbers of seabirds, walrus, sea lions, whales, fox, voles, and shrews.

Round Island, however, is the most famous of the islands, as its cobblestonelike beaches serve as one of the Pacific's largest haul-out sites for male walruses. Swarms of animals, some weighing as much as 4,500 pounds, pull themselves ashore to bask and rest between foraging excursions at sea. Biologists have tallied as many as 15,000 walruses on the island during a single day. Although walruses were hunted commercially during the 18th and 19th centuries, their populations have since rebounded and stabilized within their Pacific range while the Atlantic populations remain depleted and fragmented. It should be noted, however, that haul-out sites and their use by walruses vary greatly from year to year, so it is important that scientists pinpoint the world's haul-out sites and perform subsequent counts to arrive at an accurate estimate of walrus populations.

Round Island not only serves as prime resting and feeding grounds for walruses but also serves as a haul-out site for the endangered Stellar sea lion. Unlike the walrus, Stellar sea lions were not extensively harvested at any point in history, yet their populations have sharply declined in recent years. The rate of and reason for their decline has been a point of contention and debate among policymakers, researchers, and the general public. While global populations appear stable, Alaska's Stellar sea lion populations have declined an estimated 50 to 80 percent since the 1970s. Overfishing, climate change, shooting by anglers, exposure to contaminants leading to reproductive failure, and disease have all been implicated in the sea lions' demise.

Round Island's remote location and infrequent human disturbance make it an especially critical site for the gathering of census data. Annual population counts are preformed for both the walrus and the Stellar sea lion as well as a half dozen species of seabirds that flock to the island to breed, nest, and feed. The opportunity to consistently perform such head counts yields additional information about the animals' reproductive rates and success in addition to mortality estimates. Much of this data translate into a deeper understanding of regional and global populations and in turn influence public policy.

Six of the seven islands are open to the public; access to Round Island requires a permit that must be applied for and issued by the Alaska Department of Fish and Game (ADF&G). Although the ADF&G oversees the sanctuary and its visitor program, its inhabitants receive additional protection under the 1972 Marine Mammal Protection Act.

Further Reading

National Oceanic and Atmospheric Administration Fisheries. "Marine Mammal Protection Act." http://www.nmfs.noaa.gov/pr/laws/mmpa/.

Okonek Calamar, Diane. "Walrus Island State Game Sanctuary Annual Report." http://wildlife.alaska.gov/refuge/pdfs/ri_06report.pdf.

Appleton-Whittell Research Ranch, 24
Aravaipa Canyon, 25
Buckelew Family Lands, 27
Hassayampa River Preserve, 29
Kofa National Wildlife Refuge, 30
Sierra Vista Wastewater Wetlands, 32

ARIZONA

Although the landscape of Arizona is frequently recognized by its vast cacti-studded deserts or immense earthen fissures, Arizona is more diverse than first glances may suggest. The northern portions of the state sit on a high plateau that gives the region a significantly cooler climate than that of the southern portion of the state. Characterized by cold winters and mild summers, the northern portions of the state are home to a number of plant and animal communities that are limited, if not totally absent, in the blistering heat of southern Arizona. The mountains of the Mogollon Rim, for example, are covered with one of the world's largest stands of ponderosa pine in addition to many other plant and animal species that are indicative of the Colorado Rockies. Moving southward down the rim, the habitat transitions to that of the Sierra Madre Occidental with its Lumholtz's pine, Yécora pine, Arizona oak, and Mexican blue oak. Additional habitat transitions occur as the north becomes the south and the landscape becomes increasing dry and sparsely vegetated with drastically different species than that of the high plateau.

Southern Arizona is dominated by the desert biome and is divided in two by the Sonoran Desert in the west and the Chihuahuan Desert in the east. Each of these desert ecosystems is defined by specific vegetation: the Sonoran is characterized by the presence of the famous saguaro cacti along with a number of other types of cacti, while the Chihuahuan is defined by a handful of plants including yucca, mesquite, lechuguilla, and creosote bush. Of the two deserts, the Chihuahuan sits at a higher elevation and therefore experiences temperatures that are a bit cooler than that of the Sonoran, which averages summer temperatures of between 90° and 120° F. Surprisingly, it is the Sonoran Desert that contains the region's most populated and fastest growing cities: Phoenix and Tucson.

Population growth is at the root of many of the state's ecological and economic concerns. Urban sprawl is not only consuming the state's natural places but is overtaking its agricultural fields and rangeland as well. Securing open space is only one area of concern; the other is water. Water in the American Southwest is forever at a premium, but as populations expand along with city limit boundary lines, the state must reconsider its approach to water resource management. The added pressure has forced state leadership and private citizens to create innovative ways to not only use but actually reclaim significant amounts of gray water—or water that has already been used. Water conservation then ensures that land conservation efforts remain viable, since there is little incentive to save a riparian forest if the water is going to be diverted for municipal use. Land conservation in Arizona occurs at a pace that is somewhat different than much of the American West but is championed by a number of public and private lands trusts, the Nature Conservancy, Arizona Game and Fish Department, Sky Island Alliance, and various city and county entities that work toward sustainable growth and development across the state.

APPLETON-WHITTELL RESEARCH RANCH

The Appleton-Whittell Research Ranch encompasses roughly 8,000 acres of semi-arid grassland in southeastern Arizona and preserves one of the largest intact grasslands of its kind. In addition to vast stretches of grassland, the ranch also includes habitats of oak savanna and oak woodlands, along with several small creeks and the associated water-loving riparian habitat.

As the dominant ecosystem, the grasslands are comprised of more than 100 species of grasses, including fluffgrass, plains bristlegrass, wolftail, sprucetop grama, and green sprangletop. Collectively, these grasses provide a diverse range of cover and fed for an equally wide range of animals. Half a dozen types of sparrows along with eastern blue birds, western meadowlarks, northern harriers, and burrowing owls are common to the grasslands, as are badger, fox, rabbit, hooded skunk, and herds of Sonoran pronghorn. A plethora of insects also inhabit the grasslands and are preyed upon by nearly two dozen resident bat species.

Animals like Coue's white-tailed deer, Gould's turkey, Montezuma quail, and white-nosed coatis prefer a habitat of mixed grassland and oak forest, which is formally classified as oak savanna. Both the oak savanna and oak woodland support another assemblage of birds and mammals including squirrels, ring-tailed cats, nuthatches, owls, and wood peckers, all of which prefer the vegetative structure of woodland forest over open grasslands.

The Appleton-Whittell Research Ranch also protects areas of riparian habitat, which are most commonly found where water collects in low-laying canyons and washes. Cottonwood and willow tend to dominate the canopy, while the understory is filled with shrubbery and herbaceous perennials. The combination of water and shade along with the structural diversity of the riparian plant community makes this habitat vital to the area's wildlife. A particularly colorful bird population including blue grosbeaks, hooded orioles, yellow warblers, orange crowned warblers, and Anna's hummingbirds reside in the streamside habitat. The ranch's turtle and amphibian populations rely exclusively on the riparian zone, while other wildlife species periodically move in and out as dictated by their need for water.

The ranch not only protects this biologically diverse environment but also aims to support scientific research projects that will enhance the depth and breadth of knowledge regarding conservation biology and ecology. Dozens of scientists from various agencies and universities are currently researching topics ranging from bird dispersion and breeding to groundwater depth and soil composition, all in an effort to better understand the needs of this grassland ecosystem. These research projects have yielded dozens of publications that disseminate data-driven information to others who are working to restore and protect natural places both in the United States and abroad.

While the National Audubon Society has owned the ranch for more than 30 years, it is cooperatively managed by the National Audubon Society, the U.S. Forest Service, the Bureau of Land Management, the Nature Conservancy, and the Research Ranch Foundation. Aside from attaining the multifaceted goals of conservation, research, and public education, the management team is specifically concerned with protecting the ranch from a number of threats. Fire—or the lack thereof—has altered some of the historic grassland by allowing shrubs and woody thickets to encroach upon the open grassland. Biologists are now working to implement a series of controlled burns that would keep the grasslands open while also returning important nutrients back into the soil.

Perhaps the most unique obstacle facing wildlife conservation efforts in this region arises from the construction of the border fence between the United States and Mexico. The fence is design to reduce the flow of illegal immigrants across the border but is also impassable to Coue's deer, jaguars, pronghorn, mule deer, and white-nosed coatis, among other species, which do not recognize international restrictions but instead rely on a continuous ecosystem by which to carry out their natural life cycles.

Further Reading

Bock, Carl E., and Jane H. Bock. *The View from Bald Hill: Thirty Years in an Arizona Grassland.* Berkeley: University of California Press, 2000.

ARAVAIPA CANYON

Aravaipa Canyon holds within its canyon walls a wealth of biological diversity, including the country's most pristine desert streams and native fish communities. The canyon, which is located between the Galiuro and Santa Teresa Mountains of southeastern Arizona, forms a rugged 11-mile-long fissure bounded by steep canyon walls. Although the main feature of the area is Aravaipa Canyon, nine other canyons branch off the Aravaipa Canyon, and a large number of these ravines contain streams that flow at various times of the year. These streams run the length of their respective canyons before draining into Aravaipa Canyon and Aravaipa Creek. Aravaipa Creek eventually joins the San Pedro River, which is one of only two rivers that flow northward from Mexico into the United States. In the otherwise dry and arid American Southwest, these water features support a unique array of plants and animals. The Aravaipa region is home to five major plant communities, including Sonoran desert scrub, desert grassland, interior chaparral, evergreen woodlands, and riparian forest. Of these plant communities, the riparian forests rely most heavily on stream flow and support the highest levels of animal biodiversity in the region. In total, the Aravaipa region is home to 46 mammal species, more than 200 types of birds, 46 species of reptiles, and over half a dozen species of amphibians.

The riparian forest of Aravaipa Canyon and its associated corridors are divided into three distinct forest types: forestlands dominated by cottonwood and willow, mesquite bosques, and the alder/walnut/hackberry forestlands. These riparian ecosystems skirt the area's stream banks, thus providing a dense canopy of shade that keeps water temperatures low and reduces evaporation. A total of seven native desert fish species, including the federally threatened loach minnow and spikedace, live in Aravaipa Creek. Leopard frogs, garter snakes, great blue herons, and black hawks are also found in direct association with the canyon's aquatic ecosystem. Numerous animals including mountain lion, bighorn sheep, javelina, deer, and coyote frequent the creek for a drink of water before returning to the outlying scrublands and grasslands.

Even Aravaipa Canyon's walls, which jut upward of 1,000 feet from the canyon floor, are dotted with pockets of vegetation. Plants indicative of interior chaparral including shrub live oak, point-leaf manzanita, alligator juniper, and Arizona cypress are commonly found in this drier, rugged terrain. Tall treelike saguaro cacti can also be seen growing amid the canyon walls. The cliffs eventually discontinue their vertical rise and level out to a region called the tablelands. Contrary to the name, the tablelands are anything but flat. Large areas of exposed bedrock and frequent earthen fissures of various depths make this terrain extremely rugged. The plant life here is best classified as Chihuahuan desert

Aravaipa Canyon. (Courtesy of Michael Wifall)

scrub intermixed with desert grasslands. Yucca, jojoba, sotol, beargrass, creosote bush, palo verde, brittlebush, and triangle-leaf bursage along with a number of native grasses thrive in this desert biome. While shade and water are a scarcity atop the tablelands, the arid climate supports a plethora of insects, rodents, birds of prey, bats, lizards, and snakes.

The canyon's rich biodiversity along with its pristine water resources are protected by both the Nature Conservancy and the Bureau of Land Management (BLM). Collectively, these two agencies manage roughly 42,000 acres of desert wilderness in and around Aravaipa Canyon. The management goals are numerous, but maintaining public access, protecting both water quality and quantity, and species monitoring are priorities. Special attention is also focused on keeping the creek system free of invasive and nonnative fish species. Populations of several dozen species of concern—including the Sonoran desert tortoise, roundtail chub, Allen's big-eared bat, and western yellow-billed cuckoo—are all closely monitored in an effort to ensure their continued survival. One of the major concerns facing the conservancy and BLM as well as adjacent private landholders is the illegal use of off-road vehicles. A number of illegal roadways have been cut by motorcycles and ATVs, which lead to erosion and the spread of invasive plant species. Research also indicates that unpaved roadways can alter animal behavior, energy expenditure, and reproductive success. Monitoring the activities of the public, posting signage, and restoring illegal roadways are all dubious tasks in such rugged terrain but necessary for the continued protection of this uniquely diverse desert ecosystem.

Further Reading

Childs, Craig. *The Secret Knowledge of Water: Discovering the Essence of the American Desert*. Seattle, WA: Sasquatch Books, 2000.

BUCKELEW FAMILY LANDS

What began in 1954 as a 505-acre family farm has now transitioned into a 500-acre preserve that not only protects a key grassland corridor in southern Arizona but also safeguards the Buckelew family farm from development. In 2006, the Arizona Open Land Trust brokered a deal by which Pima County acquired both the Buckelew family property as well as 2,170 additional acres of state and federal land leases and irrigation rights. Notably, the $5 million purchase was made possible by a citizen's approved bond measure. The purchase by Pima County is only one of many such acquisitions in and around the Altar Valley that aim to conserve and restore the final remnants of southern Arizona's native grasslands.

The Buckelew farm contains a mixture of plant communities, some of which are naturally occurring while others are the result of agricultural endeavors. Those areas under cultivation have been planted to various crops such as corn and pumpkins. Other areas of the farm have been heavily grazed and are set to undergo restoration from invasive Bermuda grass and lovegrass to native perennial bunchgrasses. Other areas of the farm have been only lightly grazed or have been uncultivated in recent years and now consist of grassland intermixed with woody shrubs, including desert broom, snakeweed, chain fruit cholla, and velvet mesquite. The property also contains a small pocket of riparian habitat that has been formed via the runoff from irrigation water and is dominated by mature mesquite trees with an understory of diverse shrubs, grasses, and herbs. Whitethorn, cat-claw, and desert hackberry are also common in the desert wash community which is formally called Brawley Wash. Desert washes are characterized by seasonal flash flooding events during which rain water flushes the through low-laying channels.

Collectively, the farm's plant communities support a plethora of songbirds, raptors, bats, snakes, and lizards. The property also supports several species of plants and animals including the Tucson shovel-nosed snake, cactus ferruginous pygmy owl, western yellow bat, desert tortoise, and pima pineapple cactus, all which have been classified as priority vulnerable species by Pima County's Sonoran Desert Conservation Plan.

Although the Buckelew land will remain a working farm, the purchase by Pima County essentially protects the land from being rezoned, subdivided, and fragmented by housing and other urban developments. The purchase agreement also requires that farming practices be conducted in a manner that is conducive to habitat and wildlife preservation. Such practices include controlling the spread of invasive species, developing a permanent source of water for wildlife, restoring native grasslands, and planting vegetation that will attract and support both resident and migratory animal populations. Management plans also include the reintroduction of the western burrowing owl.

The Buckelew property is one of many key land parcels that are being pieced together so that the Altar Valley is occupied by a continuous swath of protected land. This corridor is critical to the migration of grassland species such as pronghorn, which move in herds from one grass-lined valley to the next. Uninterrupted grassland ecosystems also help to link the adjacent mountain ranges, thus giving plant and animal species an extended terrain over which to forage, migrate, and populate.

The Altar Valley is only one small part of a grassland ecosystem that stretches from southwestern New Mexico to southern Arizona and then on to northern Mexico. Collectively known as the Apache Highlands Ecoregion, the region has undergone dramatic changes that coincide with human settlement. The spread of nonnative species, fire suppression, urban development, and habitat fragmentation are included among the many factors that jeopardize the region's biodiversity. The threat is compounded by the reality that the majority of native grasslands within the southwestern United States occur on either private or state lands and thus receive no legal protection. Several agencies, including the Arizona Open Land Trust, U.S. Fish and Wildlife Service, Bureau of Land Management, Sierra Club, as well as numerous county agencies, are working to preserve and restore what is left of southern Arizona's open grasslands.

Further Reading

"Arizona's Grasslands." http://azconservation.org/projects/grasslands/.

Phillips, Steven J., and Patricia Wentworth Comus, eds. *A Natural History of the Sonoran Desert*. Berkeley: University of California Press, 1999.

HASSAYAMPA RIVER PRESERVE

From an Apache word meaning "river that runs upside down," the Hassayampa is one of the country's few subterranean rivers. For most of its 100-mile course, the Hassayampa flows underground from its headwaters in the Northern Bradshaw Mountains to where it drains into the Gila River. Along this course, there are only three locations totaling roughly 14 miles at which the Hassayampa breaks the surface, thus creating a rich biological oasis in the midst of an otherwise arid environment.

The Hassayampa River Preserve is one such oasis; the original parcel was purchased by the Nature Conservancy in 1986 and then expanded in 2004. The preserve now encompasses 660 acres of riparian habitat, mesquite bosques, marshlands, and outlying desert wash communities. Although each vegetative community is home to a unique assemblage of plants and animals, the riparian forest habitat is, in many respects, the feature attraction for wildlife as well as human visitors.

A mix of trees dominated by large Fremont cottonwood and Gooding's willow form the majority of the riparian's canopy. The leafy canopy formed by these trees not only provides protection from predators but also protects its inhabitants from the scorching heat of the day as well as the near-freezing evening temperatures. The canopy's lush vegetation is supplemented by an understory of shrubs, herbs, wildflowers, and grasses, all of which attract a variety of grubs and insects, which in turn sustain birds, rodents, reptiles, frogs, and bats.

Hassayampa River Preserve. (Courtesy of Eric Vondy)

The Hassayampa River Preserve is home to 280 species of birds and is a famous location among birders who visit in hopes of seeing such rarities as the zone-tailed hawk, Mississippi kite, yellow-billed cuckoo, Tennessee warbler, and northern water thrush. The preserve also attracts seven species of hummingbirds, including the jewel-colored Costa's hummingbird and broad-billed hummingbird. The preserve also contains a small spring-fed pond that is frequented by green herons, American bitterns, white-faced ibis, cinnamon teals, bufflehead, hooded mergansers, and pied-billed grebes.

Apart from the riparian forest and pond marshlands, the preserve also contains typical desert vegetation consisting of Hohokam agave, cow's tongue prickly pear, velvet mesquite, blue palo verde, gray thorn, and whitethorn acacia. Even the most desiccated reaches of the preserve are inhabited by birds such as roadrunners, quail, raptors, and sparrows. Other larger animals such as javelina, bobcat, ring-tailed cat, mountain lion, and mule deer also find protection within the boundaries of the preserve.

The Hassayampa River Preserve is a critical piece of land because it protects the water resources that are fundamental to supporting the region's unique ecosystems and biodiversity. Researchers estimate that the desert riparian forest habitat is one of the most endangered habitats in the United States due in part to increased need for agricultural and municipal water. Scientists also estimate that up to 80 percent of Arizona's wildlife depends on the riparian habitat at some point during its life cycle. The Nature Conservancy, therefore, manages the preserve with utmost attention to water quality and quantity. The conservancy also supports an active events calendar designed to engage the public in activities ranging from bird banding to mineralology.

Further Reading

Baker, Malchus B. Jr., Peter F. Folliott, Leonard F. DeBano, and Daniel G. Neary, eds. *Riparian Areas of the Southwestern United States: Hydrology, Ecology, and Management.* Boca Raton, FL: CRC Press, 2004.

Kingsford, Richard, ed. *Ecology of Desert Rivers.* New York: Cambridge University Press, 2006.

KOFA NATIONAL WILDLIFE REFUGE

What began in 1936 as a statewide campaign initiated by the Boy Scouts of Arizona to save the bighorn sheep led to the establishment of Kofa National Wildlife Refuge in 1939. The refuge now encompasses 665,400 acres of southeastern Arizona and preserves vast tracts of fragile desert habitat. The region's landscape is dominated by the rugged Kofa and Castle Dome Mountains, which abruptly puncture the otherwise flat desert plain with their steep slopes and deep canyons.

One of these canyons—Palm Canyon—is home to several rare plant species, including Arizona's only native palm. Located in the west end of the Kofa range, Palm Canyon is tucked between two near-vertical rock walls, which creates a microclimate of deep shade, moisture, and vegetation. The palms most likely represent a remnant ecosystem that dominated the region during the last ice age when Arizona was climatically cooler and wetter. The other theory attributes the palm grove to the work of birds and mammals spreading seeds from afar. Regardless, the palms are only one of several unique plant species that inhabit the canyon. Palo verde, ironwood, and rare Kofa Mountain barberry also grow in the canyon and, with the palms, offer a diverse array of vegetative cover for a number of birds and mammals. Canyon wrens, phainopepla, swallows, gnatcatchers, flycatchers, brown towhees, and thrashers are all common inhabitants of Palm Canyon.

A total of 185 birds occupy the refuge during various seasons; some—like the loggerhead shrike, Costa's hummingbird, great horned owl, white-winged dove, and golden eagle—breed and nest within the refuge, while others use the reserve as wintering grounds or as a migratory rest stop. Kofa is also home to an impressive number of small mammals such as bats, rodents, and rabbits, most of which go unseen by daytime visitors. As is characteristic of desert wildlife, many of Kofa's inhabitants are nocturnal, avoiding the scorching daytime heat by restricting activities to the dark of night. More than a dozen species of bats spend the day tucked away in old mining shafts, small caves, and rocky fissures; many more animals, including Merriam's kangaroo rat, the southern grasshopper mouse, Bailey's pocket mouse, the cactus mouse, the white-throated wood rat, and the desert tortoise, all utilize underground burrows for thermal protection. Underground burrows also provide protection to the region's many snake and toad populations.

For close to 70 years, the refuge, which is managed by the U.S. Fish and Wildlife Service (USFWS), has provided critical habitat for bighorn sheep. Until recently, the Kofa

Palm Canyon in the Kofa National Wildlife Refuge. (Courtesy of Curtis R. Campbell)

sheep herds have been stable enough to translocate selected individuals so that herds could be reestablished in Texas, Colorado, and New Mexico, as well as other locales within Arizona. Such translocation projects have ceased because of significant decreases in bighorn population. Biologists speculate that population declines may be the result of several compounding factors including prolonged drought, disease, and predation by mountain lions. Management activities are now focused on conducting population surveys, radio tagging, tracking female sheep, and monitoring mountain lion activity. The USFWS is also proposing to cull individual mountain lions that repetitively feed on mountain sheep. Scientists project that eliminating mountain lions will increase the survival rates of the mountain sheep, thus allowing their populations to rebound.

As it pertains to sheep management, research, and funding, the USFWS has been aided by a number of entities including the Arizona Game and Fish Department, the Arizona Desert Bighorn Sheep Society, the Foundation for North American Wild Sheep, and the Yuma Valley Rod and Gun Club.

The issues revolving around mountain lions and the management of their populations are a challenge being faced by the Kofa refuge and a handful of other refuges. Many environmental groups have challenged the legality of such hunts and have, on occasion, found support for their case in the federal court system. In addition to its efforts to manage the predatory cat population, the USFWS works to control the spread of invasive species, manage wildfires, survey wildlife populations, and restrict the use of off-road vehicles.

Further Reading

Van Devender, Thomas R. *The Sonoran Desert Tortoise: Natural History, Biology and Conservation*. Tucson: University of Arizona Press, 2006.

Whitford, Walter G. *Ecology of Desert Systems*. San Diego, CA: Academic Press, 2002.

SIERRA VISTA WASTEWATER WETLANDS

Located in the southernmost reaches of Arizona, Sierra Vista is a town working to balance population growth and water demands. True to most of the American Southwest, the Sierra Vista region is an arid landscape averaging a mere 12 inches of rainfall per year. With limited rainfall and only one major river (the San Pedro) running through the area, Sierra Vista must make the most of its water resources. City government and local organizations have, over the years, worked diligently to educate the public regarding water usage and conservation and have implemented various programs that reward savvy water usage. Recent population growth has, however, necessitated additional widespread water conservation and reclamation measures.

City officials had long recognized that a significant portion of the city's water was literally being flushed down the drain and into the city's sewage treatment facility. A large percentage of this water was then being lost to evaporation during the course of treatment. In an effort to reclaim this water while simultaneously responding to population growth and a subsequent increase in water demand, the city of Sierra Vista enrolled in a pilot project that aimed to utilize manmade wetlands as a natural filtration system by which to detoxify municipal sewage and recharge groundwater systems. The project, which was carried out via a working partnership between the city of Sierra Vista, the Bureau of Reclamation, the U.S. Geological Survey, and the Arizona Department of Environmental Quality, was closely monitored over two years. By the end of the two years, scientists had measured significant reductions in ammonium nitrogen, nitrate nitrogen, and inorganic nitrogen, all of which are benchmarks of water pollution and by-products of human waste management systems. The pilot wetlands, which consisted of two three-and-a-half-acre plots also provided new habitat for birds. A total of 49 bird species were recorded feeding, resting, breeding, or nesting within the newly constructed marshlands.

The success of the initial project led to the expansion of the wetlands system and water treatment facility into what is now called the Environmental Operations Park (EOP). The EOP is, in many respects, a typical municipal facility complete with industrial infrastructure and equipment, but the area also teems with wildlife that inhabits the facility's 50 acres of wetlands. Moreover, the EOP is now a favorite among bird-watchers who utilize the facility's 1,800-square-foot wildlife viewing platform that overlooks a dense matrix of bulrush, duckweed, three-square bulrush, and iris. A variety of waterfowl and shorebirds can be accounted for in and among the tall reeds, including ruddy ducks, mallards, northern shovelers, green-wing teals, dowitchers, herring gulls, and western grebes. Say's phoebe, yellow-headed blackbirds, marsh wrens, horned larks, yellow-rumped warblers, and rock wrens are just a few of several dozen species of songbirds that now inhabit the manmade ecosystem. The wetlands provide critical resources for resident bird species as well as hundreds of migratory birds that rest and refuel at the EOP before continuing on their way.

While the rich diversity of avian life is a major draw for visitors, the newly formed habitat is also frequented by deer, javelina, and bobcat. Moreover, the resources provided to wildlife are secondary to the main goal of recapturing water. Upon entering the facility, the water passes across several large screens that eliminate large particles and trash before flowing to several settling ponds, where bacteria and natural sunlight promote decomposition of organic wastes. Eventually, the water is flushed into the wetlands, where aquatic vegetation takes up excessive nitrogen-based nutrients. The water is then allowed to slowly percolate through the soil and bedrock. This natural subterranean filter of soil, rock, and microbes performs the final purification and returns the water to the underlying aquifer, thereby recharging what was previously withdrawn. City officials estimate that the wetlands system recaptures about 2,000 acre-feet of effluent or fouled water on an annual basis, thus helping to ensure some measure of sustainability in the face of dramatic population growth. A recent population census conducted by the Center for Economic Research at Cochise College reported that Sierra Vista's population increased by 18 percent from 2000 to 2007. Such growth carries with it widespread consequences in regard to water usage, which is further underscored by the natural scarcity of water amid the desert landscape of southern Arizona.

Further Reading
De Villiers, Marq. *Water: The Fate of Our Most Precious Resource.* New York: First Mariner Books, 2001.

CALIFORNIA

No state epitomizes the American West quite like the state of California. As a landscape of fertile valleys, mountainous peaks, mineral-rich soils, and bountiful seas, California beckoned to masses of early settlers and immigrants. Today, California supports the eighth largest economy in the world and is the nation's most densely populated state. The combination of these two facts has had a tremendous effect on California's ecological biodiversity. Despite its economic capacity, the state has not been immune to the financial crisis that began in 2008. As a result, the state's legislative body outlined a set of extensive budget cuts which would force the closure of some of the state's natural places thus leaving these areas open to vandalism, poaching, and overall ecological degradation. California's remarkable biodiversity is largely attributed to its north-south orientation, which lends itself to much climatic variation across latitudes. The northern reaches of the state are typified by coniferous forest and timber production. One of the most notable forest ecosystems of this region are the redwood forests, which contain earth's largest and tallest trees. Northern California also marks a transitional area between the southern end of the Cascade Mountains and the northernmost peaks of the Sierra Nevada. Both of these mountain ranges run in a roughly north-south direction and therefore greatly impact the state's climate. Moisture-laden clouds coming off the Pacific Ocean typically deposit their rain somewhere between the Pacific coastline and the western slope of the Cascades and Sierra Nevada, thus leaving the eastern slope relatively dry. The result (called the rain-shadow effect) characterizes almost the entire length of the state, placing arid grasslands and deserts in the eastern half of the state and milder climates in the western half. The state's ecosystems continue to shift from the northern forest lands into the fertile prairie lands and agricultural fields of the Central Valley. The valley, which spans nearly 400 miles and sits in a north-south orientation, is also bordered on all four sides by mountain ranges: the Cascades to the north, the Tehachapi Mountains to the south, the Sierra Nevada in the east, and the Coast ranges in the west. As a result of this geography, the Central Valley receives a phenomenal amount of water from the ranges' annual snowpack and subsequent streams and rivers. The region's various watersheds eventually drain into two main rivers—the Sacramento and San Joaquin—both of which support the area's agricultural interests as well as a booming population. Researchers estimate that the valley is California's most rapidly growing region, with a current population of more than 6.5 million people and some of the state's poorest air quality.

The southwestern portion of California is also heavily populated via the cities of Los Angeles and San Diego and their associated sprawl. The ecology of the region is determined by a mild Mediterranean climate, which is dominated by the chaparral biome. Chaparral is one of the world's rarest plant communities and, in the case of southern California, is plagued by development, urban sprawl, and fire suppression. Finally, the southeast portion of the state is home to the infamous Death Valley, a seemingly desolate place that is surprisingly alive with highly specialized flora and fauna and hidden water.

Increased demands for land and water are having a profound effect on the stability of California's ecosystems and have thus drawn the attention of numerous conservation groups in addition to policymakers, economic analysts, human rights organizations, public and private universities, and private landholders. No single group has been awarded top honors when it comes to conservation of California's natural places. Efforts have instead been highly collaborative and, in many cases, costly in both time and money due to frequent legal battles.

BALLONA WETLANDS

Several thousand years ago, the Los Angeles River deposited large amounts of sand, silt, and clay in the area that is now the Ballona Wetlands. Originally, this habitat stretched for 2,000 acres but has since been reduced to 190 acres as a result of urban encroachment from Marina del Rey, Venice, and West Los Angeles. These three cities form the immediate boundaries of the wetlands to the north, east, and south, while the Pacific Ocean completes the square on the western border.

In addition to tidal ebb and flow, fresh water runs into the marshes via Ballona Creek. Together, the marine and freshwater sources support five distinctive habitats: salt marsh, freshwater marsh, riparian corridor, bluffs, and dunes. All five systems are currently undergoing extensive restoration that is overseen by the Ballona Wetlands Foundation.

The salt marsh is defined by the daily rise and fall of the tides, which constantly cycles water, nutrients, wastes, and minerals in and out of the wetlands. A halophyte—or salt-loving plant—called pickleweed dominates the saline soils of this terrain. Pickleweed, in turn, provides habitat for Belding's savannah sparrow, which is listed as an endangered species with the state of California (as opposed to being federally listed). Additional plant species are also being restored in an effort to bring back the once-native Californian least tern and the clapper rail.

Perhaps one of the greatest restoration obstacles will come with the repair and subsequent monitoring of the freshwater marsh, both of which will require large investments of time, money, and technology. As it currently stands, during the rainy season, the marsh receives large amounts of runoff from driveways, gutters, freeways, and city sidewalks. As water drains from these sources, it carries to the wetlands a variety of pollutants, including oil, fertilizers, trash, and pet waste. The pollutants of past generations will, over time, be degraded by microbial activity, exposure to sunlight, and other natural processes. Future run-off, however, will be run through a filtration facility before being pumped back into the wetlands.

Adjacent to the freshwater wetlands is the riparian corridor. Riparian habitat is characterized by the presence of fresh water and plant communities that include willow, poplar, aspen, and cottonwood. Unlike the soils of a wetland, which are soft and relatively unstable, the substrate in riparian habitats is firmer and therefore supports large trees. These trees are home to a variety of birds, including both long- and short-eared owls, belted kingfishers, hermit thrushes, and mourning doves.

An entirely different set of birds utilize the sandy dunes of Ballona. The dunes mark the gateway to the Pacific and are home to a variety of shorebirds, including the snowy and semipalmated plovers, long-billed dowitcher, western sandpiper, and whimbrel. Portions of these dunes are entirely devoid of vegetation and are free to shift with the wind, while other parts are inhabited by prostrate coastal strand plant communities of sand verbena and dune buckwheat. The presence of dune buckwheat is critical to the endangered El Segundo blue butterfly.

The highest points within the Ballona Wetlands are called the bluffs. These hills, which are relatively small (50 to 75 meters high) yet steeply sloped, sit along the southern border of Ballona and overlook the four other habitats. A variety of low shrubs, bunch grasses, burrowing owls, raptors, western and side-blotched lizards, and rodents are native to the bluffs. Two invasive species also inhabit the bluff ecosystem: feral cats and the red fox. Both have had a profound impact on the reptiles and small mammals, which, in turn, are the primary food source for the bluffs raptors.

Collectively, the five habitats sustain a diverse assortment of flora and fauna, yet special attention is now being paid to five specific bird species that reside in or migrate through the Ballona wetlands: the northern pintail, greater scaup, common tern, loggerhead shrike, and grasshopper sparrow. A study conducted by the Audubon Society deemed these five species among the top 10 common birds now in decline.

Continued restoration and educational outreach conducted by the Ballona Wetlands Foundation may offer reprieve for these waning bird populations, if not for the rest of the plants and animals that inhabit this dynamic ecosystem.

Further Reading

Ballona Wetlands Land Trust. http://www.ballona.org.

Zedler, Joy B. *Handbook for Restoring Tidal Wetlands*. Boca Raton, FL: CRC Press, 2001.

CATALINA ISLAND

Catalina Island lays 22 miles offshore of the densely populated coast of southern California. The island measures 22 miles in length and 8 miles at its widest and is home to around 3,600 people. Most of its population is centered in two small towns, thereby leaving most of the island open to an impressive number of plants, insects, and both terrestrial and marine animals. The natural places of Catalina Island total approximately 88 percent of the island and are managed by the Catalina Conservancy.

The conservancy was established in 1972 by members of the Wrigley and Offield families, who deeded 42,135 acres of the island to the conservancy. The purpose of the transaction was to ensure that the island's ecosystems would remain intact for future generations. As is true of many islands, Catalina is home to a number of endemic species, which by definition are found nowhere else in the world. Six plants and 16 animals are endemic to the island. Among them are the Beechey ground squirrel, Santa Catalina Island fox, Avalon hairstreak butterfly, Catalina shield-back cricket, Santa Catalina Island shrew, along with subspecies of Berwick's wren and the California quail. These animals, along with the rest of the island's fauna, gain sustenance from over 400 species of native plants. (Native meaning that the plants were not transported to the island by humans.) Some of these native plant species are exceedingly rare; for example, the Catalina mahogany tree is not only endemic to the island but is also federally listed as endangered. The seven individual mahogany trees tucked away in Wild Boar Gully are monitored an annual basis and protected within a fenced enclosure.

Wild Boar Gully is one of 32 areas on the island that are designated as a significant ecological area (SEA). SEAs are classified by several means but in general encompass land where rare and endangered species or habitats are found. Places like the Orizaba Mountains, Avalon Canyon, the west end, and Gallagher's Canyon are just a few of Catalina's SEAs, which, in turn, protect groves of ironwood trees, oak woodlands, maritime cactus scrub, and chaparral plant communities.

Conservation of these plant communities is of high priority to the Catalina Conservancy, which not only monitors and restores the vegetation but also runs the John H. Ackerman Native Plant Nursery. The nursery, which was established in the late 1980s, propagates native species via seed collection and cuttings. The seedlings are then reared in a controlled environment and will eventually be planted as part of the island's many vegetative restoration projects.

In addition to the long list of native plants, another 180 plant species were brought in by settlers and tourists; while not necessarily invasive, introduced species are closely monitored by the conservancy to prevent their spread. A handful of nonnative mammals also persist on the island; the American bison (left behind after the filming of a movie), mule deer, and black-buck antelope are among the large herbivores that pose a constant threat to rare plant communities and are thus monitored and kept in check by the conservancy. Native animals include several species of bats, snakes, and lizards in addition to the Pacific tree frog, American bald eagle, Allen's hummingbird, California sea lions, and elephant seals. Of the island's mammals, the Catalina Island fox is arguably the most notable; not only is it endemic but it is also the island's largest native mammal. The fox is also at the center of intensive conservation effort. In the early 1990s Catalina's fox population numbered around 1,300. An outbreak of canine distemper (introduced via a domesticated pet) reduced the population to 100 by 1999. The fox was saved from extinction by a collaborative partnership between the conservancy and the Institute for Wildlife Studies. Their dynamic plan included captive breeding programs in conjunction with vaccinations against distemper. This strategy combined with continual monitoring has helped to increase the population to around 400.

The plight of the Catalina fox is one of several ecological emergencies the conservancy must respond to. Fire is another frequently human-induced catastrophe: Between 1999 and 2007 Catalina experienced three significant fires that jeopardized and, in some cases, destroyed thousands of acres of grassland, chaparral, coastal sage scrub, and oak woodland. In many cases, the denuded land sprouts anew with fresh plant communities. The conservancy then protects the new growth from hungry deer and replants those areas that are slow to rebound.

In addition to safeguarding the island's flora and fauna, the Catalina Conservancy supports a variety of scientific research and coordinates educational programs, outings, and workshops for children and adults. Volunteer vacations, eco-tours, and summer internships are also available through the conservancy. Special permits are needed for certain camping, hiking, and biking activities.

Further Reading

Catalina Conservancy. http://www.catalinaconservancy.org/.

Pedersen, Jeannine L. *Images of America: Catalina Island*. San Francisco, CA: Arcadia, 2004.

COSUMNES RIVER PRESERVE

As the last undammed river flowing from the western slope of the central Sierra Nevada, the Cosumnes River is still allowed to run its natural course. From its mountainous origin, the Cosumnes meanders some 80 miles through the Central Valley of California before joining the Mokelumne River. Unlike its dammed counterparts, the Cosumnes is allowed to undergo natural flooding cycles that occur primarily as a result of rainfall as opposed to winter snowmelt. Winter flooding in succession with hot dry summers create an ever-fluctuating environment that is as biologically rich as it is sensitive.

The preserve encompasses about 40,000 acres of land containing 442 species of plants, 247 species of birds, 30 species of mammals, and another dozen or so species of amphibians and reptiles. Such staggering biodiversity is organized amid the region's distinct plant communities. For example, the valley foothill riparian community hosts an assemblage of Fremont cottonwood, elderberry, wild grape, willow, and box elder. These water-loving trees and shrubs are situated along the river's bank and other low-lying areas and provide key habitat for songbirds, owls, mountain lions, frogs, and small mammals. The valley elderberry longhorn beetle, which is federally listed as a threatened species, also lives in the preserve's riparian zones.

The preserve's other plant communities include valley oak woodland, blue oak woodland, perennial grasslands, annual grasslands, and fresh emergent wetlands. American dogwood, interior live oak, and white alder along with the valley oak and blue oak are among the additional tree species found within the preserve. Herbs like fennel, water parsley, wild licorice, and field mint grow among annual and perennial grasses. Wild rose, buttercup, California poppy, yarrow, and clover also flourish. Such a dynamic collection of flowers, grasses, herbs, trees, and shrubs provide a wide range of habitat for other animals, including a plethora of insects, which are the dietary mainstay of the preserve's seven species of bats along with the western spade-foot toad, pacific tree frog, alligator lizard, California tiger salamander, and countless species of birds, fish, and small rodents. In turn, these animals are preyed upon by large raptors such as the osprey, bald eagle, red-tailed hawk, northern harrier, and western screech owl. Western rattlesnakes, giant garter snakes, gray fox, red fox, bobcat, mountain lion, and badger are just a few of the high-ranking predators living in the preserve.

Riparian forest along the Cosumnes River. (Courtesy of John N. Schmidt)

The stability of the preserve's complex ecosystems and subsequent food web is threatened by a number of factors such as population growth, declines in water quality and quantity, and invasive species. The Central Valley is one of California's most rapidly developing areas and in recent years has experienced population gains of almost 50 percent. Further estimates suggest that the city of Sacramento, which is just north of the Cosumnes River Preserve, will increase by 1.7 million by 2040. Demands for water have already lowered groundwater levels to such a degree that the river loses some of its water to underground water tables. Historically, however, groundwater used to seep into the river, thereby keeping the river replenished even after the long summers. Low water levels have fragmented the river in several places and severely jeopardized the fall run of Chinook salmon, which are now federally listed as endangered. Water quality has also been on the decline as pesticides and fertilizers enter the watershed from nearby agricultural fields. Other contaminates such as methylmercury are a result of old mining practices but persist in the environment and accumulate in animal tissues, which may then lead to a variety of diseases and decreases in reproductive success.

Mitigation of these threats as well as continued conservation of the Cosumnes River is a multiagency effort; the Nature Conservancy, Ducks Unlimited, the Bureau of Land Management, and the California Department of Fish and Game are a few of the agencies that, in combination with other nonprofit organizations, manage the Cosumnes River Preserve. These agencies cooperatively work toward assessing and monitoring the preserve as well as educating and introducing the public to its many wonders.

Further Reading

Carle, David. *Introduction to Water in California.* Los Angeles: University of California Press, 2004.

Naiman, Robert J., Henri Décamps, and Michael E. McClain. *Riparia: Ecology, Conservation, and Management of Streamside Communities.* San Diego, CA: Academic Press, 2005.

CRESTRIDGE ECOLOGICAL RESERVE

Located in southern California just outside of San Diego, the Crestridge Ecological Reserve is an ecological island of biodiversity virtually surrounded on every side by urban development. The property that now contains the reserve was originally part of an 1845 Mexican land grant that placed more than 48,000 acres of land into private ownership. The majority of the land was used for livestock grazing and other agricultural endeavors, yet, over time, most of the parcels were sold off and developed, leaving just a few thousand acres of open space. This open space was also set to be developed with the initial attempt being made in the early 1970s. By the 1990s, several citizen groups including the Crest Open Space Supporters, Endangered Habitats League, and the Back

Country Land Trust (BCLT) combined forces in an effort to protect the land from further development. The Nature Conservancy and the Wildlife Conservation Board also played a large role in the outright purchase of the land.

BCLT now manages the reserve with support from the California Department of Fish and Game. While both entities work together to maintain and monitor the reserve's flora and fauna, the BCLT is largely responsible for coordinating volunteer efforts and educational and community outreach programs. Numerous elementary school groups use the reserve for educational opportunities and service learning events, and some of the area's high school students conduct research projects. Student projects, which range from global positioning system mapping to controlled burn research, not only provide youngsters with the opportunity to experience field work but also benefits the reserve by adding information to its data base. The reserve is also frequented by the Urban Corps, a nonprofit organization that serves the youth of disadvantaged inner-city communities by enhancing their work skills while at the same time restoring and conserving the environment in which they live.

The natural habitats of the reserve are marked by nine plant communities: mature live oak woodland, southern mixed chaparral, scrub oak chaparral, coastal sage scrub, nonnative grassland, freshwater seep, coast live oak riparian woodland, eucalyptus woodland, and areas of disturbed vegetation. From water-loving willows and cottonwoods that grow streamside to the drought-resistant yucca plant, manzanita, and sumac that populate the canyons, the reserve's flora supply ample habitat to other life forms. A hundred or more invertebrates have been counted by the reserve's biologists; among these species are orange pallid band-wing grasshoppers, stink beetles, wide-headed cicadas, and an unidentified species of tarantula. Other invertebrates arrive as butterflies and moths; the Hermes copper and Quino checkerspot butterflies (both federally listed as endangered), along with the Pacific sara orangetip, and dainty sulphur can be found sipping the nectar of various blossoms. In all, there are 13 additional species that are listed as sensitive species within Crestridge's management plan. Most of these sensitive species are also listed as species of concern at the state or federal level. Other animals like the mountain lion and southern mule deer require room to roam, and, given the reserve's urban surroundings, nearby interstate highway, and a lack of migration corridors, these species face a very unique set of threats.

Invasive species, fire, erosion, and diminished water quality are also on the list of threats for Crestridge and its flora and fauna. Vandalism is an enormous problem for the reserve. Vandals have repeatedly destroyed fencing to gain access for off-road vehicles. In 2003, state officials discovered a dirt bike track complete with eight-foot-high berms for jumping. Such activities are both illegal and costly in many respects. Volunteers have since restored the area, and management efforts are focused on educating the public about the rules of the reserve along with increased enforcement of those laws.

Further Reading
Heath, Fred. *An Introduction to Southern California Butterflies*. Missoula, MT: Mountain Press, 2004.
Earth Discovery Institute. http://www.earthdiscovery.org/.

DEATH VALLEY NATIONAL PARK

L ocated in the southeastern corner of California, this ominously named park is famed for being one of the hottest, driest, and lowest (in elevation) ecosystems on earth. Despite outward appearances, the region has a long and ancient history of supporting life. Following the end of the last ice age, massive amounts of water filled the valley's great basins and subsequently supported large game and human habitation. Over the next several thousand years, four groups of Native Americans inhabited the region despite its progressive desertification. With an average rainfall of 2.33 inches per year, Death Valley now falls under the classic definition of a desert, which is any region that receives less then 10 inches of precipitation per year. Extreme temperatures, which may dip below freezing at night and soar to over 120° F in the day, further contribute to the desert's ruggedness.

Despite its climatic severity, Death Valley is home to more than 1,000 species of plants (23 of which are endemic—found nowhere else in the world). The valley's vegetation comes in many forms, from ephemeral wildflowers to ancient creosote bush and bristlecone pine, which may live for several thousand years. Other plant species such as the mesquite and piñon produce large quantities of nutrient-rich seeds that support birds and humans alike. Such diverse plant communities sustain approximately 400 species of highly adapted mammals, birds, reptiles, amphibians, and fish. For example, the kangaroo rat possesses a set

Creosote bushes, sand dunes, and the Amargosa Range. (Courtesy of James Paris)

of kidneys so highly evolved for water conservation that the animal never drinks. Within the plant kingdom, mesquite and creosote bush exhibit reduced leaf size, which minimizes water loss, while extensive taproots may descend 50 feet in order to access year-round groundwater. Multiple species of desert pupfish have evolved to thrive in water temperatures that reach 107° F and are several times saltier than seawater. Such specialization make desert communities especially susceptible to alterations, whether natural or manmade.

Prior to the mid 1800s, the valley was unknown to all but the Timbisha Shoshone Native Americans. However, in 1849, a group of pioneers headed for the California Gold Rush took a detour through the valley and discovered an abundance of ore and minerals. What followed was a boom of human settlement and environmental degradation as mining towns were constructed and prospectors set to work extracting copper, lead, silver, gold, salt, talc, and borax. Mining was briefly halted for just short of a year when President Hoover established the Death Valley National Monument in February 1933. With national monument status came the implementation of the National Park Service removal policy, which repetitively uprooted and relocated the Shoshone Indian camps. It was not until 1994 that the monument saw drastic change, when President Clinton signed the California Desert Protection Act on October 31, 1994. The act expanded the park by over one million acres and changed its status from a national monument to a national park. The act also authorized the secretary of the interior and native tribal leaders to begin the process of establishing a Timbisha Shoshone Reservation. Today, Death Valley National Park encompasses 3.4 million acres, 7,500 acres of which belong to the Timbisha Shoshone tribe, making it both the largest national park in the contiguous United States and the first national park to contain a reservation within its borders.

Despite protective legislation, mining continues in the valley albeit on an exceedingly limited basis; conservation efforts now revolve around water. The most immediate threat to the valley's water supply stems from Las Vegas's unprecedented expansion. The city is 100 miles from Death Valley and has, for several consecutive years, experienced the largest rates of population growth in the United States.

Further Reading

Aitchison, Stewart. *Death Valley National Park: Splendid Desolation*. Mariposa, CA: Sierra Press, 2002.

Lingenfelter, Richard E. *Death Valley and the Amargosa: A Land of Illusion*. Los Angeles: University of California Press, 1988.

Reisner, Marc. *Cadillac Desert*. New York: Penguin Books, 1993.

FARALLON WILDERNESS

Although legally incorporated into the city of San Francisco, the Farallon Islands are a place of remote isolation that bustles with crowds of seabirds and seals. The chain of small islands, which are located 27 miles west of the Golden Gate Bridge, are spread out over a distance of about five miles in a northwestern direction. The largest island measures a mere 310,406 square meters, and some of the islands are nothing more than a pile of jagged boulders. Pounding surf, harsh weather, poor soil, and scarce vegetation add to the seemingly inhospitable scenery.

Of the 18 species of native plants that do grow on the Farallons, Farallon weed is not only abundant but one of the most important since it is used as a nesting material by many of the islands' nesting bird populations. Farallon weed, clover, seaside daisy, sea rocket, and sand spurry are all examples of the low-profile to short shrubbery that is characteristic of the islands' flora. In contrast to most terrestrial ecosystems, life on the islands is supported mainly via photosynthetic plankton called phytoplankton. The phytoplankton are fed upon by larger plankton and krill, which are then food for small fishes and even whales. The fish are then preyed upon by numerous seals and sea lions, not to mention nearly a quarter of a million nesting seabirds and their hungry chicks.

The world's largest colony of ashy storm petrels nest here alongside tufted puffins, Cassin's auklets, Leach's storm petrels, back oyster catchers, and common murres. Thirteen species use the nooks, crannies, and rocky ledges of the Farallon Islands to nest and raise their young. In fact, the Farallon Islands support the largest colony of nesting seabirds south of Alaska and account for 30 percent of all of California's nesting seabirds. It has been estimated that, prior to the late 1840s, common murres alone numbered half a million. By 1881, their population had plummeted to 6,000 as a result of egging practices during which people collected murre eggs by the boatload and shipped them to San Francisco for sale and consumption. Egg harvesting began with harvesters walking through the colony, crushing as many eggs as possible. The birds responded by laying fresh eggs, which were then collected and sold. As many as 500,000 eggs could be harvested in a month, with the egging season spanning from May to July.

The plight of the common murre is by no means an isolated instance of human-induced population collapse. Both the northern fur seal and northern elephant seal were hunted to local extinction in the Farallons, yet, like the common murre, they have made a slow but steady rebound. Elephant seals, for example, were absent from the Farallons for nearly 100 years before they started to recolonize the area in 1959 and then began breeding on the islands in 1972. In the case of the northern fur seal, it was 150 years before the first pup was born on the islands in 1996.

Recovery of the flora and fauna of the Farallons first began in 1909, when President Theodore Roosevelt signed Executive Order 1043 and thus created the Farallon Island Reservation, which protected the northernmost islands. Protection was extended in 1969, when all of the islands were incorporated as a national wildlife refuge. Additional protection is afforded to the region's marine mammals under the Marine Mammal Protection Act of 1972, while the entire offshore marine ecosystem is included in the Gulf of the Farallones National Marine Sanctuary. The Farallon Wilderness is currently managed by the U.S. Fish and Wildlife Service in cooperation with the Point Reyes Bird Observatory. Together, the two agencies protect and monitor the islands' various animal populations by gathering data regarding seal and seabird reproduction, recording great white shark activity, controlling invasive plant species, assessing the impacts of climate change, and safeguarding the islands from environmental contaminants. To maintain an environment that is absent of human disturbance, the island is closed to the public; however, offshore educational boat trips are periodically conducted by commercial tour operators.

Further Reading

Casey, Susan. *The Devil's Teeth: A True Story of Obsession and Survival among America's Great White Sharks*. New York: Macmillan, 2005.

Karl, Herman A. *Beyond the Golden Gate: Oceanography, Geology, Biology, and Environmental Issues in the Gulf of the Farallones*. Menlo Park, CA: Diane, 2000.

FOOTE BOTANICAL PRESERVE

The Foote Botanical Preserve sits amid a landscape where monocultures reign and biodiversity is secondary. The preserve is located in northern California just east of the city of Napa in a region of intensive agriculture and world-renowned wine production. As decreed by the land's prior owners, Si and June Foote, the land is protected in perpetuity as a botanical preserve for native plant species. Their initial land donation was made in 1977 and simultaneously marked the founding of the Land Trust of Napa County, which now manages the preserve. The Foote family donated the second land parcel in 1995, thus incorporating 645 acres into the preserve. More than 370 plant species are arranged into numerous habitats ranging from seasonal wetlands to drought-hardy chaparral. There are also numerous places within the preserve where vegetation is sparse and rocky outcroppings abound. The soils to which these plants cling are relatively thin because of the underlying volcanic substrate. This means that spring rains quickly saturate the soils and then seep into the cracks of the underlying rocks, only to trickle out again into low-lying areas. Thirsty plants such as deer fern, western ladies tresses, marsh zigadenus, and Mexican lovegrass populate the wetlands. The botanical preserve also protects several riparian zones along the creeks that run through the property. Trees such as coast redwood, Oregon ash, American dogwood, and white alder provide dense shade and cover, which not only keeps water temperatures cool but provides ample resources for small birds and mammals as well as the preserve's frogs and aquatic insects.

For the most part, the Napa region is characteristically dry and arid, perfect for chaparral. Chaparral, which is often classified as the world's smallest terrestrial biome, consists of shrublike vegetation that is highly adapted to long, hot, dry summers and shallow, nutrient-poor soils. The chaparral of the Foote Botanical Preserve is dominated by chamise (also known as greasewood) in addition to five species of manzanita. Many of these same plant species are also well adapted to coping with fire, often resprouting from seemingly dead wood. Seeds of some chaparral species will actually lay dormant until a fire prompts them to germinate. Such is the case with the hollyleaf ceanothus; scientists estimate that, in its natural habitat, the seeds may remain viable for hundreds of years while waiting for combustion to occur. In the Foote Botanical Preserve, such events transpire every 30 to 80 years. Dozens of less-dominant species, including naked-stem buckwheat, red larkspur, pitcher sage, green coyote mint, chaparral currant, Napa dwarf flax, leather oak, and Solano morning glory, further define the Foote preserve's chaparral community.

Extensive botanical surveys have identified at least nine plant species that are listed as special status plants by the Californian Native Plant Society. Also growing on the preserve are an additional 10 species that are rare in Napa County. Assuring the viability and preservation of these botanical species is priority number one for the Land Trust of Napa. To attain this goal, the land trust focuses it efforts on the removal and control of invasive plant species, public education, trail maintenance, and provides support for botanical research. The Foote Botanical Preserve is open to the public, although visitors must either request permission beforehand or join one of the guided hikes.

Further Reading

Quinn, Ronald D., and Sterling C. Keeley. *Introduction to California Chaparral*. Los Angeles: University of California Press, 2006.

Sugihara, Neil G., Jan W. Van Wagtendonk, Kevin Eugene Shaffer, Joann Fites-Kaufman, and Andrea E. Thode, eds. *Fire in California's Ecosystems*. Los Angeles: University of California Press, 2006.

KERN RIVER PRESERVE

The Kern River Preserve is located in the central portion of California, about 57 miles northeast of the city of Bakersfield. The Kern River, after which the preserve is named, drains the southern portions of the Sierra Nevada of their winter snowmelt. What begins as two forks, aptly named the North Fork and the South Fork, merge into Lake Isabella before exiting as one larger river below the Isabella Dam and continuing toward Bakersfield. Although most of the water running through of the lower portions of the river (below the dam) is diverted to meet municipal and agricultural demands, much of the South Fork maintains its wealth of water. The Kern River Preserve, which is adjacent to the South Fork, supports California's largest lowland tract of riparian forest and protects more than 2,000 species of plants and dozens of other animals.

Prior to being purchased by the Nature Conservancy in 1979, the land had been part of a cattle ranching operation since the mid-1800s. While under conservancy management, several large vegetative restoration projects were completed, and, by the mid-1990s, the conservancy was looking for another agency to take ownership of the preserve. In November 1998, the 1,127-acre deed was passed from the Nature Conservancy to the National Audubon Society and its Californian chapter. Other milestones soon followed and included the addition of three significant land acquisitions; by 2006, the Audubon Society had expanded the preserve's boundaries to include 2,789 contiguous acres. The riparian forests that dominate this acreage are not particularly diverse in that the forest is made up of primarily two species of trees: Fremont cottonwood and red willow. Tucked between are stands of mule fat, stinging nettle, Yerba mansa, and other herbaceous plants. What these stands lack in diversity they make up for in productivity.

Their leaves, flowers, and bark support a number of caterpillars, grubs, and other insects, which then sustain a diverse population of birds, including the yellow-billed cuckoo and willow flycatcher, both of which are listed by the state as endangered. Another 40 avian species are listed as species of concern. In total, more than 240 species of birds representing nearly every major bird class are accounted for; songbirds, shorebirds, raptors, waterfowl, game birds, herons, condors, hummingbirds, woodpeckers, roadrunners, and parakeets fill the trees and grasslands with activity. Many will breed, nest, and raise their young here, while others will utilize the dense cover and plentiful resources to re-fuel during their annual migrations. Wetland areas full of cattails, horsetails, and other water-loving reeds flourish in the preserve. Even the most arid sections of the preserve support plant communities of rabbit brush, perennial grasses, saltbush, and Great Basin sage. Such contrasting landscapes accommodate great biological diversity, as seen by the vast number of snakes, turtles, frogs, lizards, toads, deer, coyote, beaver, kit fox, mountain lion, and black bear that inhabit the preserve.

Audubon California continues to pursue land purchases that will build upon the foundations already in place at the Kern River Preserve. Restoration of the preserve's plant communities is a constant process in light of the roughly 36 invasive plant species that tend to displace native varieties. Animals such as the American bullfrog, European starling, feral dog, feral cat, and white bass are a few of the introduced animal species that continually upset the natural balance of the river's ecosystems. Managing these threats as well as meeting the needs of the public is an ongoing task for Audubon California. The group runs a wide range of public outreach events ranging from reptile and amphibian celebration days to bird counting events and fundraising activities. The preserve is open from dawn to dusk every day, including holidays.

Further Reading

Audubon California. "Kern River Preserve." http://kern.audubon.org/krp.htm.
Erie, Steven P. *Beyond Chinatown: The Metropolitan Water District, Growth, and the Environment in Southern California*. Stanford, CA: Stanford University Press, 2006.

McCloud River Preserve

The McCloud River is a natural place of scenic waterfalls, pristine waterfalls, and world-famous fish. The river begins its 80-mile course through northern California in the mountain springs of the southern Cascade Mountains. As it flows southward, the McCloud runs south of Mount Shasta, passing through Lake McCloud and the Shasta-Trinity National Forest, and eventually flowing into the Shasta Lake Reservoir. In the reservoir, the waters of the McCloud mix with the Pit and the Sacramento rivers. Once these waters breach the Shasta Dam, they will flow collectively as a continuation of the Sacramento River.

Similar to many of the great rivers of the West, the flow of the McCloud has been al-tered via dams, diversions, and reservoirs. Its banks and the deep canyons through which it cuts have, however, been kept intact, due in part to over 100 years of private land ownership. One of oldest private landowners—the McCloud River Club—purchased a large riverfront parcel from the Central Pacific Railroad in 1900. It was not until 1974 that the private fishing club then donated 2,330 acres of this land to the Nature Conservancy. The Nature Conservancy now manages the area as the McCloud River Preserve and oversees a variety of scientific monitoring projects that provide valuable data regarding fish stocks, water quality, invasive species, insect populations, and the region's plant communities. Pacific yew, Douglas fir, incense cedar, and the endemic Shasta eupatory populate the sloping canyon walls, while white alder, American dogwood, horsetails, wild rose, lupine, native azalea, Shasta lily, and Indian rhubarb populate the river bank and meadows. Black bear, wolverine, elk, river otter, wild pig, and mountain lion are some of the more prominent animals found in the preserve. Amid a lengthy tally of songbirds, squirrels, newts, frogs, and snakes, there exists another long list of animals in peril. Willow flycatchers, purple martins, northern spotted owls, golden eagles, red-legged frogs, Shasta salamanders, tailed frogs, northwestern pond turtles, wolverines, and eight species of bats are a sampling of the fauna that are either listed by the state of California or the federal government as either threatened, endangered, or a species of concern. The McCloud River Preserve not only safeguards these terrestrial populations and their related habitats but also protects the key ingredient to all this biodiversity: water.

Water is as central to the preserve as it is to life on earth. Long before European settlers ventured into the region, the McCloud sustained the Wintu Indians with plentiful salmon, steelhead, and trout. Eventually, the McCloud River became nationally recognized as a prime location for trout fishing, and, by 1872, California's first fish hatchery was built on the river. Two short years later, McCloud River trout eggs were being shipped around the country and abroad. To this day, trout in the British Isles, New Zealand, Argentina, and across the United States carry the genetic legacy of the McCloud trout populations. In a sort of international fish exchange, the brown trout, which originates in Germany and Scotland, was introduced into the river in the 1930s. At that time, the river's constant flow of frigid, clean, clear water supported large populations of rainbow, brown, and bull trout, which fed on massive hatches of insects like the gold stone, salmon fly, pale morning dun, and caddis flies.

The dynamics of the McCloud River ecosystem changed forever when the Shasta Dam was built between 1938 and 1945, followed by the McCloud Dam, which was built in 1965. The two structures not only divided the river into segments but also created artificial lakes or reservoirs as water backed up behind the dam. These reservoirs—now named Lake Shasta and Lake McCloud—flooded burial and ceremonial sites of the Wintu Indians as well as valuable terrestrial habitat, while also preventing the upstream migration of bull trout. With an essential part of their life cycle inhibited, the bull trout was considered locally extinct by 1975. While not yet extinct in the region, both Chinook salmon and steelhead are also blocked from their historic natal grounds.

Although the Nature Conservancy works diligently to protect what it owns, the river is a moving body with both upstream and downstream considerations. Current water shortages throughout California in combination with a booming population are placing extreme demands on any and all available water throughout the state. This pressure has translated into the recent land sale of Bollibokka, a once private fishing club whose land was originally purchased in 1921. The controversial, $35 million purchase by the Westland Water District is viewed by many as a strategic maneuver to expedite the expansion of the Shasta Dam. Further upstream, near the river headwaters, the citizens of McCloud and the Nestlé corporation are doing battle over a proposed water bottling plant. The original contract entitled Nestlé to pump as much as 521 million gallons water from the spring. Moreover, the contract longevity was to span 100 years. Public outcry and government intervention have since pushed Nestlé back to the drawing board and the company is expected to approach the community with a scaled-down version of the original plan.

Since the McCloud River is part of one of the region's largest watersheds, it will most likely remain embroiled in a long debate regarding water usage. The Nature Conservancy, Trout Unlimited, the McCloud Watershed Council, the Environmental Justice Coalition for Water, and the Wintu are among the many groups working toward securing a healthy future for the river and those that depend on it. For now, the river runs as pristine as can be expected and continues to draw naturalists, photographers, birders, wildflower lovers, and anglers from around the world.

Further Reading

McCloud Watershed Council. http://www.mccloudwatershedcouncil.org.
Shiva, Vandana. *Water Wars: Privatization, Pollution, and Profit.* Cambridge, MA: South End Press, 2002.

MERCED GRASSLANDS

The Merced Grasslands are located in the rapidly developing San Joaquin Valley of northern California, where urban and suburban development in combination with viticulture and orchards are engulfing the grasslands. This pastoral preserve is scattered with vernal pools filled with delicate invertebrates, salamanders, and frogs. The pools and seasonal wetlands are also a life source for large flocks of wintering waterfowl and shorebirds.

The vernal (meaning spring) pools come and go with the seasons, but their occurrence nonetheless provides a window of opportunity for many organisms to carry out their life cycles. The larvae of California tiger salamander, for example, live in the pools until they metamorphose, thereby losing their aquatic gills and adapting a terrestrial life at the same time as the pools dry up. The pools are also home to a unique set of tiny shrimplike organisms that feed and breed during the wet season and then remain dormant in the dried-out pool bottoms for the rest of the year. The vernal pool fairy shrimp, California fairy shrimp, Conservancy fairy shrimp, and vernal pool tadpole shrimp are among the rare species found in the preserve. Also rare are a number of plant species that grow near the vernal pools; succulent owl's clover, Hoover's spurge, and Colusa grass are all federally listed as threatened while Greene's tuctoria is endangered.

Aside from the vernal pools and their associated wetlands, there exist several other types of habitat, including riparian, blue oak savanna, perennial aquatic, clay flats, and annual grasslands. The annual grasslands dominate the scenery, although this was not always the case. Scientists estimate that the Merced Grasslands were once dominated not by annual grasses such as bromes, wild barley, Italian ryegrass, and wild oat but by perennial bunchgrasses. The transformation is thought to have occurred around 200 years ago, with the settlement of Europeans in the American West. The introduction of exotic annual species, overgrazing, human disturbances, and drought likely encouraged the spread of the hearty annuals while displacing the perennials. Some native bunchgrasses, including purple needlegrass, one-sided bluegrass, and oldfield threeawn still grow in patchwork throughout the preserve. The tall, undulating grasses provide both food and cover for songbirds, including the California horned lark, savanna sparrow, and tricolored blackbird. Overhead, prairie falcons, Cooper's hawks, and red-shouldered hawks survey the grasslands for rodents and reptiles. The endangered San Joaquin kit fox also roams the grassland as do badger, red fox, striped skunk, bobcat, and coyotes.

What began in the 1980s as a donation of 5,000 acres of the Flying M Ranch to the Nature Conservancy has since grown into a major preserve now totaling 125,000 acres. The Nature Conservancy works with a number of public and private entities to monitor and manage the grasslands, which sit amid one of California's fastest-growing regions. Such growth prompted the recent development and construction of the University of Merced. The school is the first U.S. research university to be built in the 21st century and was done so atop vernal pools and grasslands. The Nature Conservancy has since entered an easement agreement by which the college has agreed to set aside 750 acres of its camps as a nature preserve where researchers can study the complexities of life on the Merced Grasslands.

Further Reading
Stromberg, Mark R., Jeffery D. Corbin, and Carla M. D'Antonio eds. *California Grasslands: Ecology and Management.* Berkeley: University of California Press, 2007.

MOUNT HAMILTON

The Mount Hamilton project was launched by the Nature Conservancy in 1998 with the goal of preserving one of the last significant open spaces between the Silicone Valley and Central Valley of California. The project's landscape totals 700,000 acres of pristine terrain and nearly undisturbed ecosystems. Since its inception, the Nature Conservancy has acquired nearly 100,000 acres within the Mount Hamilton project area. An additional 300,000 acres have been obtained by other agencies and nonprofit organizations, bringing the grand total to about 400,000 acres. Such collaborative efforts are continually working to bring additional easements, properties, and ranches into the collective whole. Doing so will create a continuous corridor by which animals may migrate from the southern reaches of the Diablo Mountain range northward past San Jose toward the city of Livermore.

Until recently, this corridor contained a major gap between Grant Ranch County Park in the north and Henry W. Coe State Park to the south. The land in between had been purchased in the 1950s by the Hewlett and Packard families and operated as a cattle ranch (called the San Felipe Ranch) for about 50 years. In an effort to preserve both the ranch and its open spaces, the Hewlett and Packard families donated a conservation easement on the 28,359-acre property. The easement not only fills the gap by connecting one conservation area to another but also preserves a vast array of plant and animal species that thrive on the San Felipe property and throughout the Mount Hamilton area.

Since the project area spans some 700,000 acres and thus includes the Nature Conservancy properties, Henry Coe State Park, Pacheco State Park, San Luis Reservoir State Recreation Area, Anderson Lake County Park, Coyote Lake County Park, and Joseph D. Grant County Park, it is nearly impossible to correctly assess the number of species found within the area. For example, Henry Coe State Park alone is home to 675 species of plants. Such staggering biodiversity is commonplace in the area and serves to highlight the importance of conserving these ecosystems. Plant communities including mature oak savannas, sycamore woodlands, open grasslands, seasonal wetlands, and streamside forests are all accounted for, as are healthy populations of bobcats, mountain lions, golden eagles, red-tailed hawks, badgers, rainbow trout, and tule elk. For federally endangered or threatened species such as the San Joaquin kit fox, California tiger salamander, foothill yellow-legged frog, bay checkerspot butterfly, and red-legged frog, the Mount Hamilton project offers a much-needed reprieve from human development.

The Conservancy and its many partners are now focused on acquiring easements and property around the perimeter of the Mount Hamilton project. Their primary concern, however, is the southern region of the project, which encompasses roughly 20,000 acres of the upper Pajaro River region. Once a vast riverland forest prone to seasonal floods and thus rich with life, the region is now being looked upon for urban development. Incorporating the Pajaro River region into the larger Mount Hamilton project will preserve the floodplain's flora and fauna and help to control downstream flooding while also creating a wildlife corridor between the Diablo Mountain range in the east, westward toward the Santa Cruz Mountains. Urban development, pushed by population growth in the Central Valley, Bay Area, and Silicone Valley, continue to pose the biggest threat to the not-yet-purchased portions of the Mount Hamilton project and the Pajora River. The river, however, will have to overcome a second set of obstacles regarding both water quality and quantity as it must meet the needs of a hungry and thirsty human population and the flora and fauna that also depend on it.

Further Reading

Hilty, Jodi A., William Z. Lidicker, Jr., and Adina Maya Merenlender. *Corridor Ecology: The Science and Practice of Linking Landscapes for Biodiversity Conservation.* Washington, DC: Island Press, 2006.

Nature Conservancy. "Mount Hamilton." http://www.nature.org/wherewework/north america/states/california/preserves/art6323.html.

PINNACLES WILDERNESS

Designated by a 1976 act of Congress, the Pinnacles Wilderness spans 15,985 acres of dramatic topography, rare plant communities, and caves of bats. Set within the larger Pinnacles National Monument, the wilderness area receives additional protection because of its designation as wilderness and is devoid of roads, power lines, and other manmade features. In their place, visitors will find rocky spires, rolling hills, creeks, and canyons plus 30 miles of hiking trails by which to explore them.

The Pinnacles Wilderness epitomizes the geological and seismic activity for which California is famous. According to the theory of plate tectonics, the Pacific Plate and North American Plate met up some 23 million years ago and created the San Andreas Rift Zone. The rift then filled with molten lava and subsequently formed a massive mountain, which was then worn down by eons of water, wind, and freeze-thaw cycles. What remains are the tall rock columns that give the preserve its name. Plate tectonics also had a hand in moving the pinnacles approximately 195 miles north of where they originally formed. The San Andreas Fault is still active today, as the Pacific Plate and North American Plate continue to grind and slip. This geological activity is also responsible for the formation of the talus caves that form when large boulders topple into a pile, thus leaving open spaces between adjoining rocks. The caves are home to large colonies of Townsend's big-eared bats and western mastiff bats. Fourteen species of bat live within the Pinnacles Wilderness, all of which dine on insects and spiders.

The vegetative communities at Pinnacles can be classified into five habitats: chaparral, woodland, riparian, grasslands, and rock and scree. Collectively, these habitats sustain hundreds of species of plants, each occupying a specific niche or unique ecological role within the greater ecosystem. Of these five communities, it is the chaparral that dominates and typifies the rugged beauty of this natural place. As a world biome, chaparral is very rare, occupying only tiny portions of the Mediterranean, South America, South Africa, Australia, and the United States. Relatively large swaths occur throughout California but are also concentrated in and around California's most populated areas, including San Diego, Los Angeles, Riverside, and Santa Barbara. This makes reserves like Pinnacles all the more critical for preserving the unique chaparral biome. Typically short and often sporting thorns, deep taproots, water-storing structures, and special-shaped leaves (some of which are coated in wax), the plants of the chaparral are well adapted to the region's long, arid summers. Plants such as chamise, holly-leaved cherry, manzanita, buckbrush, black sage, and mountain mahogany serve as the foundation to the rest of the ecosystem. Within the Pinnacles Wilderness, small life forms dominate: 400 species of bees, 68 types of butterflies, 36 species of dragonflies and damselflies, and thousands of other invertebrates. Nearly two dozen species of reptiles along with a number of amphibians and fish also have their place in the region's food chain. Common mammals include the previously mentioned bats, bobcat, gray fox, badger, brush rabbit, chipmunk, and black-tailed deer. The birds of the Pinnacles are represented by over 140 species ranging from raptors to hummingbirds. The most notorious bird living in the Pinnacles Wilderness is the California condor. Although still listed as endangered, the condor has been the focus of extensive and somewhat controversial conservation efforts, which began in 1987 with the capture of all remaining wild condors. These 22 birds were incorporated into captive breeding programs at both the San Diego Wild Animal Park and the Los Angeles Zoo. The program was a success, and 1991 marked the first year of the condors' reintroduction into the wild. As of May 2008, there were 152 condors living in the wild, 13 of which are known to frequent the Pinnacles. In addition to the condors, the Pinnacles Wilderness provides refuge to 27 other sensitive animal species that are listed as endangered, threatened, or a species of concern by either state of federal agencies.

The balancing act of protecting these sensitive species while maintaining an area that is open to the public is overseen by the National Park Service. Public comment on the park service's updated management plan highlights many of these issues: The public wants more trails and more boardwalks, yet they also want the place kept wild; they want controlled burns, yet do not want the park to be closed during the burn; they want to see more protection for the bats, yet want more access to the caves. It is probable that one of the greatest threats to the Pinnacles Wilderness may actually stem from the people who love it the most.

Further Reading

Halsey, Richard W. *Fire, Chaparral, and Survival in Southern California.* El Cajon, CA: Sunbelt Publications, 2004.

Moir, John. *Return of the Condor: The Race to Save Our Largest Bird from Extinction.* Guilford, CT: Globe Pequot, 2006.

POINT LOBOS STATE NATURAL RESERVE

Point Lobos State Natural Reserve sits on a picturesque peninsula of land three miles south of the city of Carmel, just off of the famously scenic Highway 1. As far as human activity goes, the land here initially sustained a group of Native American peoples collectively called the Ohlone. Inevitably, Spain and Mexico each occupied and developed the area, followed by Portuguese whaling fleets and commercial abalone harvesting, which was initiated by the Chinese. Coal mining, granite quarries, and secret U.S. military operations are also part of the peninsula's history. Despite these activities, the striking beauty of Point Lobos has remained intact and attracts a multitude of filmmakers, writers, artists, hikers, birdwatchers, photographers, and scuba divers.

Conservation of Point Lobos began in 1890, when Alexander and Satie Allan purchased 640 acres of land, which was then managed by the Allans as a sort of private sanctuary. By the mid-1920s, a conservation organization called the Save the Redwoods League rallied to save the Monterey cypress forests that grow on the peninsula. After working with the state of California, the Redwoods League purchased 348 acres from the Allan family. This original purchase was extended when the Allan family later donated 15 acres of cypress forest land to the reserve. Subsequent land additions have brought the terrestrial acreage total to 400 acres. Seven hundred fifty acres of underwater habitat were added to the reserve in 1960.

Most visitors to Point Lobos State Natural Reserve never see the submerged ecosystems that are accessible only to free divers and scuba divers. The unique abundance of life here is supported in part by a steady influx of cold, oxygen-rich, nutrient-loaded water that wells up from deep, offshore trenches. Such conditions promote the vigorous growth of phytoplankton and marine algae, which serve as the foundation of the ecosystem's food chain. From miniscule iridescent patches of reddish-purple algae to massive forests of giant kelp, the algae here are as diverse as they are colorful. The giant kelp is one of the most prominent species found in the reserve, growing 18 to 24 inches per day and reaching a height of 60 to 180 feet. The resulting kelp forest provides food and shelter for a variety of invertebrates and fish as well as sea otters and sea lions. The dense

A large tidal pool along the coastline of Point Lobos State Reserve in California. (Courtesy of Susan B. Clark)

kelp forests are punctuated by a variety of underwater features ranging from underwater crevasses to vertical walls, gapping caverns, rocky reefs, and the occasional sand flat. This diverse terrain is inhabited by a wide variety of fish ranging from wolf eels and lingcod to rockfish, gobies, leopard sharks, bat rays, and a prehistoric behemoth known as the mola mola. Point Lobos also preserves a vast collection of invertebrates including soft-bodied sea cucumbers, brightly colored sea slugs, delicate feather duster worms, blossom-like anemones, and spiny purple sea urchins.

Although not as diverse in species as the marine environment, the terrestrial ecosystems of Point Lobos are marked by a handful of unique features, one being the presence of a rare grove of Monterey cypress. Although commonly used in landscaping, there are only two natural stands left of what was once a sprawling coastal forest: one in Point Lobos and the other in Pebble Beach. A few of these surviving trees are about 2,000 years old. As one of the major plant communities at Point Lobos, the Monterey cypress forest supports minimal plant life due to the dense canopy formed by the cypress in addition to relatively shallow soils that are slight of nutrients. Outside this forest, other plant communities including northern coastal prairie, northern coastal scrub, and coastal bluff are inhabited by numerous songbirds, badger, bobcat, gray fox, dusky-footed wood rats, black-tailed deer, and pocket gophers. Point Lobos is also home to thousands of monarch butterflies, which migrate from as far away as Canada to spend the winter sipping on the blooming eucalyptus trees.

Due in part to its small size and sensitive ecosystems, public access to Point Lobos is restricted. Vehicles and passengers are welcomed on a first-come-first-served basis until the parking area is full. Divers must book a reservation and purchase a permit to dive in the reserve. Reservations should be made several months in advance as only 15 teams of two divers each are allowed in the reserve per day.

Further Reading

California State Parks. "Point Lobos State Natural Reserve." http://www.parks.ca.gov.

Hall, Howard. *The Secrets of Kelp Forests: Life's Ebb and Flow in the Sea's Richest Habitat.* Montrose, CA: London Town Press, 2007.

Pyle, Robert M. *Chasing Monarchs: Migrating with the Butterflies of Passage.* New York: Houghton Mifflin, 2001.

WADDLE RANCH

With a price tag of $23.5 million, the Waddle Ranch is often cited as one of the largest and most complicated conservation efforts in the Sierra Nevada region. Its purchase was initiated by the Truckee Donner Land Trust, a private nonprofit organization dedicated to preserving open spaces in the greater Truckee region. What began as a group of hikers and outdoor enthusiasts rallying to save the Coldstream Valley from logging grew into an agency that, as of 2007, has protected more than 12,442 acres (including the Coldstream Valley). Ultimately, it took the cooperative and financial efforts of six other major public and private entities to secure the purchase of the ranch.

The Waddle Ranch is located on 1,462 acres of prime real estate just north of Lake Tahoe on the eastern slope of the Sierra Nevada. The land has been privately owned for more than 150 years, beginning with the Waddle family, who purchased a 6,000-acre parcel in the 1880s. Over the years, the Waddles sold some of the land to the Army Corps of Engineers and the neighboring airport but kept intact the most biologically valuable terrain. The Waddle family sold the rest of the ranch in 1971 to the Pritzker family, who would sell it to the Truckee Donner Land Trust in 2007. Prior to its sale, the property, which sits in the Martis Valley, was slated to undergo major development plans that included 600 housing units and a golf course. Other sections of the valley were also marked for development; these plans included shopping malls, hotels, resorts, and 6,000 additional homes. A subsequent legal battle followed by court-ordered negotiations resulted in an agreement that allowed construction to progress in a southerly direction while restricting northward expansion. Furthermore, it was decided that a set of open-space fees were to be charged to developers who decided to build in the valley. The revenue from these fees eventually added up to roughly $10 million, which was used to purchase the Waddle Ranch. Its acquisition has benefited both people and wildlife: The old "No Trespassing" signs have been removed, and the ranch is now open to the public for mountain biking, snowshoeing, cross-country skiing, hiking, photography, and wildlife viewing opportunities.

Now under protection, the ranchland will continue to serve wildlife as a corridor spanning eastward to Nevada. Bear, cougar, bobcat, coyotes, and deer will all benefit from the added space. An unusual mix of plant life populates the ranch due in part to its location in a transition zone between the pine forest–dominated Sierra Nevada and the sagebrush-dominated Great Basin. Mature stands of coniferous forests, sagebrush flats, open grasslands, marsh lands, and riparian forest are set in patchwork formations across the ranch. Vernal pools and Dry Lake (which actually holds plenty of water) provide lush habitats for invertebrates as well as nesting and feeding grounds for a myriad of duck species in addition to geese, loons, sandhill cranes, and bald eagles. To further protect the unique biodiversity of the Waddle Ranch and the greater Martis Valley, the land trust and its partners are in continuous negotiations with neighboring landowners. The Waddle Ranch adjoins 2,200 acres of open space to the west, which is owned by the federal government, while another large swath of open space to the southeast is owned by a forest products company called Sierra Pacific Industries. Purchasing or gaining easements to these two properties would further extend the wildlife corridor and help to preserve an area that is a hotbed of urban development.

Further Reading

Johnston, Verna R. *Sierra Nevada: The Naturalist's Companion.* Los Angeles: University of California Press, 2000.
Truckee Donner Land Trust. http://www.tdlandtrust.org/.

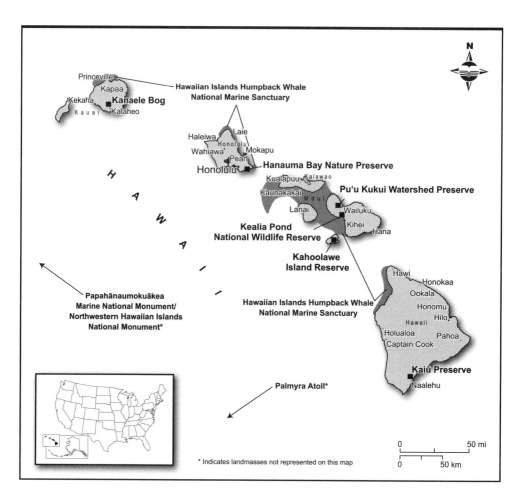

Hanauma Bay Nature Preserve, 60

Hawaiian Islands Humpback Whale National Marine Sanctuary, 62

Kahoolawe Island Reserve, 63

Kanaele Bog, 65

Ka'ū Preserve, 66

Kealia Pond National Wildlife Reserve, 68

Palmyra Atoll, 69

Papahānaumokuākea Marine National Monument/Northwestern

Hawaiian Islands National Monument, 71

Pu'u Kukui Watershed Preserve, 72

HAWAII

Hawaii is in many respects an ecological anomaly compared to the rest of the United States. While holding the title of the world's most isolated islands, Hawaii's flora and fauna evolved independently from mainland species, eventually giving rise to a set of uniquely adapted plants and animals. Scientists estimate that, of the 21,388 species of plants and animals that inhabit the island, 8,759 of them are endemic—meaning that they are found nowhere else in the world. Many of these same species are not only endemic to Hawaii, but some are found only on particular islands within the Hawaiian chain. The Oahu 'elepaio bird, for example, is endemic to the island of Oahu, which measures a mere 596 square miles.

Habitat destruction and fragmentation are one of the biggest challenges facing the state's biotic communities. The installation of sprawling golf courses, beachfront condos, high-rise resorts, and intensified agricultural endeavors not only subtract from available habitat but fragment migration corridors and introduce a variety of manmade disturbances. While traffic, pollution, and water quality and quantity issues all take their toll, none has been more devastating to native populations than the introduction of nonnative species. Ranging from cats and dogs to rats and ornamental garden plants, researchers estimate that Hawaii is now home to more than 4,200 exotic species. Nonnative plants frequently outcompete native flora by spreading more quickly and thereby monopolizing both space and nutrients. These invasive plants also thrive in the absence of predatory insects that might otherwise keep populations in check. Animals such as the domestic cat and nonnative rat continually wreak havoc on native bird populations, destroying nests, eggs, and chicks along with adult birds.

These factors and others have led to the extinction of an estimated 271 species of plants, insects, snails, and birds from the Hawaiian Islands. Unfortunately, this statistic also earns Hawaii the title of extinction capital of the world. Formal conservation of Hawaii's landscapes has, until recently, lagged behind the rest of the continental United States. Although the reasons for delay are numerous, the state did not join the Union until 1959; therefore, the U.S. Fish and Wildlife Service, National Marine Sanctuaries Program, National Refuge System, and other protective laws were not applicable. This is not to say, however, that Hawaii had not protected any of its natural landscapes prior to statehood. Native Hawaiians have for thousands of years preserved not only their most sacred natural places but also the knowledge of the region's flora and fauna. In fact, separating native Hawaiian culture from the environment would diminish the understanding of both.

Conservation groups such as the Nature Conservancy, Hawaii's Audubon Society, the Sierra Club, and the Trust for Public Land are just a few of the more prominent groups working in Hawaii. They are aided by a number of public agencies, private alliances, and landowners, all of which aim to preserve Hawaii's unique biodiversity. In doing so, the state has protected a number of delicate ecosystems including alpine bogs, coral reefs, dry land forest, tropical rainforest, wetlands, and offshore atolls. The state has also protected its open water ways in an effort to secure the breeding and birthing grounds of humpback whale. As of 2006, the state of Hawaii has earned yet another title and is now home to the world's largest marine reserve, a title that is both indicative of Hawaii's progressive conservation policies and its deeply rooted cultural history.

HANAUMA BAY NATURE PRESERVE

Located just 10 miles east of Waikiki on the southeastern shores of Oahu, Hanauma Bay may easily be one of the most frequently visited marine preserves in the United States. Its white sandy beaches and aquamarine waters have long been an attraction to residents and tourists alike. From the 1930s to the 1940s, the deeply arched cove was a popular place to picnic and fish but was devoid of the massive crowds that would eventually descend upon the picturesque bay. In 1956, the city of Honolulu decided to make way for the new trans-Pacific undersea telephone cables and sold easement rights along Hanauma Bay to the Hawaiian Telephone Company. This development project resulted in the blasting and removal of several tons of coral rock from the central portion of the reef. Such alterations were, at the time, thought to be improvements—for example, the gaping hole left in the remaining reef was to serve as a swimming hole.

By 1967, Hanauma Bay had been severely overfished and was subsequently closed to fishing. The fishing closure did little to deter visitors, and, by 1970, the city called for another set of improvements at Hanauma Bay. Again the reef was blasted to make a second swimming hole. The blasted reef rubble was then dredged out of the bay and buried on the beach. An additional 4,000 cubic feet of sand was trucked in from the north shore of Oahu so that the debris could be fully covered. To protect the enhanced beach from erosion, several large basalt boulders were placed in strategic locations in an effort to reduce wave and current action.

It is estimated that, by the 1980s, three million people were visiting Hanauma Bay every year. Parking problems, congestion in adjacent neighborhoods, and solid waste

Hanauma Bay Nature Preserve. (BruceandLetty)

management were among the terrestrial problems that plagued the bay. Water quality and reef health were, however, the main area of concern at this time. Several factors contributed to the fouling of the bay. Water analysis indicated that people were not using the public restrooms but relieving themselves in the bay. Compounding the problem was visitors' persistent feeding of bread to the fish. Estimates suggest that, during peak season, over half a ton of bread entered the water on a daily basis. The coral reefs of Hanauma Bay dwindled not only as a result of poor water quality but also due to being stood on by swimmers and snorkelers.

Finally, in 1990, steps were taken to assess, monitor, and control the number of people visiting the bay. The following decade brought much-needed change to Hanauma Bay. Admission and parking fees and the restriction of commercial use helped to reduce the number of visitors to a more manageable one million per year. Educational programs and public outreach worked to increase visitors' knowledge and appreciation of Hanauma Bay's marine habitat. Today's tourists still enjoy the swimming holes and soft sand beaches that were molded by human hands, but they are also able to enjoy the natural wonders of the coral reefs, which are making a gradual comeback.

Further Reading
Precht, William F. *Coral Reef Restoration Handbook*. Boca Raton, FL: CRC Press, 2006.
Scott, Susan. *Exploring Hanauma Bay*. Honolulu: University of Hawaii Press, 1994.
State of Hawaii, Department of Land and Natural Resources. http://hawaii.gov/dlnr.

HAWAIIAN ISLANDS HUMPBACK WHALE NATIONAL MARINE SANCTUARY

The Hawaiian Islands Humpback Whale National Marine Sanctuary is one of 13 national marine sanctuaries that are overseen by the National Oceanic and Atmospheric Administration (NOAA). Originally proposed by NOAA in 1982, the Hawaiian Islands Humpback Whale National Marine Sanctuary met stiff opposition from community members who feared that such a measure would negatively impact fishing access and reduce shipping lanes. The proposal was initially rejected, only to resurface again in the early 1990s. After working in close partnership, Congress, NOAA, and the state of Hawaii designated the Hawaiian Islands Humpback Whale National Marine Sanctuary in 1992. The project did not receive formal approval from Hawaii's governor until 1997. The delay was again due to regulatory concerns in addition to a largely divided public; some community members were adamantly for the sanctuary while others stood adamantly against it.

Although the goals of the sanctuary are multifaceted, its primary mission is to protect and educate. Protection comes in the form of regulations to limit the distance at which people and ships can approach the whales, restrictions on the discharge of waste water and altering the sea floor via dredging or bottom trawling, for example. In total, 1,370 square miles of water have been incorporated into the sanctuary's boundaries. The area is, however, not continuous but is split into five parcels that run adjacent to six of the major Hawaiian Islands. The largest of the five sections (which equate to about 685 square miles) partially encircles the islands of Maui, Lanai, and Molokai.

These protected waters extend from the shoreline to depths of up to 600 feet and encompass a diverse set of habitats. Shallow beds of sea grass and complex coral reef systems are home to hundreds of species of marine animals, including the endangered Hawaiian monk seal, green sea turtles, parrotfish, lobster, stony corals, and sharks. Scientists estimate that 25 percent of Hawaii's marine species are endemic, meaning that they do not naturally occur anywhere else in the world.

Humpback whales, on the other hand, can be found in all of the world's major oceans, typically spending summer months feeding in cool polar waters and then migrating great distances to tropical and subtropical waters to breed and calve. It is estimated that two-thirds of the north Pacific humpback whale population uses the waters off of Hawaii to reproduce and give birth. The sanctuary, therefore, protects a vital stage of the great mammals' life cycle and helps to ensure the continued growth of humpback whale populations. Humpback populations suffered losses upward of 70 percent due to whaling, a practice that was not commercially banned until 1986. Since then, the humpback has made a slow but steady recovery; in recent years, global populations of humpbacks have increased on average of 7 percent per year. Scientists now estimate that 80,000 humpbacks cruise the oceans today. Still a far cry from their historic prewhaling numbers, the humpback continues to be threatened by various human endeavors. The International Whaling Commission (IWC) is an international governing body that sets the rules and regulations regarding whale harvest worldwide. In recent years, the IWC has been embroiled in controversy surrounding the issuance of scientific permits that allow various countries to harvest a set number of whales for scientific study. Japan has specifically faced severe criticism because its annual scientific harvests allow for the killing of 850 Antarctic minke whales, 220 common minkes, 50 humpbacks, 50 fin whales, 100 sei whales, and 10 sperm whales. Critics charge that the scientific data gathered from such studies is redundant and contributes very little to the understanding of whale biology and population structure. The Japanese whaling fleets have been met with intense international protest, particularly from Australia. Japan had originally planned to fill its humpback quota off the coast of Australia but was eventually deterred via public outcry and harassment by environmental groups.

Although whaling is certainly not permitted within the Hawaiian Islands Humpback Whale National Marine Sanctuary, the sanctuary aims to further reduce casualties due to ship strikes and entanglement in commercial fishing gear. Ship strikes are a frequent occurrence worldwide, and, on occasion, they even occur within the sanctuary. Therefore, the sanctuary works to limit the incidence of ship strikes within its borders by posting speed limits and by strategizing with ferry and other boat operators to minimize risk and ensure the safety of both passengers and whales. Sanctuary personnel also work to rescue humpbacks that are entangled in commercial fishing gear. When these non-biodegradable fishing lines become entangled around flippers, heads, and tails, they can restrict movement and inhibit feeding and often cut large fissures into the animals' tissues, thus leaving them open to infection. In both instances, the best solution to reduce entanglement and ship strikes is to prevent them in the first place; therefore, education and public awareness is central to the humpback sanctuary's mission.

Further Reading

Gales, Nick, Mark Hindell, and Roger Kirkwood. *Marine Mammals: Fisheries, Tourism and Management Issues*. Collingwood, Victoria, Australia: CSIRO, 2003.

International Whaling Commission. http://www.iwcoffice.org.

National Oceanic and Atmospheric Administration. "Hawaiian Islands Humpback Whale National Marine Sanctuary." http://hawaiihumpbackwhale.noaa.gov/.

KAHOOLAWE ISLAND RESERVE

The island of Kahoolawe is the smallest of the eight main Hawaiian Islands, measuring 11 miles in length and 6 miles at its widest point. Despite its diminutive size, the island has withstood a long and somewhat ugly history of ecological degradation. It has been only recently, under the careful management of the Kahoolawe Island Reserve Commission (KIRC), that the island has undergone a process of both ecological and spiritual renewal.

Archeological evidence dating back to about A.D. 400 suggests that Kahoolawe Island served as an important cultural and religious center for early settlers from Polynesia. Since then, the island has been the site of an adze quarry, penal colony, sheep and cattle ranch, and a U.S. Navy bombing range. From 1858 to 1941, the Hawaiian government issued a series of ranch leases on the island, thus opening it to livestock grazing. By 1890, about 15,000 sheep, 900 cattle, and an untold number of goats roamed the island, grazing at will. Collectively, the livestock stripped the island of most of its native vegetation, trees, shrubs, vines, and grasses, leaving behind barren, exposed soil. Devoid of any roots to hold it in place, the soil quickly eroded, washing into the sea with the rain or blowing away in the wind. Even today, with restoration underway, it is estimated that nearly two million tons of soil are washed from the island on an annual basis. So much topsoil has been lost that one-quarter of the island has eroded down to hardpan, a soil layer that is impervious to water and roots.

By 1941, most of the sheep and cattle had been transported off the island due to repetitive droughtlike conditions, and there was no substantial amount of vegetation left. The goats, however, were left behind to multiply, and, by the 1980s, there were 50,000 of the sure-footed beasts. The year 1941 also ushered in a new era for Kahoolawe. Following the attack on Pearl Harbor, the United States declared martial law and began using the island as a bomb testing range. The end of World War II was of little consequence to Kahoolawe Island, and, in 1953, President Eisenhower transferred the title to the island over to the U.S. Navy, provided that it be returned to the state in a condition suitable for habitation. It was not until 1976 when the grassroots organization Protect Kahoolawe Ohama (PKO) filed a lawsuit to stop the bombing. A year later, the navy was ordered to begin restoration projects, including revegetation, soil conservation, and goat eradication. In 1990, President Bush closed the bombing range on Kahoolawe. Congress then approved $400 million to be spent to clear the land of its remaining ordnances. The funding was enough to clear about 74 percent of the island's surface of unexploded materials, and 9 percent of the island was cleared to a depth of four feet. Because many of the ordnances were buried and many more have been washed into gullies and canyons, much of the island is still unsafe.

Despite these obstacles, efforts to restore the land are in full swing. The KIRC has concentrated its efforts on replanting 820 acres of the most severely eroded areas and rehabilitating the island's patchwork of wetlands. In addition to the wetlands, the Kahoolawe Island Reserve is home to five other plant communities, each of which is typified by a distinct shrub or grass such as the 'ilima, ma'o (also known as Hawaiian cotton), and pili. These plant communities support a number of invertebrates including the Koa butterfly and the endangered Blackburn's sphinx moth. A number of migratory birds as well as nesting Hawaiian petrels, band-rumped strom petrels, and endangered bristle-thighed curlews all depend on the island's natural resources. The KIRC hopes to reintroduce other animals that inhabited the island prior to its environmental decline; the endemic and critically endangered Laysan duck and the Hawaiian hoary bat will likely be reintroduced along with a variety of native invertebrates and marine reptiles.

Conservation of the marine ecosystem is another focal point of the KIRC. The Kahoolawe Island Reserve extends seaward for two miles from the island's coastline and harbors a number of species of corals, green sea turtles, monk seals, pelagic fish, and an untold number of other invertebrates. Like its terrestrial counterpart, the marine habitat here is also undergoing assessment and monitoring. Invasive algae, marine debris, and sedimentation due to erosion are among the list of threats to Kahoolawe Island Reserve's marine ecosystems.

Further Reading

Coles, S. L., R. C. DeFelice, J. E. Smith, D. Muir, and L. G. Eldredge. *Determination of Baseline Conditions for Introduced Marine Species in Nearshore Waters of the Island of Kahoʻolawe, Hawaii.* Honolulu, HI: Bishop Museum Press, 1998.

State of Hawaii, Department of Land and Natural Resources. http://www.state.hi.us/dlnr/dofaw/cwcs/.

KANAELE BOG

L ocated in the mountains of southern Kauai, Kanaele Bog is the last intact low-lying bog land in the state. Its counterparts have long been drained for their water, developed, or planted as agricultural lands. This makes the 80-acre parcel that is Kanaele Bog all the more critical for the preservation of Hawaii's bog land plant communities.

Kanaele is home to a variety of rare plant species that are highly adapted to living in soggy bog lands. Bogs are categorized as a type of wetland that acquires most of its water via precipitation and lack any significant flow of water either into or out of the system. The ground is therefore consistently saturated with relatively stagnant water. These conditions leave the soil highly acidic and devoid of oxygen, which in turn prevents the complete decay of dead plant materials and retards the cycling of nutrients within the ecosystem. (The accumulated dead plant material is called peat.) In Kanaele Bog, carnivorous plants such as the sundew gain supplemental nutrition by luring small gnats to their glittery dew-dropped leaves. Dwarfed trees and several species of endangered plants including the bog violet, Kauai island aster, naʻenaʻe, and haha also inhabit Kanaele Bog. It is estimated that 27 rare plant species populate the bog land area. The area's plant communities have historically supported several species of birds that are endemic to Kauai or the greater Hawaiian Islands. In the past, bird surveys have recorded the presence of ʻapapane, ʻiʻiwi, ʻanianiau, akekeʻe, Kauai ʻamakihi, and Kauai ʻelepaio; however, recent population counts have found that only the apapane and elepaio can be accounted for. Researchers theorize that the reduction in bird diversity is the result of compounding factors including habitat disruption, invasive species, and disease.

The soil and plant communities of Kanaele Bog are extremely fragile and easily disturbed. Wild pigs, in particular, are attracted to the soft spongy soil that is easy to root through. These feral animals not only mar the soil but uproot established native plants, thereby making it easier for invasive species to take hold. Other nonnative animals including rats and cats have, along with the feral pigs, transported foreign plant seeds in

Lobeliads of Kanaele Bog. (Courtesy of Nicolai Barca)

and among the bog lands. Plants such as eucalyptus, strawberry guava, downy rose myrtle, and Asian melastome all threaten to crowd out native plants.

To better protect Kanaele Bog, the McBryde Sugar Company (which owns the land) and the Nature Conservancy established a management agreement under which the Nature Conservancy would be charged with preserving the bog land. The agreement, which was signed in 2003, is to last for 10 years, during which the Nature Conservancy hopes to build a wire fence around the bog to keep out wild pigs and construct a boardwalk from which to monitor plant life without having to tread on it. The conservancy also plans to control and monitor invasive species while maintaining a population census of the bog's flora and fauna.

Further Reading
Denny Jim. *The Birds of Kaua'i*. Honolulu: University of Hawaii Press, 1999.

KA'Ū PRESERVE

Located on the southern end of the island of Hawaii, Ka'ū Preserve encompasses 3,500 acres of nearly pristine native 'ōhi'a forest. While similar tracts of forest have given way to agriculture, housing developments, resorts, logging, and disease, Ka'ū Preserve protects the largest and most intact stretch of native forest land in the state. The forest land, which was privately held until 2002, skirts the adjoining Ka'ū Forest Reserve, which is owned and managed by the state of Hawaii. In 2002, the Nature Conservancy purchased the land in an effort to protect the area's old-growth trees and endangered plants and animals and to allow the state freer access to its own lands, which had been previously encircled by private landowners. The Ka'ū Preserve and Ka'ū Forest Reserve may now be viewed as a cohesive ecological unit.

The plant community within Ka'ū is as strangely beautiful as it is rare. The forest canopy is often dominated by the 'ōhi'a tree. Reaching heights of 40 to 60 feet, its gnarled branches often span the space between neighboring trees, thus forming a closed canopy. The understory formed by the 'ōhi'a serves to protect yet another endemic species, the koa tree. Prized for its hard wood, the koa was once a popular resource for making canoes, bowls, floors, and jewelry. Although it is now illegal to cut down a living koa, there are enough dead koa trees to support the jewelry industry in Hawaii. (There are, however, no koa left that are large enough to carve out a traditional Hawaiian canoe.)

The rest of the 'ōhi'a forest understory is populated with a lush variety of tree ferns, which may reach upward of 40 feet high, in addition to the rare nuku 'i'iwi. The nuku 'i'iw, with its gracefully curved red blossoms, is not native to the islands, yet Hawaii may end up serving as a final holdout for the plant, which is rapidly disappearing from its native Philippines.

The koa and 'ōhi'a trees are critically important to a number of rare birds that are listed as endangered and are also endemic to Hawaii. The 'elepaio, 'amakihi, and 'akepa are among the songbirds that breed, nest, feed, and/or raise their young in the 'ōhi'a woodlands. The Hawaiian hawk (also known as 'Io) is the state's only raptor. It, too, is endangered and specifically endemic to the island of Hawaii; it breeds only in the 'ōhi'a forest. Efforts to rehabilitate hawk populations are, however, in conflict with attempts to reintroduce the Hawaiian crow (also known as 'alala), which is now considered extinct in the wild. In 1993, more than two dozen Hawaiian crow fledglings that had been bred and raised in captivity were released into the preserve; by 1999, all but six had died or disappeared. The mortality rate of the crow was largely blamed on the hawk, since the Hawaiian hawk tends to prey on young crows.

The race to save species from extinction is in full swing at Ka'ū. Decades of human disturbances in the form of cattle ranching, sugar cane plantations, water diversion, and timber harvest combined with the introduction of invasive species including feral pigs, cats, rats, and an assortment of habitat-altering weeds have already led to the extinction of several species of birds and plants and have thus profoundly altered the delicate balance of this ecosystem.

Further Reading

Walters, Mark J. *Seeking the Sacred Raven: Politics and Extinction on a Hawaiian Island.* Washington, DC: Island Press, 2006.

KEALIA POND NATIONAL WILDLIFE RESERVE

Kealia Pond National Wildlife Reserve sits in a lowland basin along the southern coast of central Maui. The pond and its surrounding banks, mudflats, and dunes are among the last of Hawaii's natural wetlands. Its unique location, ever-fluctuating water characteristics, and large size sustain a high level of biodiversity ranging from large flocks of birds to the smallest of minnows.

Measuring roughly 691 acres, the reserve serves as a final water catchment for a 56-square-mile watershed that funnels seasonal runoff from the nearby mountains and hills into the basin and finally out to sea. In fact, the Pacific Ocean is close enough to the pond that the two occasionally mix, thereby creating brackish water. The pond's salinity also fluctuates on a seasonal basis. Winter rains flush the pond with fresh water, thereby decreasing its overall salinity. The rainy season also causes the pond to expand, covering nearly 200 acres in knee-high water. The onset of summer, however, leads to a drop in water levels and a steady increase in salinity as the water evaporates. The salts left behind eventually form a crystalline crust around the bank but dissolve again as the pond fills with the winter rains.

At one time, birds flocked to Kealia Pond by the thousands; prior to the 1900s, some 40,000 ducks wintered at the reserve compared to recent counts of 2,000. Still, half of Hawaii's population of endangered Hawaiian stilts (also known as ae'o) use the costal wetland for breeding, nesting, and raising young. Hundreds of endangered Hawaiian coots also live here alongside Hawaiian ducks, which are also federally listed as endangered. The northern pintail, greater scaup, and common tern not only rely on the refuge for wintering grounds but are listed among the Audubon Society's top 20 common birds in decline. Approximately 110 species of birds utilize the refuge either as nesting and breeding grounds, as wintering grounds, or as a resting spot during migration from summer breeding grounds in Alaska.

Of the flora and fauna inhabiting the pond, it is estimated that 90 percent of the species have been introduced. Pickleweed, Florida mangrove, and Indian marsh fleabane are among the alien species that tend to outcompete native plants such as salt grass, sea purslane, and makai sedge. Mongoose, feral cats, and rats are among the invasive predators that take their toll on local bird populations, eating both eggs and young. Yet another foreign species—a fish called tilapia—was left behind after a failed aquaculture endeavor. Tilapia populations explode during the wet winter months, only to die off as the pond shrinks in the summer heat. The massive die-off fouls not only the water, but the smell permeates the air and drifts into nearby neighborhoods. The boom-and-bust cycle of the tilapia population also leaves native fish stocks with unfavorable living conditions.

Invasive species are only one of the many threats to Kealia Pond. Environmental contaminants from upland agricultural lands and urban settlements flow down the watershed and enter the pond. These contaminants may include herbicides, pesticides, fertilizers, and sediments. Sedimentation alone has had a profound effect on the pond's topography; it is estimated that the pond once had an average depth of six to eight feet, but sedimentation has reduced the depth to one or two feet. The pond does, however, prevent these sediments from entering the nearby ocean and subsequently smothering the area's coral reefs.

The U.S. Fish and Wildlife Service oversees the management of Kealia Pond, but the agency also depends on a number of volunteers and community groups that donate time, money, and materials to maintain and enrich the ecosystem. The pond is open to the public and attracts around 2,700 visitors each year. Access may be restricted during stilt and coot breeding seasons.

Further Reading
Hawaii Audubon Society. http://www.hawaiiaudubon.com/.
U.S. Fish and Wildlife Service. "Kealia Pond National Wildlife Reserve." http://www. fws.gov/kealiapond/.

Palmyra Atoll

Palmyra atoll is located in the Pacific Ocean, about 1,052 miles southwest of Hawaii—a position halfway between Hawaii and American Samoa. By definition, an atoll is an oceanic island that has sunk beneath the ocean's surface. The dry land portion of an atoll forms as a result of eons' worth of accumulating sand and sediments formed by the surrounding barrier reefs. Aerial photos of Palmyra display typical atoll features: a myriad of small, sandy white islands arranged in a loose ring. In the center of the island circle sits a shallow lagoon, while the seaward side is encircled by a vast system of coral reefs.

Palmyra has a long and complicated history of ownership that formally started in 1862, when the fourth king of Hawaii, Kamehameah IV, laid claim to the atoll. Until its purchase by the Nature Conservancy in 2000, Palmyra had changed hands several times and yet managed to remain largely undeveloped and uninhabited. Prior to its purchase by the Nature Conservancy, Palmyra had been the proposed site for several ventures, including a casino, a nuclear waste dumping ground, and a fish processing center.

The protective boundary line includes the 680-acre atoll and all of it terrestrial inhabitants and extends 12 miles out to sea, thereby encompassing the area's coral reefs. The reef systems consist of 125 species of corals, rare giant clams, pilot whales, tiger sharks, and manta rays, along with hundreds of species of brightly colored reef fish. Several endangered species, including the Hawaiian monk seal, hawksbill sea turtle, and green sea turtle, also utilize the atoll. Yet another rarity exists crawling amid the coconut trees. The coconut crab, which feeds on coconuts and grows to be two and a half feet across, still thrives in Palmyra, though it has virtually been wiped out of the rest of the Pacific due to overharvesting by people.

The Palmyra Atoll. (Courtesy of Ethan Roth)

The tally of biodiversity escalates further when taking count of Palmyra's seabird populations: 29 species in all adding up to millions of individuals. Sooty terns, red-footed boobies, white-tailed tropic birds, and black noodies are just a few of the colorful bird species found on Palmyra. Another noteworthy species is the bristle-thighed curlew; several hundred of the existing 6,000 birds use Palmyra as their first stopping point on their migratory route from Alaska (which is 4,000 miles away) to French Polynesia.

Plentiful rainfall keeps the land here lush and green with coconut palms, ferns, and the largest remaining stand of Pisonia beach forest in the Pacific. Widely logged elsewhere for their timber, the Pisonia forest of Palmyra hosts trees that approach 100 feet tall and are important shelter for many of the island's bird species.

Palmyra Atoll not only supports a vastly diverse population of terrestrial and marine animals but also functions as a laboratory for biologists and researchers who are studying the region's ecosystems. Palmyra's corals, for instance, are giving scientists a glimpse into the earth's climactic history. More impressively, it is considered to be one of the few places on earth where an intact ecosystem can be studied. (Most ecosystems have, at one time or another, experienced mass disruptions by humans.)

Further Reading

U.S. Department of the Interior, Office of Insular Affairs. http://www.doi.gov/oia/Island pages/palmyrapage.htm.

Papahānaumokuākea Marine National Monument/Northwestern Hawaiian Islands National Monument

The planet's largest fully protected marine reserve was established with the signing of Presidential Proclamation 8031 on June 15, 2006. The Northwestern Hawaiian Islands National Monument is several hundred miles northwest of the main chain of Hawaiian Islands and encompasses some 140,000 square miles of land and ocean. Spanning an area nearly 100 times larger than Yosemite, the monument serves as a remote oasis for countless terrestrial and marine animals as well as a cultural mecca for native Hawaiians and a maritime heritage site. Although the monument was renamed the Papahānaumokuākea Marine National Monument on March 2, 2007, the refuge is commonly referred to by its original name.

Conservation and management of the Papahānaumokuākea Marine National Monument is overseen by a multiagency network consisting of eight state and federal agencies. Among these agencies, the National Oceanic and Atmospheric Association is tasked with chief jurisdiction over the monument's marine waters, while guardianship of terrestrial habitats is vested with the U.S. Fish and Wildlife Service and the state of Hawaii's Department of Land and Natural Resources.

The Papahānaumokuākea Marine National Monument is home to approximately 7,000 species of plants, animals, and insects, over one-quarter of which are endemic to Hawaii. Endemic species are species that are exclusively native to a particular area and therefore do not naturally occur outside of the given region. Since endemic species tend to be highly adapted to a specific environment, they are particularly sensitive to habitat alterations and prone to endangerment. Among the endangered endemic species found within the Papahānaumokuākea Marine National Monument are the Hawaiian monk seal, Hawaiian green sea turtle, three types of songbirds, six plant species, and the world's rarest duck—the Laysan duck. The monument also serves as primary nesting ground for most of the world's Laysan and black-footed albatrosses—in fact, all but three species of Hawaiian birds use the reserve for breeding and nesting grounds.

Just beyond the terrestrial environment are more than 4,000 square miles of the world's most pristine coral reefs. Coral itself consists of a fragile colony of animals (typically several thousand animals per colony) that secrete a hard calcium-based substance, thus giving protection to the colony. Vast networks of coral form the reefs, which in turn support numerous species of algae, invertebrates, and fish and thereby establish the foundations for extensive yet delicate food webs. The reefs of the Papahānaumokuākea Marine National Monument, are home to a variety of fish that were once common on the main Hawaiian Islands but whose numbers have severely declined due to sale to the aquarium industry. The monument's robust fish populations, in turn, support a healthy stock of larger predatory fish such as jacks, grouper, and sharks. These top predators are used by scientists as indicator species, meaning that their abundance is indicative of a stable and thriving ecosystem. For comparison, half of the biomass (or weight) of the monument's reef ecosystem is made up of top predators compared to the main Hawaiian Island's 3 percent.

Most scientists adhere to the thinking that the Papahānaumokuākea Marine National Monument is one of the last places on earth where coral reef systems and ecology can be studied without having to consider large-scale human disturbances. Human influence on this area is, however, not completely absent. Marine debris and invasive species are among the greatest source of concern for those departments charged with the management and preservation of the region. Every year, converging ocean currents heap 40 to 80 tons of marine debris on the area. Two main constituents comprise this marine trash: household plastics such as toothbrushes, jugs, lighters, and bottle caps and derelict fishing gear. Every year, dozens of animals, many of which are endangered, die after ingesting plastic or becoming entangled in the discarded fishing nets.

Invasive species pose yet another serious and immediate problem for the Papahānaumokuākea Marine National Monument. By definition, invasive species are nonnative species that pose economic or environmental harm. As many as 125 invasive insects and spiders have made their way to the region; it is thought that most of these species arrived in clothing and supplies brought in by people working and visiting the islands. To limit the introduction of invasive species and to preserve the fragile ecosystems of this area, access to the monument is highly restricted. Permits must be obtained by anyone wanting to visit, whether for recreational, educational, cultural, or research purposes.

Further Reading

National Oceanic and Atmospheric Administration. "Papahānaumokuākea Marine National Monument." http://hawaiireef.noaa.gov/.

Rauzon, Mark J. *Isles of Refuge: Wildlife and History of the Northwestern Hawaiian Islands.* Honolulu: University of Hawaii Press, 2001.

Safina, Carl. *Eye of the Albatross: Visions of Hope and Survival.* New York: Macmillan, 2003.

Pu'u Kukui Watershed Preserve

Located in the mountains of western Maui, the Pu'u Kukui Watershed Preserve is the largest privately owned preserve in the state of Hawaii. The 9,881-acre property was purchased by the Maui Land and Pineapple Company Inc. (ML&P) in 1988 and is currently managed via a working partnership between ML&P and the Nature Conservancy of Hawaii. Although ML&P's main business ventures are based in pineapple production and other agricultural endeavors and in the operation of Kapalua Resort, the company also supports a number of environmentally friendly projects and business practices.

Western Maui was once dominated by a large active volcano; however, time and weather have now sculpted the terrain into a series of steeply graded mountains and deep valleys. The summit that sits above the preserve is the highest peak in the western mountain range and one of the wettest places on earth. As warm air from the Pacific Ocean converges with the cool, alpine air of Maui's western mountain range, the air vapors condense to form dense rain clouds. The resulting rainfall averages 350 inches per year and is enough to satisfy all of the industrial, agricultural, and urban water requirements for the western, central, and southern portions of Maui. The mountains of western Maui and, by extension, the Pu'u Kukui preserve serve as a major water catchment for this precipitation, thereby allowing the water to gradually trickle and flow toward the sea. As the water percolates downward, it saturates the soil, creating a soft spongy substrate that holds little oxygen and has a relatively acidic pH. As a result, the plant communities here are highly specialized and include a number of species of mosses, lichens, greenswords, lobelias, dwarf 'ohi'a trees, and native hydrangea and geraniums. The dark-rumped petrel, nene goose, and hoary bat are a few of the endangered animal species that find protection within the Pu'u Kukui Watershed. For each of these endangered animals, there are several dozen more life forms, ranging from insects and crustaceans to fish and birds, that are listed by the U.S. Fish and Wildlife Service as either a candidate for the endangered species list or as a species of concern.

The Pu'u Kukui Watershed Preserve not only protects these species by safeguarding their habitat but also gives scientists and researchers a pristine laboratory in which to monitor and assess this ecosystem. (This is especially important to species like the hoary bat and Hawaiian owl, because much of their biology and population status are unknown.) ML&P and the Nature Conservancy have put forth a variety of efforts to preserve this unique habitat. For example, preserve personnel have collected seeds from plants already growing in the preserve so that they may be cultivated by hand and later used to rehabilitate areas that may have had their vegetation damaged. Feral pigs tend to be the biggest culprit when it comes to destroying plant communities within Pu'u Kukui, but the axis deer is also a concern. Preserve staffers estimate that feral pig populations have decreased by 80 percent in recent years. Other invasive species such as rats and feral cats have proven harder to control and are especially harmful to nesting birds.

On behalf of the Pu'u Kukui Watershed Preserve, ML&P also founded the West Maui Mountain Watershed Partnership, which works to coordinate both public and private landowners' efforts to protect Maui's main water sources. Safeguarding Pu'u Kukui and other similar watersheds not only translates to habitat conservation and increased biodiversity but also makes good business sense. The University of Hawaii Economic Research Organization estimates that a single Hawaiian watershed is worth $7.4 billion to $14 billion. The financial rewards come in the form of sustainable agriculture, ecotourism, groundwater, climate control, and subsistence.

To protect its environmental assets, the Pu'u Kukui Watershed Preserve is not open to the public. Access is limited in an effort to reduce the introduction and spread of invasive species, which can be transported in the form of seeds and insect larvae that may arrive on visitors' clothing, shoes, and sack lunches. Admission is occasionally open through special events put on by ML&P.

Further Reading

Cox, George W. *Alien Species in North America and Hawaii: Impacts on Natural Ecosystems*. Washington, DC: Island Press, 1999.

Maui Land and Pineapple Company Inc. http://www.mauiland.com/.

Nevada

The landscape of Nevada is strikingly barren, with scant rainfall to support vegetative life; the state is relatively devoid of the biodiversity that is characteristic of the rest of the Pacific and West region. The state is, however, not without its natural places; the northern portions of Nevada are characterized by the Great Basin and its associated sagebrush and juniper plant communities. The southern half of the state, which is even drier than its northern counterpart, is covered by the Mojave Desert. This desert ecosystem is frequently defined by the presence of Joshua trees and, although seemingly bereft of life, supports an estimated 1,800 species of plants and animals.

Conservation in Nevada faces some unusual obstacles that go back to the Homestead Act and the settlement of the West. Due the extreme environment and an acute lack of densely vegetated grazing lands, it was not feasible for homesteaders to settle in Nevada. The few who did settled near an available water source and then leased government land for grazing their livestock (a practice that is still in place today and poses additional threats to Nevada's native flora and fauna). The majority of Nevada's land (86%) is still owned by the federal government and has been subject to various uses, many of which have precluded these lands from conservation.

The deserts of Nevada have long been subject to nuclear testing. Beginning in 1951 and continuing to 1992, the U.S. government performed both atmospheric detonations and underground weapons testing in an area known as the Nevada Test Site. While testing in this site seems to have desisted, the state is now at the center of a major push to store the nation's nuclear waste in the Yucca Mountains of the Mojave Desert. Public opposition and legal charges have so far waylaid the attempt.

Conservation efforts have focused on Nevada's water-based ecosystems leading to the protection of its rivers, streams, wetlands, marshes, meadows, and lakes. Although the vast majority of the state's flora and fauna are highly adapted to the desert environment, none can survive in the absence of water. Moreover, thousands of migrating birds rely on Nevada's wetlands and marshes as a place of refuge to rest and refuel before continuing their journey between

Alaska and South America. Water is not just a pivotal issue as far as wildlife conservation is concerned but a matter of urgency for the entire population of Nevada. Several consecutive years of below-average snowpack in the Colorado Rockies have translated into dire water shortages for southern Nevada in particular, which gets 90 percent of its municipal water from the Colorado River. Water from the Colorado is stored behind Hoover Dam and subsequently fills the Lake Mead reservoir. As of October 2007, Lake Mead is filled to only 47 percent of its capacity, thus leaving the state in search of another more immediate source of water. The problem is further compounded by population growth: Las Vegas tops the U.S. Census Bureau's list of America's fastest growing cites.

Amid growing pressure, Nevada's leading conservation groups including the Nature Conservancy, Eastern Nevada Landscape Coalition, U.S. Forest Service, U.S. Fish and Wildlife Agency, the Bureau of Land Management, the Trust for Public Land, the Audubon Society, Trout Unlimited, and the Sierra Club have already begun to tackle the state's most urgent issues. Assisting are an equally savvy group of farmers, ranchers, business owners, and grassroots citizen groups, all of which have a vested interest in the environmental health and economic stability of their home state.

Ash Meadows National Wildlife Refuge

Ash Meadows National Wildlife Refuge springs to life in a very unusual location. In the midst of the parched Mojave Desert and just 90 miles west-northwest of the city of Las Vegas, the refuge is one of the West's last remaining examples of a desert oasis. The almost supernatural presence of water in an otherwise desiccated environment is the result of geological fault, which acts as an underwater dam. A massive amount of water is backed up behind the formation and is subsequently forced to the surface, where it marks the landscape with numerous springs and seeps. All together, the refuge's seven major springs gush at a rate of more than 10,000 gallons per minute. Scientists estimate that this water entered the groundwater system several thousand years ago before making its way to the surface of the Mojave—hence, the name fossil water.

This wealth of water brought an onslaught of development in the 1960s and early 1970s. Water diversion, road development, large-scale earth moving, livestock grazing, and crop irrigation severely impacted native wildlife and was further exacerbated by the introduction of more than 100 nonnative plants and animals. During this same time, a large wetland area tucked in the northwest portion of the soon-to-be refuge called Carson Slough was drained and mined for peat moss. The threat of urban development loomed large in the early 1980s as the land was slated to be divided into a 20,000-lot subdivision. However, a 1984 purchase by the Nature Conservancy with help from the Bureau of Land Management, U.S. Fish and Wildlife Service, Nevada Senator Paul Laxalt, and the Richard King Mellon Foundation placed 23,000 acres of this remarkable landscape into protection. The reserve, which is now managed by the U.S. Fish and Wildlife

Shallow water and reeds in Crystal Lake in Ash Meadows National Wildlife Refuge. (Courtesy of Muriel Areno)

Service, harbors a number of species that are not only endemic to the region but are also federally listed as endangered or threatened. Threatened plant species include, Ash Meadows milk vetch, spring-loving centaury plant, Ash Meadows sunray, Ash Meadows gum plant, Ash Meadows ivesia, and Ash Meadows blazing star. Four species of endangered fish inhabit the area's springs, and include the Ash Meadows Amargosa pupfish, warm springs pupfish, Devil's Hole pupfish, and Ash Meadows speckled dace. The Devil's Hole pupfish measures a mere three-quarters of an inch and, until recently, lived in one specific spot on earth. The fish's indigenous waters are located in a 500,000-year-old cave measuring about 300 feet deep and filled with 86° F spring water. Although relatively small in size, these fish have been at the center of numerous conservation efforts and legal battles, some of which have made it all the way to the Supreme Court. The 1976 case of *Cappaert v. United States* was one such example which also set legal precedence in regard to water rights by ruling that the neighboring landowners and developers did not have the right to pump and use water that would have otherwise drained into Devil's Hole. This ruling helped to ensure that water levels in Devil's Hole would continue to sustain the endangered pupfish.

Water exploitation continues to be one of the largest threats to Ash Meadows. Population growth in Las Vegas and surrounding cities continues to deplete underground aquifers, thus altering the flow of the meadow's springs and channels. Protecting the Ash Meadows aquifer and reestablishing historical flow levels are just one of the goals of the U.S. Fish and Wildlife Service. The agency is also working to control invasive species such as largemouth bass, tropical fish, crayfish, and bullfrogs. These species prey upon native animals and compete for similar living space among other resources.

Further Reading

Kuletz, Valerie. *The Tainted Desert: Environmental Ruin in the American West*. New York: Routledge, 1998.

BLACK ROCK DESERT

Located in northwestern Nevada is a vast conservation area called the Black Rock Desert—High Rock Emigration Trails National Conservation Area. The area was signed into protection in 2000 by President Clinton and encompasses 799,163 acres of public land that is managed by the Bureau of Land Management. Much of this public land (roughly 751,847 acres) is classified as wilderness area and therefore garners additional protection. The Black Rock area in the southern half of the greater conservation area is split into two arms by the Black Rock Mountain Range. The east arm contains the Black Rock Wilderness and is therefore managed by a different set of rules than the rest of the Black Rock Desert. As a wilderness area, all mechanized modes of transportation and machinery are prohibited; this includes everything from mountain bikes to airplanes to chainsaws. What may initially seem like a trivial set of differing laws makes for an interesting contrast between east and west.

The wilderness to the east is a place of perpetual solitude and isolation. Bound by the Jackson Mountain range in the east and the Black Rock range in the west, the wilderness in between is accessible only by foot or horseback. The terrain here is classic basin and range habitat, with hills covered in sagebrush, balsam root, bitterbush, mountain mahogany, and sporadic bunchgrasses. The higher elevations support trees such as aspen and Utah juniper, while low-lying water-gathering depressions are home to isolated stands of riparian woodlands, open meadows, and wetlands. A variety of big game including mule deer, pronghorn antelope, and bighorn sheep can be sighted roaming both open sage lands and steep canyons. The wilderness also provides critical habitat for sage grouse, which have recently experienced dramatic declines in population due to habitat loss. Most scientists agree that the sagebrush communities on which the birds depend have been dying off due to an extended period of drought in the Great Basin area. As a result, the birds are now candidates for the endangered species list. Wrens, warblers, sparrows, hummingbirds, falcons, owls, and eagles are among the other avian inhabitants. People visiting the Black Rock Wilderness may hike, hunt, camp, and rock climb or immerse themselves in stargazing, rock hounding, and photography.

Although similar activities draw visitors to the west arm of the Black Rock region, this desert playa sits in stark contrast to its easterly neighbor. The playa of the Black

Black Rock Desert. (Courtesy of Jeremiah Galli)

Rock Desert was once the bottom of a massive prehistoric lake called Lake Lahontan. At one time, this lake covered most of northwestern Nevada as well as parts of southern Oregon and northeastern California. However, over thousands of years, the lake dried, leaving northwestern Nevada pocked with leftover lake beds. The Black Rock Desert playa covers more than1,600 acres and is one of the largest playas in the United States. The flat-as-a-pancake surface is covered in deep alkaline silt that is devoid of vegetation and nearly bone dry for most of the year. In spring, however, if precipitation is plentiful, the playa may fill with several inches of standing water. This phenomenon induces the mass hatching of millions of tiny crustaceans called fairy shrimp, which, in turn, feed flocks of migrating waterfowl and shorebirds. The arid Nevada sky eventually reclaims the water, and, as it does, the fairy shrimp reproduce, lay eggs, and die. The eggs will lay dormant in the salty soil until the water returns, which may not be for several years. During the interim when the playa is dry, it serves as a testing ground of human ingenuity. It was here in 1997 that the world land speed record of 763 miles per hour was set by Andy Green, and several amateur rocket clubs regularly use the Black Rock playa as a launch site and have set records of their own. As if fairy shrimp, speed records, and rocketry were not enough, the desert playa is also home to the annual Burning Man Festival. The 30,000-plus people who attend the week-long celebration of art and self-expression are incorporated into a temporary community known as Black Rock City (BRC). For that week, BRC ranks as Nevada's seventh largest city.

The commotion inflicted on Black Rock playa is intense but sporadic, and when the people clear and the dust settles, there are still many sights to be appreciated. Starry skies free of light pollution, wild horses and burros, sand dunes and hummocks dotted with greasewood and wildflowers, and geothermal hot springs are among the many wonders that survive.

Further Reading
Burning Man. http://www.burningman.com.
Goin, Peter, and Paul F. Starrs. *Black Rock*. Reno: University of Nevada Press, 2004.

JARBIDGE WILDERNESS

Compared to the rest of Nevada with its arid landscape of sagebrush and rock, the Jarbidge Wilderness is a breath of fresh air. Located in the northeastern corner of the state, the Jarbidge Wilderness and its surrounding mountains receive seven to eight feet of snow on an annual basis. The spring snowmelt then fills several lakes and dozens of streams that drain into the Jarbidge River, all the while sustaining plant and wildlife communities found nowhere else in the state. The topography of the region is spectacularly rugged, hosting 10 peaks that measure over 10,000 feet above sea level. These impressive summits are also paired with equally stunning canyons. Jarbidge Canyon, for example, reaches a depth of more than 4,800 feet, which is nearly equal to the depth of the Grand Canyon. For all its jagged terrain, there are 150 miles of trails that can be explored by hiking, cross-country skiing, or horseback. Despite such opportunities, Jarbidge is one of America's least visited wilderness areas, so it offers profound seclusion to an abundance of wildlife and a handful of adventuresome people.

Originally founded in 1964 and covering 64,667 acres, the Jarbidge Wilderness was Nevada's first wilderness area. The area was expanded by the Wilderness Protection Act of 1989 and now spans 113,167 acres. In sharp contrast to many of America's natural places, the Jarbidge Wilderness has not been subject to extensive human influences. Aside from a brief burst of mining activity during the Gold Rush, the area has remained virtually untouched. Such conditions not only encourage a great abundance of flora and fauna but also support high levels of biological diversity. The biological diversity of the region is due to the unique position of the Jarbidge Wilderness, which sits at the junction between the southern boundary of the Snake River Plains and the northern reaches of the Basin and Range Province. The dry plateaus support sagebrush and bunchgrasses, while the river and stream banks are lined with cottonwood, alder, mountain ash, and willow. Tress such as aspen, mountain mahogany, cedar, limber pine, white-bark pine, and subalpine fir can be found growing in canyons as well as at higher elevations. Hundreds of species of grasses have adapted to nearly every nook and cranny and soil type in the Jarbidge region. Even the vertical faces of rocky

Jarbidge Wilderness. (Courtesy of Mary-Austin & Scott)

outcroppings and tree trunks are encrusted with plant life in the form of lichens and mosses. Many herbaceous or nonwoody plants are also strewn about the wilderness area and are most noticeable in spring when they are in full bloom. Lupine, monkshood, penstemon, evening primrose, Indian paintbrush, and mule's ear are a handful of the wildflowers that dot the spring landscape in hues of blue, yellow, orange, and red. Diverse vegetation gives rise to diverse animal life, including pronghorn antelope, elk, cougar, bobcat, pika, ferrets, western marmots, rainbow trout, rubber boas, and a plethora of bird species.

Yet another notable feature of the Jarbidge Wilderness is its designation by the Environmental Protection Agency as a Class I Airshed. The pristine air of the Jarbidge Wilderness is one of more than 150 such sites in the United States and receives the highest level of protection offered by the Clean Air Act, which was established by Congress in 1963 and subsequently amended in 1977 and 1990. Clean air, plentiful water, and high levels of biodiversity make Jarbidge an outdoor enthusiast's paradise but are also unique in a state that is otherwise dominated by arid landscapes.

Further Reading
McPhee, John. *Basin and Range*. New York: Noonday Press, 1990.

McCarran Ranch

The 305-acre McCarran Ranch is located 15 miles east of the city of Reno and was purchased in 2002 by the Nature Conservancy. The ranch, which is bisected by the Truckee River, supports a variety of wildlife including deer, mountain lion, turtles, frogs, trout, carp, raptors, and songbirds. The ranch also hosts a number of educational outreach programs, birding events, and other public recreational activities. Most of the recent activity on the ranch has been due to its multimillion dollar facelift that included the restoration of native wetlands and riparian forests and reconstruction of the river bed. Restoration of the McCarran Ranch was of particular importance because the venture was an initial pilot project for a larger-scale ($40 million) restoration of the Lower Truckee River. Since the work at McCarran was to eventually be repeated along other sections of the river, the Nature Conservancy and its many conservation partners were careful to gather baseline data regarding fish populations, algae growth, water chemistry, and available habitat so that before-and-after comparisons could be made.

Restoration efforts focused on a specific mile-long river section that had been straightened in 1962 in an attempt to control localized flooding. Prior to being straightened, the river slowly meandered through a serpentine path, saturating adjacent low ground, which provided the water necessary to sustain rich habitats of wetlands and riparian forest. Like water shooting through a straight tube, the new river course did not allow time for water seepage and led to the demise of the area's natural habitats. The new water corridor also expanded the dimensions of the river from its original width of 75 feet to 200 feet. Its swift flow additionally scoured away about three feet of bottom substrate. Such dramatic changes have occurred up and down the 110-mile-long Truckee River and contributed to some staggering statistics: Estimates suggest that the number of nesting migratory songbirds has declined by 70 percent, while Truckee's riparian forests have regressed by 60 percent. Threatened species such as the Lahontan cutthroat trout, northern leopard frog, and western pond turtle are also faced with extirpation or localized extinction. The process of restoring the historical river path began in fall 2003 and enlisted the help of commercial excavating equipment to raise the river bed and narrow its width from 200 feet to 120 feet. Several bends were also put back into the river in an attempt to reconnect the river to its original floodplains. The next several years were devoted to restoring native vegetation by planting stands of cottonwood and willow and creating rearing ponds for turtles and frogs. The location and structure of the rearing ponds were specifically designed to protect developing leopard frogs from nonnative predators including bullfrogs and crayfish. Artificial underground dens, brush piles, rock piles, bird perches, and nesting boxes and platforms were also added to encourage species to utilize the restored habitats. While revegetation projects are ongoing, the bulk of the job was completed in December 2006.

For now, the McCarran Ranch project appears to be a success; side-by-side aerial photographs show a prerestoration river lined by only thin margins of plant life, while the postrestoration photo shows a sprawling green landscape of mixed vegetation. The work here is not done, however, as the conservancy and its partners will continuously monitor and gather data regarding the health and abundance of both aquatic and terrestrial life as well as water quality. Such data will help conservation specialists better understand and predict the outcomes of additional restoration projects that are scheduled for other portions of the Truckee.

Further Reading

Dawson, Robert, Peter Goin, and Mary Webb. *A Doubtful River.* Reno: University of Nevada Press, 2003.

MOAPA VALLEY NATIONAL WILDLIFE REFUGE

The Moapa Valley National Wildlife Refuge is a relatively small 117-acre parcel located in southeastern Nevada just outside the town of Glendale. The refuge is divided into four units, each of which were acquired at different points in time and each of which contains its own separate stream system. The founding unit, the Pedersen Unit, was acquired in 1979, followed by the Plummer Unit in 1997, the Apcar Unit in 2000, and finally the Pederson #2 Unit in 2006. These parcels are managed as a collective whole with the main goal of protecting the endangered Moapa dace. In fact, the Moapa preserve was the first national wildlife refuge to be created for the sake of an endangered fish. The Moapa dace is also endemic to Nevada, meaning that it is found nowhere else in the world. Furthermore, the fish is confined to the geothermal springs and streams that drain into the Muddy River and later Lake Mead. These spring waters are characteristically high in calcium carbonate and very warm with an average temperature of 90° F. Since the dace's habitat requirements are so specialized, it does not relocate or transplant well and is especially sensitive to changes in its environment. Habitat loss, degradation, modification, chemical runoff, and invasive species such as mosquito fish, tilapia, and shortfin mollies, have all taken a toll on the Moapa dace.

The U.S. Fish and Wildlife Service (USFWS), which manages the refuge, is working to reverse some of this damage by restoring habitat, monitoring water quality as well as quantity while also conducting research and public outreach. A major focus of the USFWS efforts have been on the Pederson and Plummer Units, because this land had previously been operated as vacation resorts complete with swimming pools, bath houses, and extensive plantings of nonnative palm trees. Since 2006, nearly all artificial structures have been removed, and the Pedersen Unit has been rid of its nonnative fish. Palm trees and invasive thickets of cattails, Canadian thistle, and salt cedar have also been removed to make way for natives like willows, mesquite, salt grass, spike rush, pondweed, and watercress. Such improvements have brought the dace population up from an estimated few hundred in 1977 to well over 1,000 according to a 2005 census. In addition to the Moapa dace, several other species of concern inhabit the refuge, including the Moapa pebblesnail, Moapa warm spring riffle beetle, Moapa White River spring fish, desert tortoise, loggerhead shrike, and phainopepla. Zebra-tailed lizards, western whiptail lizards, red-tailed hawks, barn owls, bats, American kestrels, mourning doves, belted kingfishers, and white-crowned sparrows are among the commonly encountered fauna.

Although the USFWS has made great strides toward reestablishing this natural place, there is still significant work to be done. Many of the projects are not yet complete, and it is truly an area under environmental construction. As such, the Moapa Valley National Wildlife Refuge is not yet open to the public. Like the rest of Nevada, the Moapa region is in the midst of a water crisis. Increasing population growth directly translates into an increased need for municipal water. In the case of Moapa National Wildlife Refuge and the greater Moapa Valley, it has been proposed that the valley's groundwater be pumped and diverted to Las Vegas. The consequences of such actions are, for the most, part poorly understood but likely to be fiercely debated in America's courtrooms.

Further Reading

Moore, Roberta, and Scott Slovic, eds. *Wild Nevada Testimonies on Behalf of the Desert.* Reno: University of Nevada Press, 2005.

PAHRANAGAT NATIONAL WILDLIFE REFUGE

Located in the southeastern corner of Nevada, the Pahranagat National Wildlife Refuge extends down the southern half of the Pahranagat Valley. The valley is bound by the Irish Range and Pahranagat Range to the west and by the Hiko Range to the east and bisected by two major highways. Although much of the valley and its surrounding landscape typify Great Basin vegetation with its saltbush and sagebrush, the Pahranagat National Wildlife Refuge is nothing short of an oasis. Several bodies of water are in and around the refuge support unique assemblages of water-loving vegetation. The majority of the refuge's water originates from several large springs situated north of the refuge. These same springs also support local agriculture and ranching endeavors. It is theorized that the flow of the White River has also been impacted by irrigation demands, and it might have, at one time, contributed significant amounts of water to the refuge. The flow of the White River is now intermittent and is permanently dry to the south of Lower Pahranagat Lake. In addition to Lower Pahranagat Lake, there is also an Upper Pahranagat Lake and a Middle Pond, all of which hold open water habitat. Several marshlands including the Middle Marsh and North Marsh also hold pockets of water interspersed with reeds, cattails, and other herbaceous plants.

Although a number of different animal species inhabit the refuge, it arguably serves its most important role as a bird sanctuary. Tens of thousands of birds use the refuge as a rest stop during their long migration from South America to Alaska via the Pacific Flyway. Many more call the refuge home, breeding, nesting, and raising fledglings within its 5,380 acres of habitat. Over 230 bird species use the Pahranagat Refuge during some phase of their life cycle. Large flocks of waterfowl and shorebirds congregate in the marshlands during various seasons. Great blue herons, egrets, cinnamon teals, and sandhill cranes in spring; mallards, Canada geese, Clark's grebes, canvasbacks, and American coots abound in summer. Fall peaks with increases in waterfowl populations, while winter brings raptors including osprey, bald eagles, and migrating northern harriers. While other habitats are not necessarily home to flocks of thousands, they are home to other plant communities and yet another diverse array of birds. Riparian habitats dominated by cottonwood and willow give songbirds like warblers, finches, flycatchers, and orioles a place to nest and raise their young. Several species of sparrows inhabit the drier uplands, as do roadrunners, ring-necked pheasants, and Gambel's quail.

Since the refuge is a matrix of starkly different environments and occupants, its management requires practices specifically tailored to each of the habitats. Separate vegetation programs are in place for desert, wetland, and grassland communities. Invasive species also differ among habitats, as do the methodologies of control. The refuge also runs various educational, research, and student intern programs. Waterfowl management, population surveys, water quality monitoring, and prescribed burns are among the additional responsibilities of the refuge's two-person staff. Limited staff and budget constraints are just a few of the obstacles to managing Pahranagat. Water, or the lack thereof, is the most prominent threat to the refuge and its inhabitants. Water will always be at a premium since most of Nevada receives less than 10 inches of rain per year and is therefore classified as a desert. The problem is further exacerbated by unprecedented population growth. For example, in 2007, the U.S. Census Bureau ranked the city of Las Vegas among the top 10 population-gaining cities in America. In many cases, urban demands for water are being met by diverting water from rural sources, and the Pahranagat Valley is no exception. A 2008 agreement between the Southern Nevada Water Authority and a number of other state agencies has already paved the way for such water usage. Numerous safeguards are written into such contracts in an effort to protect both wildlife and the ecosystems that sustain them. Although it is impossible to tell how contracts and nature will coexist, it is inevitable that water will continue to be at the center of both.

Further Reading
Red Rock Audubon. http://www.redrockaudubon.org.

Pyramid Lake

Pyramid Lake is all that remains of ancient Lake Lahontan. Its prehistoric shorelines once stretched as far east as California and into southern Oregon and, in doing so, submerged most of northwestern Nevada as well. The ancient lake's surface has dwindled over the past 12,000 years from 8,500 square miles to roughly 188 square miles. Like a giant mud puddle drying in the desert, its deepest point remains and is now called Pyramid Lake. As the waters receded, they left behind a geological wonderland that would inspire both the native Paiute as well as modern scientists. Even the water itself is unique due to the lack of outflow. Water flows into the lake via the Truckee River, but there is no additional river by which water drains from the lake. Water leaves only by evaporation or seepage into the ground and subsequently causes the water to be saline in nature.

The lake was central to the life and times of the northern Paiute people, which consisted of a multitude of separate tribes that were settled near some body of water or wetlands environment. The tribe that lived along the shores of Pyramid Lake were known as the Cui Ui Ticutta (meaning cui-ui eaters) since this fish was a staple of their diet. As with any native homeland, its landscape and wildlife sustained the Paiute both physically and spiritually for thousands of years prior to the arrival of European settlers. It is thought that contact with white settlers began in the early 1840s. As the number of settlers coming into the area increased, the Paiute quickly realized that a living could be made by harvesting and selling fish from the lake. The cui-ui (for which the Pyramid Lake tribe is named) and the Lahontan cutthroat trout were both heavily exploited. Settlers' preferences for trout over the cui-ui, which is a sucker fish, put additional strain on the species. Although estimations vary, it is thought that, at the fishery's peak, more than a million pounds of Lahontan cutthroat trout were harvested on an annual basis. Unsustainable fishing was not the only factor that led to the trout's extirpation or local extinction. Two dams—one in the Mason Valley and the other on the Truckee River—blocked the spawning runs of both fish species and altered water flow. On several occasions, water levels were lowered to such an extent that spawned eggs were left high and dry in the river beds. By 1930, the fishery could not even sustain subsistence living, and, by 1945, the Lahontan cutthroat was deemed to be locally extinct.

Both fish are now federally listed; although biologists estimate that as many as one million cui-ui now live in Pyramid Lake, the species remains listed as endangered due to its highly unpredictable reproductive rates and extreme sensitivity to changes in water quality, including flow rate and temperature. Understanding the recovery of the threatened Lahontan cutthroat is more complex because the species is further divided into subspecies and these subspecies frequently mate with one another, thus creating hybrids. Genetic research has shown the Lahontan cutthroat has hybridized with both rainbow trout and Paiute cutthroat trout and has thus lost some of the distinctive characteristics of a pure Lahontan trout. It is now debatable whether the original Pyramid Lake strain of Lahontan cutthroat still exists. (Some claim that, prior to their demise, the Pyramid Lake strain where used to stock several Nevada streams and that the pure strain still exists in these streams.) The Lahontan cutthroat that are now raised in the tribe's fish hatchery and used to stock Pyramid Lake are originally from the waters of nearby Summit Lake but are thought to be the closest genetic match to the original species.

Pyramid Lake is completely contained within the Pyramid Lake Paiute Tribes' reservation, therefore the management and monitoring of the lake and its wildlife is done by the tribe. Three fish hatcheries, also administered by the Paiute Tribe, help to ensure the continued survival of both the Lahontan cutthroat trout and the cui-ui. Preservation efforts also secure nesting habitat for white pelicans and a number of other shorebirds that use the lake as a stopping point during their migrations. Several of the lake's most sensitive bird habitats are closed to the public, and violators are subject to steep fines. The lake, located 35 miles northeast of Reno, is open to the public for seasonal hunting, fishing, camping, and boating, although each activity requires a permit.

Further Reading

Reeve, Paul W. *Making Space on the Western Frontier: Mormons, Miners, and Southern Paiutes*. Champaign: University of Illinois Press, 2006.

Wheeler, Sessions S. *The Desert Lake: The Story of Nevada's Pyramid Lake*. Caldwell, ID: Caxton Press, 2003.

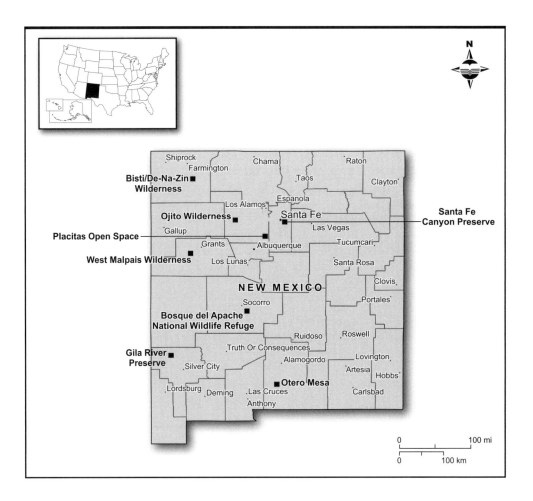

Bisti/De-Na-Zin Wilderness, 90

Bosque del Apache National Wildlife Refuge, 91

Gila River Preserve, 93

Ojito Wilderness, 94

Otero Mesa, 95

Placitas Open Space, 97

Santa Fe Canyon Preserve, 99

West Malpais Wilderness, 100

New Mexico

New Mexico is a landscape of striking contrast where the southern edge of the Rockies gives way to shimmering grasslands which then dissipate into the Chihuahuan Desert. New Mexico, like much of the American Southwest is an arid environment that is given to dramatic vistas whenever water flows through its otherwise parched landscape. A vast majority of New Mexico's surface water drains from the Sangre de Cristo Mountains, which are a subrange of the Rockies and are located in the northernmost portion of the state. Several notable rivers flow from the Sangre range, including the Canadian River, Rio Grande, Santa Fe, and Pecos. In a story so familiar to the West, these and most of New Mexico's other rivers have been dammed and diverted to supply both municipalities and agriculture with water. Population growth, climate change, and seasonal droughts have continued to plague many of New Mexico's rivers, and, in some instances (as is the case with the Santa Fe River) they intermittently run dry.

The Rio Grande and Pecos, however, continue their flow in a southerly direction, crossing through the Chihuahuan Desert, which occupies both central and southern New Mexico, and eventually flowing past the United States–Mexico border. The Chihuahuan Desert not only characterizes most of New Mexico's environment but is also one of the world's least explored and least studied deserts. This desert ecosystem is remarkably different from other desert ecosystems, because it sits at a higher elevation and is therefore defined by a markedly cooler climate. Another rarity among deserts exists here in that the Chihuahuan is dotted with small mountains. The mountains provide a further temperature buffer and are inhabited by a unique assemblage of plants and animals. Due to its unique geography and climate, scientists estimate that the Chihuahuan may be the planet's most biologically diverse desert.

As far as conservation efforts are concerned, the state is particularly focused on water issues. The state is addressing water conservation issues from a number of directions ranging from sustainable city planning and public education to legally securing and protecting existing sources from pollution. New Mexico also has some interesting decisions to make in regard to both its groundwater supply and potentially rich deposits of natural gas. Extraction of these deposits stands to be extremely profitable and yet threatens to contaminate one of New Mexico's largest remaining untapped aquifers. A number of active and well-organized associations—including the Coalition for Otero Mesa, the Nature Conservancy, the Trust for Public Land, New Mexico Wilderness Alliance, and the Chihuahuan Desert Conservation Alliance—are working to protect the state's water resources and the region's native flora and fauna.

BISTI/DE-NA-ZIN WILDERNESS

The skeletonized topography of the Bisti/De-Na-Zin Wilderness occupies the northwestern corner of New Mexico and is contained within the greater San Juan Basin. Much of its 45,000 acres is devoid of topsoil and water and therefore lacks the biological diversity typical of most wilderness areas. For the most part, the Bisti/De-Na-Zin Wilderness is a natural place of scenic vistas, a place where the eyes may be stretched for miles until they finally meet the horizon. Some striking and bewildering views are found in the badlands of the Bisti/De-Na-Zin Wilderness. The badlands are a geological phenomena resulting from the sandwichlike configuration of three earthen layers; of these deposits, the middle layer—or Fruitland Formation—dominates the badlands landscape and lies atop the Pictured Cliffs Sandstone layer. The third and most recent stratum caps the bottom two layers and is called the Kirtland Formation. Because the geology of each layer is unique, they tend to erode at different rates. Wind, rain, and freeze-thaw cycles work away at softer sediments such as sandstone and mudstone and leave harder deposits in place. Over the course of eons, the earth's natural forces have sculpted out massive sandstone pillars topped with giant, precariously overhanging slabs of shale. These dramatically strange stone formations, commonly called hoodoos, dot the badlands and are also intermixed with sandstone spires. Collectively, the three geological layers contribute to the Martian-like landscape and are also a testament to an era when the badlands were anything but a dry, life-deprived wasteland. Fossilized plant leaves of palm and cypress and petrified tree stumps suggest that the Bisti region was once a lush, swampy rainforest. The teeth of *Tyrannosaurus rex, Dromaeosaurus, Troodon,* and *Richardoestesia* along with a dozen or more types of dinosaurs hint at a once biologically diverse ecosystem. Although life in the Bisti/De-Na-Zin Wilderness is not as abundant as it once was, a handful highly adapted plants and animals manage to thrive under very harsh conditions.

In addition to the badlands, the wilderness contains regions of sagebrush, grasslands, and piñon-juniper forest. Additional plant species including yucca, saltbush, ponderosa pine, cacti, Indian ricegrass, Basin daisy, Mormon tea, and Bisti fleabane provide the necessary food and shelter to support several species of birds, mammals, and reptiles. Rabbits, coyotes, badgers, doves, jays, quail, golden eagles, ferruginous hawks, rattlesnakes, and an assortment of lizards are among the wilderness' few inhabitants. With rainfall limited to about eight inches per year, the Bisti/De-Na-Zin Wilderness fits the classic definition of a desert and is remote and rugged. Its arid terrain lacks both a trail system and signage, so visitors must be careful to pack and dress accordingly. The wilderness is open, free of charge to the public for primitive use only, meaning no motorized vehicles are allowed. Its designation as wilderness has saved the beautifully sculpted terrain from off-road vehicles and prevented the drilling and extraction of coal-based methane (CBM) from its underlying sediments. The San Juan Basin is considered one of the world's largest CBM fields, and the Bisti Wilderness is surrounded by drilling and methane extraction. Since CBM is a valuable energy source, the Bureau of Land Management, which oversees the Bisti/De-Na-Zin Wilderness, considered opening the area to drilling in the late 1990s; however, public outcry quickly tabled the proposal. Several environmental concerns surround the process of CBM extraction; most notable is a reduction in groundwater levels and a lack of consensus among scientists about the rate at which these underground reservoirs recharge or refill. The tug-of-war between a thirsty wilderness and its energy deposits and a nation that needs both will likely have some impact on both the wilderness and the San Juan Basin at large. Change, however, is nothing new to the Bisti/De-Na-Zin Wilderness.

Further Reading

Energy Justice. "Coal-Bed Methane." http://www.energyjustice.net/naturalgas/cbm/.

Howe, Wesley M. *From Basin to Peak: An Explorer's Companion to Colorado–New Mexico San Juan Basin.* Lubbock: Texas Tech University Press, 1998.

BOSQUE DEL APACHE NATIONAL WILDLIFE REFUGE

The Bosque del Apache National Wildlife Refuge encompasses a diverse terrain consisting of wetlands, farmlands, riparian forests, and mesas. The area, which is managed by the U.S. Fish and Wildlife Service (USFWS), covers 57,191 acres of central New Mexico and is intersected by the Rio Grande. The river is the lifeblood of the refuge and quenches the otherwise arid state along its 1,885-mile course from the foothills of the Canby Mountains in Colorado to the Gulf of Mexico. Approximately 3,800 acres of the refuge are part the Rio Grande's floodplain and are subject to periodic flooding. These moisture-laden areas are prime habitat for Rio Grande cottonwood, Gooding's willow, coyote willow, honey mesquite, and four-wing saltbush along with a wide assortment of wildflowers, grasses, and other herbaceous perennials.

Together, the floodplains and bottomlands serve as critical breeding and nesting ground for numerous bird species, some of which—like the southwestern willow flycatcher—are federally listed as endangered. Thousands of other birds utilize the area as a stopover along their migrations between South and North America via the Central and Rocky Mountain Flyways. Scientists estimate that more than 340 avian species, including sandhill cranes, snow geese, American white pelicans, wood storks, mountain chickadees, purple martins and red-naped sapsuckers, use the Bosque del Apache National Wildlife Refuge in one capacity or another. The Bosque's bird list also includes 14 of the 20 species listed in the Audubon Society's 2007 report of the top 20 common birds in decline. The refuge serves as a breeding ground for six of these dwindling populations: the least bittern, northern pintail, rufous hummingbird, loggerhead shrike, lark sparrow, and black-throated sparrow.

The lush vegetation of the floodplains and bottomlands eventually gives way to parched scrublands and piñon-juniper woodlands. These characteristically dry landscapes are dotted with highly adapted desert vegetation that commonly includes mesquite and creosote bush alongside rarer flora such as tall bitterweed, Plank's catchfly, San Antonio bluestar, and Mogollon whitlowgrass. Reptiles abound in this environment; checkered whiptails, desert grassland whiptails, and New Mexico whiptails, although relatively common, are noteworthy due to the fact that their populations are entirely female. Reproduction in these species is parthenogenic, meaning that eggs are laid and hatch without fertilization, and offspring are genetically identical to the parent. These lizards and the greater earless lizard and side-blotch lizards commonly feed on insects, spiders, and scorpions and in turn become prey for snakes and raptors.

Several threats loom over the Bosque del Apache refuge. Invasive species and wildfires threaten native species and jeopardize the overall stability of the area's ecosystems. Three invasive plant species—salt cedar, Russian knapweed, and perennial pepperweed—pose a constant threat by crowding out native plants and hoarding water. Controlling the spread of these weeds is only one facet of the problem, because herbicidal applications and mowing or disking via heavy tractor equipment carries its own set of risks and can be costly. Bare or disturbed ground must then be immediately reseeded or replanted with native species to prevent erosion while giving native plants the chance to take root before the nonnative flora reestablish themselves. In recent times, wildfire has unintentionally eradicated large stands of invasive salt cedar but also left vast amounts of acreage relatively devoid of vegetation and thus subject to severe erosion and entirely open to settlement by invasive plants. In response to these challenges, the USFWS has developed management plans that guide rehabilitation efforts following the event of a wildfire. The USFWS in conjunction with numerous volunteers, including groups like the Friends of the Bosque, work to rehabilitate and monitor both the flora and fauna of the Bosque and work with the surrounding community. In addition to the annual Festival of the Cranes, a variety of educational events and public outreach activities connect the public with the natural wonders of the Bosque.

Further Reading

Friends of the Bosque del Apache National Wildlife Refuge. http://www.friendsofthe bosque.org.

Horgan, Paul. *Great River: The Rio Grande in North American History*. Middletown, CT: Wesleyan University Press, 1991.

GILA RIVER PRESERVE

From its headwaters on the western slope of the Continental Divide, the Gila River transverses the lower half of New Mexico and bisects the surrounding desert with its generous water supply. Along the river's meandering course springs a lush riparian habitat that has long been a source of reprieve for many. Several Native American tribes inhabited the region along with Spanish settlers, trappers, miners, and other pioneers of the West, not to mention a plethora of plants and animals. In addition to its long and colorful history, the river holds further significance as one of the West's last free-flowing rivers. This is not to say, however, that the river is entirely undammed. The Gila flows unabated through New Mexico before crossing into Arizona and encountering Coolidge Dam, which is the only major dam on the river. Several other Arizona-based water diversion projects reduce the flow of the Gila to a trickle by the time it joins the Colorado River.

New Mexico has, on the other hand, been quick to appreciate the value a pristine Gila River ecosystem and has responded by establishing several preserves along its length. The Gila River Preserve protects more than 1,000 acres of riparian forest habitat that is dominated by Fremont's cottonwood, Gooding's willow, and narrow-leaf cottonwood. Collectively, these tall, dense trees form a thick canopy under which cool, deep shade is plentiful. Scientists estimate that nearly 400 species of plants grow within the preserve. Additional examples include Arizona sycamore, mule fat, sandbar willow, box elder, honey mesquite, Carruth's sagebrush, canyon grape, and ponderosa pine. Such varied plant growth provides ample and diverse resources, which, in turn, support hundreds of birds, mammals, amphibians, reptiles, and countless insects. Although a large number of bird species live primarily within the preserve's riparian zone, a myriad of other desert-dwelling birds dart in and out, taking advantage of its tempered climate and constant water supply. Bell's vireo, Cassin's kingbird, yellow-billed cuckoos, scaled quail, white-winged doves, curved-billed thrashers, Rivoli hummingbirds, cliff swallows, common mergansers, green herons, and roadrunners are just a few the preserve's inhabitants. Raptors are also a common sight and include zone-tailed hawks, turkey vultures, American kestrels, elf owls, and golden eagles. The preserve also protects several rare birds, including the common black hawk, Gila woodpecker, and southwestern willow flycatcher. The river is also home to several species in peril; the loach minnow and spikedace are both federally listed as threatened, while the Gila chub has been listed as endangered by the federal government. A long list of fauna continues with small-mouthed bass, several species of catfish, 12 species of bats, hog-nosed skunks, mountain lion, bobcat, collared peccary, Texas horned lizards, several species of whiptailed lizards, spiny soft-shelled turtles, diamondback rattlesnakes, Arizona coral snakes, and desert king snakes.

Wildlife viewing, birding, photography, botany walks, and volunteer opportunities are all major attractions of the Gila River Preserve. The preserve is located 30 miles west of Silver City and may be accessed via Highway 293. Although the Gila River Preserve is cooperatively managed by the Nature Conservancy and the state of New Mexico, its long-term health and stability are reliant on the river and its free-flowing nature. Attempts to dam the river are one of the most prominent threats not only to the Gila River Preserve but to the entire riparian corridor, its flora and fauna, and the citizens of the state of New Mexico, who stand to foot the bill for such projects. So far, the three major water diversion efforts—Hooker Dam, Conner Dam, and the Mangas Diversion project—have been thwarted, yet the proposals keep coming. The last proposes to divert 14,000 acre-feet of water from the Gila on an annual basis—this is twice the amount already diverted for industry and agriculture. The Gila Conservation Coalition estimates that transporting the water to Silver City would cost significantly more than simply drilling new wells and purchasing additional water rights. Furthermore, the coalition points out that lost revenues from tourism and added costly ecological impacts must also be added into the project's final price tag.

Further Reading

Baker, Malchus B., Peter F. Folliott, Leonard F. DeBano, and Daniel G. Neary, eds. *Riparian Areas of the Southwestern United States: Hydrology, Ecology, and Management.* Boca Raton, FL: CRC Press, 2003.

Glennon, Robert. *Water Follies: Groundwater Pumping and the Fate of America's Fresh Waters.* Washington, DC: Island Press, 2004.

OJITO WILDERNESS

From fossilized dinosaur remains to prehistoric human dwellings and right up to the fulfillment of its modern-day designation as a wilderness area, the Ojito Wilderness has preserved millions of years of earth's history. The region is, in many respects, a typical representation of a New Mexican desert: dry, hot, and lacking significant water. Despite these conditions, the wilderness is home to a wealth of highly adapted plants and animals that live among a backdrop of spectacular geological formations, including sandstone hoodoos, steep mineral colored mesas, box canyons, deep arroyos (dry stream beds), and high bluffs. Among the rarest of the plants here are grama grass, cactus, Townsend's aster, and Knight's milk vetch. Old ponderosa pine, piñon, hedgehog cactus, juniper trees, and a variety of bunchgrasses also grow in the Ojito. The scant vegetation is enough, however, to support mule deer, American antelope, elk, and mountain lion, along with a number of songbirds. This desert region is especially suitable for a wide range of reptiles, including gopher snakes, diamondback rattlesnakes, short horned lizards, and prairie lizards. In fact, the Ojito has a long history of sustaining reptilian life.

One of the most extraordinary natural geological features found in the wilderness area is the presence of the Morrison Formation. This formation is a vast layer of sediment that dates back 150 million years to the Jurassic era and covers large parts of New Mexico, Colorado, the Dakotas, and Montana. While the formation covers an extensive amount of the United States, only isolated portions are exposed, as is the case in Ojito. Fossils recovered from the Ojito Wilderness hint at an environment that was once a lush oasis dominated by riparianlike vegetation consisting of tree ferns, ginkgo, and cycads. During this time, the Ojito was most likely part of a large floodplain based on the presence of fossilized crocodiles, salamanders, fish, turtles, and mollusks. The wilderness has also produced hundreds of dinosaur fossils, including the large herbivorous *Camptosaurus* and the heavily armored *Stegosaurus*. One of the most impressive discoveries was made by two hikers who accidentally stumbled upon a large set of bones. Once unearthed and reassembled, the find yielded one of the largest dinosaurs skeletons ever discovered. The *Seismasaurus* measured 125 feet long and weighed an estimated 110 tons. The age of the dinosaurs eventually gave way to the age of the mammals, and several eons would pass before humans would make their mark on this land.

A number of archeological sites within the wilderness document various periods of human inhabitation starting some time during the Archaic period, from 8000 B.C. to roughly 1000 B.C. Eventually, the Navajo and Pueblo Indians would inhabit the region, living off the land's resources and leaving behind petroglyphs, pottery fragments, pueblo ruins, and small fireplaces called kivas. Ancestors of these people still inhabit the region and live in the neighboring Pueblo of Zia. Although the Bureau of Land Management oversees the 11,000-acre wilderness, the Pueblo of Zia has also worked to ensure that their ancestral home remains open to the public.

Further Reading

Foster, John. *Jurassic West: The Dinosaurs of the Morrison Formation and Their World.* Bloomington: Indiana University Press, 2007.

OTERO MESA

The Greater Otero Mesa stretches across 1.2 million acres of south central New Mexico and is considered to be North America's largest and most intact Chihuahuan Desert grassland. The land here is a spectacular arrangement of undulating black grama grassland, canyons, mountains, and cacti-studded desert. In contrast to its wild beauty, the Otero Mesa has, in recent years, been embroiled in a battle involving the Bush administration, the Bureau of Land Management (BLM), the state of New Mexico, and various conservation groups. Oil is central to the conflict, with one side wanting to drill and extract the Mesa's oil reserves and the other wanting the wilderness protected. Charges of back-room deals, obstruction of scientific evidence, and a slew of federal lawsuits continually mire the Otero Mesa in the worst of human nature.

Humans have, however, inhabited the mesa for thousands of years, leaving behind archeological sites consisting of petroglyphs, remnants of pottery, and stone artifacts. Scientists estimate that the landscape that sustained these early inhabitants remains largely intact today. Herds of pronghorn wander through grasslands of blue and black grama, bur-rograss, dropseed, and fluffgrass. Grasslands give way to a variety of highly adapted desert plants: mesquite with its 100+-foot taproots, creosote bush (possibly the oldest living organism in existence) with its reduced leaf structure and extreme longevity, as well as cacti like the fishhook barrel cactus and cholla, which are armed with unpalatable spines. Tarbush, Mormon tea, yucca, mountain mahogany, piñon, juniper, silktassel, shrub live oak, netleaf hackberry, desert willow, and cottonwood add to the region's plant diversity. The mesa is also home to a number of mammals, including mountain lions, badger, gray fox, ringtail cats, black-footed ferrets, desert mule deer, and black-tailed prairie dogs. The biodiversity of the Otero expands further when the box turtles, toads, frogs, salamander, skinks, whiptail and horned lizards, geckos, and snakes are accounted for. Additionally, some 200 species of birds also call the Otero Mesa home. When the vertebrate roll call is complete, about 282 species of animal life fill every nook and cranny of the mesa, from its canyons to its isolated mountain springs and on to the Otero's famous grasslands and deserts.

Beneath its teeming surface lies the source of all life: water. Scientists estimate that the aquifer beneath the Otero Mesa holds New Mexico's largest untapped freshwater resource. Protecting this water resource is a central aim in efforts to halt oil drilling in the mesa. Concerns regarding groundwater contamination, protocols for disposing of

Looking west-southwest to the San Andres and Organ Mountains. (Courtesy of Joe Adair)

contaminated water, and the blatant wasting of such a resource have been a few of the concerns posed by the state of New Mexico and several conservation groups such as the Wilderness Society, the Coalition for Otero Mesa, New Mexico Wilderness Alliance, the Sierra Club, and Earth Justice. The collective force of these organizations have repetitively requested that the BLM rescind its current drilling plans on the basis that the proposal offers inadequate protection for the mesa's wildlife, water, and cultural heritage. The state of New Mexico has taken the BLM to court over the matter, and, as of fall 2008, no ruling has been made. Regardless of the legal ruling, the turmoil surrounding the precious resources of Otero Mesa is likely to continue. Ironically, for now, there is no better place to find quiet solitude than amid the mesa's vast and waving grasslands or atop its worn volcanic peaks.

Further Reading
Coalition for Otero Mesa. http://www.oteromesa.org.
McNamee, Gregory. *Otero Mesa: Preserving America's Wildest Grassland.* Albuquerque: University of New Mexico Press, 2008.

PLACITAS OPEN SPACE

Conservation of the Placitas Open Space is an exemplary case of community action and long-term planning. Preservation efforts were initiated in 1966, when the city of Albuquerque purchased a 640-acre parcel from the Bureau of Land Management. A subsequent land deal reduced the acreage to its current 560 acres. It was not until the mid-1990s, when development loomed over Placitas, that community members formed two grassroots conservation groups that would eventually merge and become the Las Placitas Association. Today, the association works as a liaison between various governmental agencies and the general public to safeguard the flora and fauna of the area and, by extension, preserve its watershed while at the same time ensuring public access and promoting community outreach. The Las Placitas Association also works with the city of Albuquerque to coordinate various scientific surveys of the area's wildlife and cultural resources. Data gathered from these studies have guided the drafting and implementation of the Placitas Open Space Master Plan, a document that details both the accomplishments and goals for this open space.

The Placitas Open Space is 23 miles north of Albuquerque and three miles northwest of the village of Placitas. Although the region is a semidry climate with average precipitation rates of 12 to 13 inches of rain per year, most of it falls during July and August. Such concentrated rainfall results in seasonal flood cycles, which in turn shape many of the area's plant communities and soil profiles. For example, both the riparian and floodplain grassland communities are frequently inundated with water as the Las Huertas Creek swells and overflows during the wet season. Las Huertas Creek begins as a mountain spring and runs a mere 14.5 miles before joining the Rio Grande. En route, the creek also bisects the Placitas Open Space and provides the water necessary to sustain a variety of life forms. There are four distinct vegetative communities within this open space: the riparian and floodplains grasslands, piñon-juniper woodlands, and juniper grasslands. The majority of Placitas is covered in piñon-juniper woodland, which is visibly dominated by piñon and one-seed juniper and interspersed with joint-fir, Bigelow sagebrush, yucca, and other shrubs. The juniper grasslands are composed of a dense patchwork of black grama, New Mexico feathergrass, and galleta grass. As the name implies, these grasslands are also dotted with one-seed juniper. The remaining two plant communities are closely associated with Las Huertas Creek. The coyote willow, Fremont cottonwood, rubber rabbit brush, and Apache plume that grow streamside are a few of the species that dominate the riparian community. The adjacent floodplains are especially noteworthy since they are given to periodic flooding and yet own the distinction of having the highest plant diversity. Rabbit brush, Indian ricegrass, needleleaf dogweed, spike dropseed, one-seed juniper, four-wing saltbush, fluffgrass, and desert marigold are all common amid the floodplains. In total, roughly 200 additional plant species may be found in the Placitas Open Space, thus providing a myriad of resources for reptiles, mammals, and birds.

The list of birds is as diverse as it is lengthy: 75 species in total, ranging from massive birds of prey like the golden eagles to broad-tailed hummingbirds. Placitas is especially critical to Say's phoebes, Cassin's kingbirds, loggerhead shrikes, the juniper titmouse, Crissal thrashers, mountain bluebirds, and black-throated sparrows, all of which breed and nest within this protected area. Scientific surveys have reported that the Placitas Open Space is also home to 40 species of mammals, including black bear, mule deer, mountain lion, and bobcat in addition to several dozen types of reptiles and eight species of amphibians. Species surveys are one tool used to design the management plan for Placitas Open Space. Scientists have also gathered data regarding stream flow rates, water quality, soil profiles, and invasive species so that management decisions may be based on scientific data. Meanwhile, community volunteers are busy maintaining and establishing hiking trails, installing signage, restoring native plant communities, and working to control erosion. At the same time, government entities like the city of Albuquerque, Sandoval County, and the state of New Mexico work to provide some of the funding that is needed for daily operations and maintenance.

Further Reading

City of Albuquerque Open Space Division. "Placitas Open Space Master Plan." http:// www.cabq.gov/openspace/pdf/placitasmasterplan.pdf.

Middleton, Beth A. *Flood Pulsing in Wetlands: Restoring the Natural Hydrological Balance*. New York: John Wiley and Sons, 2002.

SANTA FE CANYON PRESERVE

The Santa Fe Canyon Preserve is a unique urban sanctuary located in New Mexico's capital city of Santa Fe. Originally established in 2000, the preserve was born of a 190-acre land donation from the Public Service Company of New Mexico to the Nature Conservancy. In 2007, the preserve was expanded by another 77 acres via a private land donation from Ralph and Janice Brutsche. The Nature Conservancy continues to work to incorporate neighboring land parcels into the preserve with the ultimate goal of doubling its total acreage. The emphasis on expanding the Santa Fe Canyon Preserve stems from its abundant assemblage of plants and animals (especially songbirds) along with its constant source of water.

In an otherwise arid climate, the preserve holds several ponds that sustain groves of willow and cottonwood. These two tree species dominate the riparian plant community and are often found near perennial water sources. Moving away from the riparian zone, other plant communities take precedence, including piñon-juniper woodlands and ponderosa pine. Sagebrush, herbaceous perennials, reeds, and rushes further enhance the area's overall plant diversity and provide the necessary food and shelter for more than 140 species of birds. Wetland areas provide a thicket of dense reeds and grasses that provide coverage for eared grebes, red-winged blackbirds, great blue herons, Virginia rails, and yellow-headed blackbirds. Mallards, northern shovelers, buffleheads, blue-winged teals, and lesser scaups also stay close to the preserve's water sources. Songbirds such as western bluebirds, Bewick's wren, yellow-breasted chats, and canyon towhees are joined by hummingbirds, swallows, jays, and quail. From time to time, visitors may also spot osprey, red-tailed hawks, merlin, and northern pygmy owls. Although the preserve is widely visited because of its avian diversity, a host of other animals—including deer, beaver, black bear, and an occasional mountain lion—also find refuge within the Santa Fe Canyon Preserve.

The preserve, as well as the city of Santa Fe, are sustained by the Santa Fe River, which cuts through both on its way to the Rio Grande. Within the preserve, the remnants of two old dams still persist: Old Stone Dam built in 1881 and the Two-Mile Dam, which was completed in 1893. These, along with other modern dams, have continually altered the flow of the Santa Fe River by storing its waters in manmade reservoirs backed by large dams. Today, the McClure and Nichols reservoirs hoard the vast majority of the river's water, thus reducing the Santa Fe River to less than a trickle. In fact, on most days, a trip to the river will yield a view of a barren and, in some places, weed-choked channel dotted with smooth, dry river rocks and bordered by an eroding bank. On occasion, an especially wet spring or heavy mountain snowmelt will temporarily restore the river's flow, with much of this water being released from the upstream reservoirs when they reach capacity. In a sense, the Santa Fe River is now more of a drainage ditch than a river.

These water management practices have been detrimental not only for wildlife but for small towns and private landowners as well. As the city of Santa Fe held back water for its growth and development, the people and land downstream began to experience shortages. Agricultural fields of alfalfa and corn as well as orchards waned and perished. Private wells had to be drilled even deeper to reach an ever-dropping aquifer.

The culmination of these factors prompted the American Rivers conservation group to list the Santa Fe River as America's most endangered river in 2007. The annual report calls attention to the river's history and economic and social value and outlines some of its most immediate needs. Among the top priorities is a long-range water plan; initiated by city leaders with input from citizens, the plan needs to establish a river-friendly approach to growth and development while making a long-term water resource management plan that includes the needs of the Santa Fe River.

Should the Santa Fe River be allowed to flow on a continual basis, its ecosystems will, over time, renew themselves, and the riparian plant and animal communities will return. For now, the Santa Fe Canyon Preserve serves as a reminder of what once was and what may be again.

Further Reading

Stanton, Paul, ed. *Rivertown: Rethinking Urban Rivers*. Cambridge, MA: MIT Press, 2007.

Wohl, Ellen E. *Disconnected Rivers: Linking Rivers to Landscapes*. New Haven, CT: Yale University Press, 2004.

WEST MALPAIS WILDERNESS

When translated from its Spanish name, Malpais (bad country), might initially deter visitors and conjure images of an ominously doomed landscape. The terrain of the West Malpais Wilderness is, indeed, strikingly unfamiliar when compared to the rest of the continental United States. The region that now contains the West Malpais Wilderness has a lengthy history of volcanic activity with the most recent eruptions and lava flows occurring 2,000 years ago. Lava tubes, rows of cinder cones, and fissures testify to a recently formed environment that is still undergoing primary ecological succession, a process by which newly formed land is inhabited by plant and eventually animal communities. The youngest lava formations that oozed from beneath the earth's crust now sit like frozen globular piles of black glass, shiny and largely devoid of plant life. Eventually, these rocks will be settled upon by various lichens. Lichens are usually the first vegetative forms to inhabit new terrestrial surfaces and will eventually grow, reproduce, die, and decay, thus contributing to the first smidge of soil. Over time, decayed material will accumulate, often filling cracks and crevices into which other plant seeds will settle. Grasses, wildflowers, and other small forbs will be the next to establish themselves. As these first vegetative communities complete their life cycles and as time wears on, the soils will accumulate, deepen, and eventually support larger shrubs and ultimately trees. Primary succession is by no means fast; it takes thousands of years.

The West Malpais Wilderness is at various stages of succession; areas of black, bare lava rock contrast with neighboring ancient cinder cone formations, some of which are well forested by piñon and juniper. Due to its diverse geology, the West Malpais

Wilderness hosts a variety plant of communities. In addition to the piñon-juniper forest, stands of ponderosa pine and Douglas fir are also common. These forests eventually give way to open grassland mesas and shrub communities as well as deciduous oak woodlands and aspen groves. Elk, mule deer, coyote, bear, bobcat, pronghorn antelope, and cougar are among the large mammals of Malpais. Golden eagles, red-tailed hawks, roadrunners, quail, mountain bluebirds, wild turkeys, mountain plover, loggerhead shrikes, and great horned owls are just a few of the approximately 190 bird species that inhabit the various ecosystems in the West Malpais Wilderness. Also notable are several species of bats, which find ample refuge in the area's caves, lava tubes, and earthen fissures.

The area's flora and fauna have been attracting people to the region for thousands of years, from early Native Americans who left behind petroglyphs to modern visitors who aim to leave no trace. Two of the most frequently visited natural features include a 6,700-acre area called Hole-In-The-Wall and a row of cinder cones called Chain of Craters. Contrary to its name, Hole-In-The-Wall is anything but a void of space; it is more suitably referred to as a *kipuka,* meaning fertile ground in Hawaiian. This particular swath of land was nearly encircled by the region's most recent lava flows, thus forming an island of deep soils and ample vegetation and wildlife. While Hole-In-The-Wall is located in the northeastern corner of the wilderness area, the Chain of Craters dots the western border. The string of 25 cinder cones are lined up along a zone where the earth's crust was relatively thin. Under building pressure, the earthen seam split, spewing bits of rock and hot lava, which eventually formed the cone-shaped mountains, some of which are well over 7,000 feet high.

The Malpais Wilderness covers roughly 40,000 acres and is included within the greater El Malpais National Conservation Area, which was established in 1987 and is managed by the Bureau of Land Management. Under the designation of wilderness, the region is open to the public for primitive recreation only, meaning that motorized transportation is not allowed. The exception to the rule applies to farmers and ranchers who maintain herds of grazing livestock. Although grazing has occasionally been an issue as far as wilderness conservation goes, most debate has centered around vehicle and equipment use. Ranching operations frequently use motorized equipment to shuttle livestock and to maintain fences, pipelines, and watering locales. Ranching under a wilderness designation requires numerous permits and subsequent processing time before many of these activities may take place. Such oversight is aimed at preserving a degree of wildness that will benefit both wildlife and nature enthusiasts; however, it has also created some skepticism among those who are leery of supporting the wilderness designations lest it should interfere with daily business operations.

Further Reading

Cawley, McGreggor R. *Federal Land, Western Anger: The Sagebrush Rebellion and Environmental Politics.* Lawrence: University Press of Kansas, 1993.

Mutz, Kathryn, and Doug Cannon. "El Malpais Area: National Monument, National Conservation Area and the West Malpais and Cebolla Wilderness Areas." Natural Resources Law Center. http://www.colorado.edu/law/centers/nrlc/projects/wilderness/ElMalpais.pdf.

OREGON

O regon is a state bisected by the Cascade Range and thus divided into strikingly different eastern and western halves. The climate of western Oregon is heavily regulated by offshore weather patterns that bring copious amounts of rainfall. In some coastal areas, annual rainfall may average more than 200 inches per year. This damp environment supports lush, old-growth forest; numerous rivers, streams, and estuaries; and oak woodlands and rare coastal prairie lands.

A vast majority of Oregon's population lives on the rainy side of the state, specifically within the Willamette Valley. The valley's fertile soils support an agricultural industry based on grass seed, beer hops, Christmas trees, hazelnuts, wine grapes, and blueberries. Although Oregon's population and economic centers are very much concentrated this half of the state, conservation efforts have certainly not lagged. The city of Portland, for example, is not only the state's most populated city but also boasts a lengthy history of environmentally friendly city planning dating back to the early 1900s. This trend has continued, making Portland one of the nation's greenest cities; from its early recycling programs to allocation of urban green spaces and restoration projects, Portland and, by extension, western Oregon have set forth exemplary conservation measures. The state also recognized the importance of its marine ecosystems, extending protection to the hundreds of offshore islands that dot the entire length of the Oregon coast. Such efforts have been made to protect western Oregon's native flora and fauna and enhance the state's livability for its citizens.

The drier eastern half of Oregon, although less populated, is no less important as far as conservation goes. It is here in western Oregon that geological time becomes most relevant; sculpted badlands, mineral-rich sediments, and 50-million-year-old fossil beds bearing bones of hippo and camel tell of a landscape very different from today. Western Oregon also contains one of the West's last remaining native grasslands, several critical trout fisheries, vernal pool habitat, and rare Rogue Valley chaparral.

Conservation of Oregon's natural places have, like much of the Pacific and West, been the undertaking of both state and federal governments as well as private nonprofit groups such as the Nature Conservancy, Connecting Green, the Urban Greenspaces Institute, and Portland Audubon. Another 11 private land trusts continually work with landowners to protect the natural environment and the rural lifestyle that define so much of Oregon.

AUDUBON SANCTUARY

From its inception in the early 1900s, the Portland Audubon Society has adhered to its primary mission "to use any and all lawful means for the protection of the wild birds and animals for the State of Oregon and elsewhere." Over the decades, Portland's Audubon chapter has been a motivating voice for conservation in both the political arena and the community at large. In addition to supporting and publicizing the creation of the Ankeny, Baskett Slough, William L. Finley, Three Arch Rocks, Klamath, and Malheur National Wildlife Refuges, the Portland Audubon Society also established its own 150-acre preserve.

Audubon Sanctuary is located five miles from downtown and offers the public free access over four miles of trails. These trails form several large loops and encompass a diverse assemblage of lush plant life. Western red cedar, bigleaf maple, vine maple, red alder, and western hemlock provide a dense, cool canopy under which a variety of shrubs and ferns grow. The verdant understory is comprised of vanilla leaf, maidenhair fern, fringecup, miner's lettuces, and yellow wood violet, among others. Many more of the preserve's plants are host plants for various butterfly larvae; Nootka rose, for example, is the caterpillar host plant for western checkerspot, morning cloak, and gray hairstreak butterflies. A large number of berry-producing shrubs, including serviceberry, salmonberry, red huckleberry, creeping snowberry, salal, and thimbleberry, dot the landscape and sustain a variety of birds and other mammals, including black bear. Additional mammal species include montane shrews, big brown and silver-haired bats, northern flying squirrels, eastern cottontail rabbits, striped and spotted skunks, elk, mule deer, bobcat, red fox, and cougar. Aquatic species including beaver and river otter, native cutthroat trout, red-legged frogs, western painted turtles, pacific giant salamanders, and roughskin newts inhabit the preserve's pond and several creeks that crisscross through the area.

True to the Audubon name, the preserve also protects vital habitat for a diverse number of birds, ranging from nectar-sipping hummingbirds, to Steller's jays, mourning doves, Swainson's thrushes, pileated woodpeckers, and mighty birds of prey. The Audubon Sanctuary protects the habitat upon which these birds depend and comes to the aid of sick and injured birds. The sanctuary's wildlife rehabilitation program began about 70 years ago and is currently one of Oregon's oldest and largest rehabilitation facilities, taking in an average of 3,500 animals each year, from ordinary crows to the federally threatened northern spotted owl. The center has also amassed a large data base regarding cause of injury: Among the top four causes are being caught by cats, human interference, being hit by cars, and being orphaned. Most cases of orphaning involved mother mallard ducks being hit by cars and adult songbirds being killed by cats while protecting their young. The care center also takes the opportunity to track banded birds that are brought in for treatment, as the band can provide valuable information about the migration and behavior of the species.

The commitment of the Audubon Sanctuary reaches far beyond land conservation. The work of well over 100 volunteers not only sustains the operations of the rehabilitation center but also provides the public with opportunities to attend lectures, guided tours, workshops, and day camps for both adults and children.

Further Reading

Ozawa, Connie P. *The Portland Edge: Challenges and Successes in Growing Communities*. Washington, DC: Island Press, 2004.

Portland Audubon Society. http://www.audubonportland.org.

Boardman Grasslands

Located in north-central Oregon just outside the town of Boardman, the Boardman grasslands are the epicenter of a dizzying array of activity. Spanning more than 69,000 acres, the area encompasses the Boardman Conservation Area, the Boardman Bombing Range, and an additional 22,642 acres that are subleased to the Nature Conservancy via Threemile Canyon Farms. The farm is by no means a small operation, producing 200,000 tons of potatoes on an annual basis and maintaining 16,000 head of dairy cows. The Boardman Grasslands are also home to a coal-fired electric plant, a radar trial site, and several feedlots and are fringed by agricultural fields. Despite such development, the grasslands remain one of the largest continuous blocks of native shrub steppe and grassland habitats in Oregon State.

Remarkably, some areas within the grasslands have not been grazed in over 50 years, thus preserving the soil's delicate biological crust. These crusts are a conglomerate of bacteria, lichen, and mosses that form a thin layer over the soil and thus prevent erosion, retain moisture, and aid in seed germination. With healthy soil in place, natural vegetation prevails. Western juniper, antelope bitterbrush, basin big sagebrush, Wyoming big sagebrush, needle-and-thread grass, bluebunch wheatgrass, downey wheatgrass, and Sandberg's bluegrass all thrive in the semiarid environment and create a specialized habitat for a number of animals. Birds flock to the area in such numbers that the Audubon Society recognizes the Boardman Grasslands as an Important Bird Area (IBA). The IBA program aims "to identify and conserve areas that are vital to birds and other biodiversity." In doing so, the Audubon Society brings attention to the wide range of avian species, including grasshopper sparrows, horned larks, loggerhead shrikes, long-billed curlews, western kingbirds, savanna sparrows, western meadowlarks, sage thrashers, and ring-necked pheasants, all of which rely on the grassland habitat. American kestrels, burrowing owls, prairie falcon, Swainson's hawks, northern harriers, and ferruginous hawks are among the birds of prey commonly seen patrolling the open terrain. Other top predators include bobcat, badger, and coyote. White-tailed jackrabbits, mule deer, sagebrush lizards, and a number of small rodents are also common. The Boardman Grasslands also serve as critical habitat for the Washington ground squirrel, and the squirrels, in turn, play a major role in the grasslands ecosystem. As the squirrels dig, they are constantly mixing soil nutrients, scattering seeds, increasing the soil's ability to hold water, and deterring soil compaction. Even abandoned burrows are utilized by other animals such as snakes, lizards, and burrowing owls. This small squirrel spends a great deal of its life underground, so large portions of its life cycle are not well understood. Studies suggest that the squirrels form social bonds in small groups and have limited periods of fertility followed by one litter per year. Ground squirrel survival rates are relatively low due to predation—especially by birds of prey—although ecologists also think that starvation during hibernation is a major mortality factor. Due to their subterranean lifestyle, researchers have found it impossible to accurately count ground squirrel populations and so instead monitor active colonies. Recent decreases in active colonies in combination with habitat loss and fragmentation have been the motivating forces behind the ground squirrel's listing by the state as an endangered species and its current status as a candidate for listing at the federal level.

Washington ground squirrel recovery efforts have created some unlikely partnerships between the U.S. Navy, the Nature Conservancy, Threemile Canyon Farms, Portland General Electric, and the Oregon Department of Fish and Wildlife. These organizations and others are working to balance agriculture, space and aeronautical development, and energy needs with conservation practices. Of particular importance is the spread of invasive plant species, especially cheatgrass. This invasive grass spreads quickly, thrives in nearly all soil conditions, and takes special advantage of areas where the biological crusts have been damaged or destroyed. Furthermore, studies suggest that areas that have been taken over by cheatgrass are more prone to fire, burning every 3 to 5 years compared to every 20 to 100 years for native sagebrush-bunchgrass ecosystems. Such frequent burns perpetuate the spread of cheatgrass and debilitate native sagebrush and bunchgrasses, which take longer to grow and mature. Although the ground squirrel will eat cheatgrass, its diet is typically very diverse, consisting of flowers, seeds, bulbs, buds, and grasses. Cheatgrass is of low nutritional value, and some researchers theorize that the ground squirrel's diet is shifting to include more and more cheatgrass as the invasive plant spreads. This change in diet may be contributing to die-offs via starvation during winter hibernation. With so much still unknown about the biology and behavior of Washington ground squirrels, it is only reasonable that great emphasis be placed on conserving their native habitat.

This task will be no small feat since the Boardman Grasslands' fertile soils hold promise of being highly productive agricultural fields, and existing developments are critically tied to national security, energy, and food production.

Further Reading

Belnap, Jayne, and Otto L. Lange, eds. *Biological Soil Crusts: Structure, Function, and Management*. New York: Springer, 2002.

Lindenmayer, David, and Joern Fischer. *Habitat Fragmentation and Landscape Change: An Ecological and Conservation Synthesis*. Washington, DC: Island Press, 2006.

CASCADE HEAD EXPERIMENTAL FOREST AND SCENIC RESEARCH AREA

Cascade Head Experimental Forest and Scenic Research Area boasts a long history of conservation in the name of science. In 1934, the Cascade Head Experimental Forest was designated under the charge that the area would be utilized for scientific research. Even prior to 1934, scientists had already begun observing and recording the growth patterns of the region's native Sitka spruce, western hemlock, Douglas fir, and red alder. The installation of a climate station in 1936 then allowed scientists to correlate climatological data with forest growth and productivity. The measuring and monitoring continued over the decades and today yields more than 70 years' worth of data, thus giving scientists an unprecedented long-term case study of a working forest ecosystem.

In 1974, an act of Congress combined the western half of the experimental forest with adjacent land parcels to create the 9,670-acre Cascade Head Scenic Research Area. The goals of the scenic area are similar to that of the experimental forest in that they support a variety of scientific endeavors ranging from seed dispersal to timber harvest techniques, nutrient cycling, understory vegetation, soil composition, and salt marsh restoration, among others. The scenic area, however, carries an additional responsibility to also promote human relationships with the environment. In addition to open public access, volunteer programs, and educational outreach, the Cascade Head Scenic Area is home to the Sitka Center for Art and Ecology. The center provides a place for artists and scholars "to expand the relationships between art, nature and humanity through workshops, presentations, and individual research projects; and to maintain a facility appropriate to its needs that is in harmony with the inspirational coastal environment of Cascade Head."

The biodiversity of Cascade Head is astounding due in part to the different ecosystems that are found within a relatively small area. The combination of prairie grasslands, estuaries, salt marshes, freshwater streams, and coniferous forest support an estimated 300 species of wildlife and more than 400 species of plants. Elk, deer, snowshoe hare, Pacific giant salamanders, bald eagles, and great horned owls are some of the more commonly sighted wildlife species. Common plants include red fescue, wild rye, Pacific reedgrass, coastal paintbrush, and lupine, in addition to the previously mentioned tree species. Also abundant, although somewhat less appreciated, are the lichens and mosses that thrive in the damp Oregon coast climate. Over 90 types of lichen and 180 moss species can be found clinging to various substrates. Less common(but closely monitored by area scientists) are the federally threatened coho salmon, spotted owl, marbled murrelet, and Oregon silverspot butterfly.

The Oregon silverspot is arguably the most famous of Cascade Head's inhabitants due in part to the multitude of organizations that are working toward saving the butterfly from extinction. The Nature Conservancy, Woodland Park Zoo, U.S. Fish and Wildlife Service, Lewis and Clark College, and the Oregon Zoo, along with countless volunteers are all working to preserve and enhance silverspot populations by via captive breeding programs and habitat protection. One of the biggest challenges surrounding recovery of the Oregon silverspot butterfly involves the feeding preferences of its larval caterpillar stage. As a caterpillar, its primary food source is the tiny purple violet, *Viola adunca*, commonly known as early blue violet or hooked-spur violet. The violet is also suffering declines due to development along the coastal grasslands where it grows. Invasive species and fire suppression are also allowing denser woodland shrubs and nonnative plants to encroach upon the violet's habitat. Scientists are experimenting with controlled burns and various methods of invasive weed control in an effort to promote violet growth and thereby give the Oregon silverspot caterpillars a dependable food source. A violet nursery also provides stock plants that are utilized in various captive breeding programs, which rear the larvae and then release the adults into the wild.

Given the area's high level of biodiversity and long history of ecological research and preservation, the United Nations Educational, Scientific and Cultural Organization (UNESCO) named Cascade Head a Biosphere Reserve in 1976. Cascade Head was added to UNESCO's Man and Biosphere program to acknowledge previous scientific work and encourage the continuation of scientific research that works to reduce biodiversity loss while improving social conditions, encouraging education, and creating environmental sustainability.

Further Reading

Agee, James K. *Fire Ecology of Pacific Northwest Forests*. Washington, DC: Island Press, 1996.

Wondolleck, Julia M., and Steven Lewis Yaffee. *Making Collaboration Work: Lessons from Innovation in Natural Resource Management*. Washington, DC: Island Press, 2000.

JOHN DAY FOSSIL BEDS NATIONAL MONUMENT

The John Day Fossil Beds National Monument protects one of the country's largest paleontological sites and, in doing so, brings to life eons of ecological biodiversity. The area is not only rich in fossilized specimens but its layers of rock and sediment (also called strata) were laid down in such a manner as to provide an uninterrupted timeline of fossilized plants and animals dating back some 50 million years ago. As a result, scientists and paleontologists have been able to reconstruct and document changes in the region's prehistoric climate and ecosystems

The fossils of the John Day Basin are embedded in four formations or strata, each of which is named and associated with a different time period. The oldest and deepest layer represents a time period ranging from 54 to 37 million years ago and is called the Clarno Formation. Fossils embedded in this layer represent animals that are extinct and evolutionary dead ends, meaning that they did not give rise to any modern species. *Patriofelis*, for example, was a large catlike animal with broad feet and short legs. This possibly semiaquatic catlike creature lived among the heavy-skulled doglike *hyaenodontids* and *amynodonts*, which were reminiscent of hippos. Water was apparently plentiful, as evidenced by a large and diverse number of plant fossils including palms, yew trees, bananas, dogwoods, pistachios, violets, and an assortment of fruits, nuts, and seeds.

The next layer is the John Day Formation. Dating from 30 to 18 million years ago, this layer contains more fossils than any of the other formations and testifies to a climate that was becoming increasingly cool and dry. The lush palms and bananas of previous eons were replaced with fossils of walnut, pine, buckthorns, roses, horse chestnut, and maples. Remnants of more than 100 animal species, including rhinos, horses, camels, false saber-toothed cats, and giant pigs, have also been exhumed from this layer. The John Day Formation is also marked with numerous ash layers, indicating an increase in nearby volcanic activity.

Volcanic activity continued well into the next stratum, which is called the Mascall Formation. The beginning of this layer dates back 15 million years ago and is marked by solidified layers of basaltic lava. Sediments and fossils sitting above the basalt layer hint at a climate that was moderately warm and wet and an ecosystem that was especially diverse. Lakes, streams, hardwood forest, and open grasslands supported a plethora of animals, including turtles, weasels, camels, deer, and the unusual bear-dog. The Mascall Formation includes all specimens dating from between 15 to 12 million years ago and gave way to the most recent layer, the Rattlesnake Formation.

Compared to the other strata, the Rattlesnake Formation contains relatively few fossils. The sediments of this stratum, which date from eight to six million years ago, point to further climatic changes. Fossil finds in this layer are dominated by grazing animals such llama, pronghorns, camels, and horses, thus indicating that grassland habitats had come to dominate the landscape. The drying trend that is indicative of the Rattlesnake Formation has continued well into modern times. John Day Basin now receives an annual rainfall of only 9 to 16 inches and is marked by drastic seasonal temperature fluctuations ranging from summer highs above 100° F to below zero during the winter. The landscape is equally dramatic, with its rough-and-tumble badlands, shimmering grasslands, cacti-studded deserts, and meandering creeks. A number of plant species including bee plant, bitterroot, John Day chaenactus, greasewood, and rabbitbrush are specifically adapted to the area's unique volcanic soils, some of which are severely devoid of nutrients. Large swaths of bunchgrasses, sagebrush, juniper, cottonwood, sedges, and berry-producing shrubbery provide ample resources for wildlife. Although the camels and hippos are long gone, the John Day Fossil Beds National Monument protects an extensive list of insects, spiders, mammals, reptiles, amphibians, birds, and fish. A short list includes more than a dozen species of bats, rubber boas, painted turtles, three species of rattlesnake, badger, gray wolves, black bear, mink, elk, and dozens of songbirds.

The monument and all its natural wonders, both extinct and extant, are protected and managed via the National Park Service, which is overseen by the U.S. Department of the Interior. Current management activities are focused on restoring the natural role of fire in this ecosystem. Scientists and researchers blame decades of fire suppression for the steady conversion of grasslands to juniper scrublands. Junipers, being particularly thirsty plants with extensive roots, readily decrease regional plant and animal diversity if not kept in check. Restoring a more natural fire regimen within a destination area for hikers, photographers, birders, and other outdoor enthusiasts is not without its risks and controversies but is necessary to preserve the biodiversity for which the area is famous.

Further Reading

Bishop, Ellen M. *In Search of Ancient Oregon: A Geological and Natural History.* Portland, OR: Timber Press, 2006.

St. John, Alan D. *Oregon's Dry Side: Exploring East of the Cascade Crest.* Portland, OR: Timber Press, 2007.

Oaks Bottom Wildlife Refuge

Oaks Bottom Wildlife Refuge is Portland's first formally designated wildlife refuge and is a prime example of an urban wasteland turned wildlife sanctuary. At one time, part of the refuge was used as a sanitation landfill; after being heaped with more than 400,000 cubic feet of construction waste, the area was capped off with a layer of soil. The soil used to bury the debris was claylike and not conducive to plant growth nor native vegetation. It would be many years and thousands of dollars later before this mistake could be remedied and restoration efforts would begin.

The Oaks Bottom Wildlife Refuge is best characterized as an urban wetland, sitting in southeast Portland along the east bank of the Willamette River. The refuge's skyline of oak and madrona is backed by the tracing of the city's skyscrapers. At 140 acres, the refuge, which is complete with trickling streams, lush thickets, looping trails, and mature moss-laden trees, attracts a number of visitors, both human and otherwise. Oaks Bottom is especially important for migratory birds, with an estimated 200 species either living in the refuge or using the refuge as stopover during migration along the Pacific Flyway. In May 2003, the city of Portland signed the Urban Conservation Treaty for Migratory Birds, thereby pledging to work in partnership with the U.S. Fish and Wildlife Service to effectively manage and enhance urban wildlife areas such as Oaks Bottom. The treaty's focus is to protect, create, and restore native habitat; educate the public; reduce hazards; and manage invasive species. As of fall 2008, Portland is one of only seven U.S. cities— and the only city west of the Rocky Mountains—to be participating in the program. Prior to signing the conservation treaty, the city of Portland was already working to restore the soils atop the old landfill area and remove several illegal dumping grounds that were piled high with household appliances and furniture.

Soil restoration and revegetation of the landfill began in the spring of 1993 with the removal of invasive blackberry thickets and stands of cottonwood. A soil analysis was done to gauge the depth and condition of the topsoil. Several years of heavy disking with a tractor followed by herbicide applications were necessary to rid the area of invasive plants, including garlic mustard, butterfly bush, prickly lettuce, giant knotweed, and ivy. The soil was eventually supplemented with 6 to 10 inches of a topsoil/compost mix and seeded with native grasses, herbaceous perennials, and other shrubs and trees such as red-osier dogwood, twinberry honeysuckle, Oregon grape, Pacific ninebark, cluster rose, red elderberry, rose spirea, and common snowberry. Special emphasis was placed on planting berry-producing natives that provide essential nutrients for migrating birds. Among the most colorful and commonly viewed birds are white-crowned sparrows, Bullock's oriole, rufous hummingbirds, western tanager, yellow warblers, red-winged blackbirds, American goldfinch, belted kingfishers, and great blue herons. Oak Bottom's more stealthy avian inhabitants include barred owls, great horned owls, Virginia rails, downy woodpeckers, spotted towhees, northern harriers, Cooper's hawk, and a large assortment of well-camouflaged sparrows. In line with its treaty obligations, the city of Portland organizes several public outreach events including the springtime International Migratory Bird Day Festival of the Birds. Oak Bottom is also popular among school groups, various Audubon chapters, hikers, photographers, botanists, and other outdoor enthusiasts. This natural area is well known throughout the Portland area as being easily accessible and kid-friendly, often cited as a great place for youngsters to explore their natural surroundings.

The Oaks Bottom Wildlife Refuge. (Courtesy of Donna M. Storz)

Further Reading
Adams, Clark E., Kieran Jane Lindsey, and Sara J. Ash. *Urban Wildlife Management.* Boca Raton, FL: CRC Press, 2006.
Weidensaul, Scott. *Living on the Wind: Across the Hemisphere with Migratory Birds.* New York: North Point Press, 2000.

OREGON ISLANDS NATIONAL WILDLIFE REFUGE

The Oregon Islands National Wildlife Refuge spans 320 miles from north of Tillamook to the Oregon-California border; it protects 1,853 offshore rocks, islands, and reefs along with two coastal headlands. The refuge, which was created in 1935 by the federal government, is largely off limits to the public due in part to the sensitive nature of its inhabitants. Coquille Point is, however, the exception; located in southern Oregon near Brandon, this mainland segment is open to the public and is complete with trails, beach access, and interpretive signage. The point overlooks an assemblage of craggy offshore rocks that are fairly representative of the rest of the coastline and that teem with breeding and snoozing harbor seals, California sea lions, Stellar sea lions, and northern elephant seals, along with a nearly unimaginable density of seabirds.

These rocky formations are home to 15 species of nesting seabirds including tufted puffins, rhinoceros auklets, pigeon guillemots, fork-tailed storm petrels, Leach's storm petrels, common murres, and three species of cormorants. Seabirds like these and others spend the majority of their lives out at sea, feeding and resting out on the open ocean. Breeding time, however, brings these birds ashore, where they congregate in large colonies to nest and raise their young before returning to sea. The numerous islands that dot the Oregon coast are prime nesting habitat; surrounded on all sides by the ocean, the islands are protected from most terrestrial predators and human disturbances. The islands also provide easy access to feeding grounds rich in herring, sardine, anchovy, smelt, and squid in addition to crustaceans like krill and copepods. This habitat, although relatively devoid of vegetation, supports an estimated 1.3 million breeding seabirds that cluster into large colonies, some of which consist of more than 100,000 individual birds.

Since the islands play such a critical role in the life cycle of these birds, special attention has been paid to monitoring and documenting population numbers as well as mapping colony locations. The U.S. Fish and Wildlife Service, which manages the refuge, publishes the survey data in a *Catalog of Oregon Seabird Colonies,* which provides both recent and historical data to biologists, researchers, regulatory agencies, and the general public. This information is critical to the health and stability of all seabird populations as they are faced with a number of growing threats. Overfishing, for example, not only depletes food resources but alters the food chain and contributes to increased bycatch mortalities that occur when birds become ensnared in fishing gear. Pollution is another growing concern and can take the form of floating plastics, oil, heavy metals, herbicides, pesticides, and other chemicals. These pollutants occasionally kill seabirds outright but

Haystack Rock, at 235 feet high, is the third largest coastal monolith in the world. Haystack Rock is protected as part of the Oregon Islands National Wildlife Refuge. (Courtesy of Timothy Heinse)

can also lead to changes in fertility, egg quality and quantity, and fledgling success—all subtle changes that, unless monitored, may go unnoticed.

Further Reading

Clark, Robert B. *Marine Pollution*. New York: Oxford University Press, 2001.

Oregon Birding Trails. "Oregon Coast Birding." http://www.oregoncoastbirding.com.

U.S. Fish and Wildlife Service. "Oregon Islands National Wildlife Refuge." http://www.fws.gov/oregoncoast/oregonislands/.

OWENS FARM

Prior to European settlement, the area that would someday become Owens Farm was tended to by the native Kalapuya. By setting fire to open grasslands, the Kalapuya were able to simultaneously roast and harvest the numerous seeds and nuts that were critical to their diet. These controlled burns also enhanced the soil's nutrients and increased food production for subsequent harvests. The presence of fire, both intentionally set and naturally occurring, also kept saplings and other shrubs from encroaching upon open prairie habitat, thereby maintaining the region's biological diversity. However, as Europeans settled the fertile Willamette Valley, fire suppression became the trend, and with it came drastic changes in habitat. The prairie lands that were once commonplace became more rare as the decades passed and trees and shrubbery crept into the once-open grassland. Today, the prairie habitat is one of the rarest ecosystems in the Willamette Valley.

Despite its long history as an agricultural landscape, Owens Farm contains remnants of prairieland and hosts areas of hardwood forest, wetlands, and riparian forest. The farm, which sits on the outskirts of Corvallis, has been managed since the 1850s for the production of grass seed, hay, livestock, and other crops. In 2000, the Owens Farm was sold and subdivided into three main parcels that were purchased in a three-way partnership. Samaritan Health Services now owns 85 acres of the original farm and will most likely develop the land via extension of its hospital facilities. Samaritan has, however, been willing to work with the Greenbelt Land Trust (which purchased 95 acres of Owens Farm) in the development of a trail system that may cross into the hospital's property. The city of Corvallis purchased the remaining 132 acres and is working with the Greenbelt Land Trust to conserve and restore the property, with the ultimate goal of establishing a system of trails and educational programs for the public.

Owens Farm encompasses a diverse matrix of vegetative communities. Low-lying lands adjacent to Frazier and Jackson Creeks support riparian forestlands consisting of willow, Oregon ash, creek dogwood, ninebark, and white alder. A series of sloughs, channels, and beaver ponds branch off the main creek beds and provide additional wetlands habitat and hold excess water during flooding. Large tracts of the farmland have been left uncultivated and are therefore covered with forests of Oregon white oak, bigleaf maple, and scattered ponderosa pine. The understory of these forest tracts have been invaded by highly invasive Himalayan blackberry, which grows in nearly impenetrable thickets. Woodland restoration has focused primarily on the removal of the blackberry via herbicidal application and mowing followed by seeding of native grasses and forbs. Wetland areas are also plagued by invasive species such as brome, reed canarygrass, tall fescue, orchard grass, and poison hemlock. These are just a few of a long list of nonnative plant species that the Greenbelt Land Trust has targeted for removal and continuous monitoring. Containment of invasive plant species is particularly important for a number of rare plants, including meadow checkermallow, Nelson's checkermallow, Kincaid's lupine, and Bradshaw's lomatium.

The farm's plant communities support a variety of wildlife, including a handful of federally listed species of concern such as the coastal cutthroat, northern red-legged frog, olive-sided flycatcher, Oregon vesper sparrow, yellow-breasted chat, acorn woodpecker, and band-tailed pigeon. The farm's more common residents include beaver, garter snakes, black-tailed deer, brush rabbits, eastern cottontails, nonnative bullfrogs, Pacific tree frogs, and western gray squirrels. Birds are also plentiful, with 76 species accounted for in recent biological surveys. It is estimated that 43 of these species breed and nest amid the various plant communities at Owens Farm, thereby further highlighting the importance of the Greenbelt Land Trust's conservation efforts.

While much of the Greenbelt Land Trust's work is done via coordinated management plans and dialogue within the greater Corvallis community, a great deal of its work involves navigating the legalities of city zoning laws. Zoning laws play a critical role in the development and taxation rates of the Owens Farm parcels and adjoining natural areas and stand to either enhance or inhibit preservation of the farm and greater Jackson-Frazier Wetland. The Greenbelt Land Trust is also partnering with neighboring landowners to ensure that the farm stays ecologically connected to adjacent habitats—especially the Jackson-Frazier Wetlands, McDonald Forest, Chip Ross Park, and other privately held lands. Maintaining ecological connectivity provides open migration corridors though which plants and animals may migrate, establish new populations, and enhance their genetic diversity.

Further Reading

Greenbelt Land Trust. *Owens Farm Management Plan*. http://www.greenbeltlandtrust. org/stewardship/owensFarm.html.

Krech, Shepard. *The Ecological Indian: Myth and History*. New York: W. W. Norton & Company, 1999.

SOUTH SLOUGH NATIONAL ESTUARINE RESEARCH RESERVE

By definition, an estuary marks the location where rivers and streams meet the ocean. The dynamic mixing of salt and fresh water combined with ocean tidal cycles and seasonal fluctuations in river flow make for a constantly changing environment. The plants and animals that inhabit estuaries are as diverse as they are well adapted; in fact, estuaries are some of the planet's most productive ecosystems, providing critical habitat to migrating and nesting birds; spawning as well as juvenile fish; invertebrate larvae; and a host of mammals, insects, and plants. South Slough National Estuarine Research Reserve (South Slough NERR) is no exception; established in 1973, South Slough NERR holds the title of the country's first national estuarine research reserve. The program is administered by the National Oceanic and Atmospheric Administration and protects 27 estuarine environments in the United States. South Slough is comparable to the other 26 reserves in that its protection allows for long-term research and monitoring of water quality, weather patterns, and plant and animal diversity while providing numerous education opportunities.

Located in southern Oregon along the Pacific coast, the South Slough is part of the larger Coos Estuary adjacent to Coos Bay. While large portions of the Coos Estuary have been developed by both industry and residential projects, South Slough protects 4,771 acres of open water, submerged meadows of eelgrass, mudflats, wetlands, salt marshes, ponds, riparian zones, and upland forests. A vast majority of the slough's biodiversity is submerged and hidden among beds of eelgrass or buried in the mudflats. A number of fish—especially juvenile salmon and ling cod, along with shiner perch, surfperch, English sole, striped bass, and starry flounder—find cover in the tall, dense blades of eelgrass, as do juvenile crab, snails, clams, and a variety of other invertebrates. Invertebrates also dominate the soft tidal mudflats, which experience varying cycles of submersion and emersion. Harbor cockles, littleneck clams, mud shrimp, ghost shrimp, juvenile Dungeness crab, bent-nose clams, and an extraordinary assortment of worms inhabit the muddy sediments. These same invertebrates attract a large number of predators, mainly in the form of shorebirds that probe the mud, sand, and shallows for food. Harbor seals and sea lions also cruise in and out of the estuary to feed on the fish and an occasional shrimp.

Collectively, the mudflats and the adjoining open water and marshlands are vital habitat to migrating birds that stop in the thousands to refuel and rest during their migrations. In fact, annual winter counts performed by the Audubon Society estimate that more than 21,000 birds representing 89 species utilize the reserve. Large flocks of ducks, gulls, and brown pelicans utilize the open water, while shorebirds such as great blue herons, greater yellowlegs, and American egrets are commonly seen along the shoreline. Bald eagles, osprey, red-tailed hawks, and kingfishers frequently perch in tree limbs scanning the terrain for prey.

The Coos River, South Slough National Estuarine Research Reserve. (Courtesy of Francis Eatherington)

The transition from the algae-covered mudflats to inland plant communities yields a mix of both freshwater wetlands and saltwater marshes. The saltwater marshes are close enough to the shoreline that they are impacted by tidal cycles and often cut with channels that fill during high tide, thereby flushing the marsh with fresh sea water and nutrients. These marshes are characterized by salt grass, Lyngby's sedge, seaside arrowgrass, pickleweed, gumweed, and tufted hairgrass.

The slough's freshwater wetlands are located in and around the various creeks and streams that drain into the marshy basin from inland mountains. These plant communities are defined by the presence of cattails, soft rush, bulrush, spike rush, and skunk cabbage. The low-lying wetlands and marshlands give way to upland plant communities dominated by Sitka spruce, Douglas fir, Port Orford cedar, Pacific wax myrtle, bigleaf maple, willow, and red alder. The forest understory is also rich with plant life that includes blackberry, salmonberry, salal, evergreen huckleberry, and thimbleberry along with several species of fern. Wildlife abounds in these diverse plant communities; black bear, skunk, bobcat, porcupine, elk, beaver, river otter, black-tailed deer, and dozens of species of birds and amphibians find refuge here. South Slough is especially important for several species of rare and endangered flora and fauna. For example, flocks of federally endangered brown pelicans and western snowy plovers find both the shelter and food necessary to support continued migration and nesting activities. Sea-run cutthroat trout, coho salmon, American bald eagles, and the peregrine falcon are also among the region's most sensitive species. Scientists are also monitoring three rare plants: the carnivorous California pitcher plant, sea lavender, and salt marsh bird's beak, all of which grow in the slough's lowland areas.

South Slough faces several threats common to nearly all of the nation's estuaries and are thus the focal point of ongoing research and monitoring at the reserve. Diminished water quality stemming from industrial and residential runoff is of widespread concern, especially during the rainy season, when storm water containing bacteria, phosphate, heavy metals, and other chemicals are flushed into the estuary. These contaminants may then enter the food web and alter vegetative growth and thus change the entire ecosystem. Invasive species are another common problem. South Slough is monitoring two particularly invasive species—the European green crab and common eelgrass—both of which threaten to displace native crabs and eelgrass and consequently alter the area's food chain. South Slough NERR must also contend with the industrial activities that occur beyond its borders. Since the greater Coos Bay is an important shipping port, there is an ever-present risk of an industrial accident. The 1999 wreck of the *New Carissa* is one such example. Although the oil-carrying freighter spilled relatively little oil, with most of the oil washing ashore outside of the South Slough reserve, the incident highlights the permeability of even our most closely guarded natural places.

Further Reading

Oregon Fish and Wildlife Office. "New Carissa Oil Spill from Response to Restoration." http://www.fws.gov/oregonfwo/Contaminants/Spills/NewCarissa/default.asp.

Oregon.gov. "South Slough National Estuarine Research Reserve." http://www.oregon.gov/DSL/SSNERR/FOSS.shtml.

Weinstein, Michael P., and Daniel A. Dreeger. *Concepts and Controversies in Tidal Marsh Ecology*. New York: Kluwer Academic, 2000.

Steens Mountain Wilderness

Spanning 20 miles and reaching a height of over 9,000 feet, Steens Mountain is one of the most prominent features in southeastern Oregon. Although easily seen from afar, its true wonder is nestled in its deep glacier-carved gorges, broad desert plains, and massive aspen groves. This dynamic terrain supports a number of plant-based habitats and associated fauna, all of which are protected under the Steens Mountain Cooperative Management and Protection Act of 2000 (the Steens Act). This piece of legislation aimed to protect the mountain and its flora and fauna and extend to the public the opportunity to enjoy this unspoiled natural place for generations to come. The Steens Act also preserved over 29 miles of waterways ranging from trickling streams to the Donner und Blitzen River. The Redband Trout Reserve also garnered protection as a result of the Steens Act and is the first such reserve in the country. Additionally, the act created the nation's first livestock-free wilderness area while simultaneous prohibiting the use of off-road vehicles as well as the construction of any new roads. The 425,550-acre wilderness is managed by the Bureau of Land Management via an advisory council made up of tribal members, private landowners, representatives from environmental groups, and other individuals who have a vested interest in the recreational and business prospects the wilderness offers.

The Steens Mountain Wilderness is exemplary of a high mountain desert. Dramatic weather patterns result in heavy winter snowpacks—especially in the higher elevations—which will eventually melt off and sustain the land through the dry, hot summers. The vegetation varies greatly but is dominated by shrub steppe habitat that includes several varieties of sagebrush and a diverse array of bunchgrasses. Characteristic of many high deserts, springtime brings a profusion of blooming wildflowers, including wild blue flax, toothed balsam root, scarlet paintbrush, common camas, and golden bee plant. Vegetation changes drastically alongside the area's waterways, which are bordered by a number of thirsty trees; among them are narrow-leaved cottonwood, quaking aspen, black cottonwood, and 16 species of willow. The deep shade provided by these trees keeps the water cool and provides suitable habitat for redband trout and Lahontan cutthroat. Although the term *redband trout* is occasionally used to describe a rainbow trout, the redband is, in fact, a subspecies found specifically in southeastern Oregon. Due in part to climate change, habitat fragmentation, irrigation, and introduction of nonnative fish species, populations of redband trout are on the decline, but the fish has yet to be listed as threatened or endangered. These same riparian habitats are also home to a wide selection of herbs, forbs, nectar-rich flowers, and berry-producing shrubs.

Wildhorse Canyon in the Steens Mountain Wilderness. (Copyright © 2007 LiefPhotos.com)

The plant diversity of the Steens Mountain Wilderness sustains large herbivores, including Rocky Mountain elk, pronghorn, mule deer, bighorn sheep, and wild horses. Struggling populations of pygmy rabbits live side by side with snowshoe hares, jack-rabbits, and cottontails. Inevitably, these rabbits and area rodents become prey for coyotes, red fox, kit fox, bobcat, cougar, golden eagles, and other raptors. The wilderness is also brimming with songbirds, sage grouse, and hummingbirds, some of which use the area as a resting point during migration and some of which breed and nest within its protected borders.

Despite the seemingly loophole-free law that created the Steens Mountain Wilderness, there are considerable venues by which this wilderness could potentially be mismanaged. Recent controversies surrounding resort developments, wind farms, and general management practices have tested the Bureau of Land Management, the advisory committee, and the general public about their vision for the future of this high desert landscape.

Further Reading

Hunter, Christopher. *Better Trout Habitat: A Guide to Stream Restoration and Management.* Washington, DC: Island Press, 1990.

Langston, Nancy. *Where Land & Water Meet: A Western Landscape Transformed.* Seattle: University of Washington Press, 2003.

Oregon Natural Desert Association. http://www.onda.org/.

TABLE ROCKS

Table Rocks is a landscape rich in flora and fauna as well as geological and cultural history. The towering table formations jut upwards of 800 feet from the valley floor and contrast sharply against the surrounding hills. Prevailing theory suggests that Table Rocks was formed seven million years ago, when a shield volcano erupted and spewed forth a 44-mile-long river of lava. This lava flow eventually solidified and formed a thick, hard crust of andesite atop the original sediments. In the millions of years that followed, the Rogue River cut its way through the slab of andesite, and, as the eons continued, freeze-thaw cycles, wind, flooding, earthquakes, and vegetative growth whittled away over 90 percent of the original lava bed, reducing it first to rubble and then to soil. What remains of this ancient formation are two horseshoe-shaped mesas with nearly vertical walls and flat tops that are named according to their position along the Rogue River: Upper Table Rock sits upstream, and Lower Table Rock sits downstream.

There are four major habitats in the area, each distinguished by one or more dominant plant species. The white oak savanna habitat is characterized by the acorn-producing tree for which it is named and is also dotted with the occasional ponderosa pine. Historically, the space between these massive oaks was filled in with native bunchgrasses; however,

Table Rock in autumn. (Courtesy of Greg Badger)

these grasses have since been replaced by nonnative species largely due to agricultural practices and grazing. The oak lands are also rich in wildflowers, herbs, and other forbs including desert parsley, common camas, and southern Oregon buttercup. The mixed woodland habitat is just that—mixed. Dominant trees include ponderosa pine, madrona, and Douglas fir. This habitat is further diversified by the presence of California black oak, Oregon grape, serviceberry, incense cedar, common snowberry, and mountain mahogany. The third habitat in Table Rocks is a unique form of chaparral (somewhat different than the chaparral for which southern California is famous) called Rogue Valley chaparral. The signature plants of this community are white-leaf manzanita and buckbrush. As is typical of chaparral, these plants are well adapted to a hot, arid environment and exhibit small, tough leafs that are often coated with a waxy substance to help reduce evaporative water loss. Last, the mounded prairie/vernal pool habitat is arguably the most unique of all the Table Rock environments due in large part to its seasonal water resources. This habitat supports two rare species: The dwarf wooly meadowfoam, which is usually found growing around the edges of Table Rock's vernal pools, is listed by the state as an endangered species and is found nowhere else in the world. The federally threatened vernal pool fairy shrimp also depends on the seasonal water puddles for carrying out its brief life cycle. Wildlife of all sizes abounds throughout the Table Rock area. Turkey vultures, lazuli buntings, ringtail, dusky-footed wood rats, bobcat, black-tailed deer, gopher snakes, common king snakes, western toads, and pacific tree frogs are just a sampling of the birds, mammals, reptiles, and amphibians that inhabit Table Rocks.

Prior to modern conservation efforts and long before European settlement, the Table Rock region was home to the Takelma Indians. The Takelma are most famous for their use of fire as a tool for managing their surrounding environment and thus ensuring a constant food supply. For example, prescribed burns cleared areas of young ponderosa, therefore allowing acorn-producing oaks to thrive. Similarly, the Takelma purposefully set fire to brush land areas to clear dead undergrowth and encourage new vegetative growth. The tender shoots of these new grassy meadows were favored by the grazing black-tailed deer, which the Takelma then hunted.

Today, management of Table Rocks is divided among the Nature Conservancy, which manages about 1,881 acres of Lower Table Rock, and the Bureau of Land Management, which manages 1,280 acres of both Upper and Lower Table Rocks. Although other portions of both the Lower and Upper Table Rocks are privately owned by the Rogue River Ranch, the ranch keeps its Table Rock property open to the public and excludes cattle from grazing on the Lower Table Rock parcel. As part of a working collaboration, each of the involved parties works to not only protect the area's flora and fauna but to maintain public access and conduct educational outreach activities. Table Rocks is a popular natural place, with 10,000 visitors hiking its trails and participating in community lectures, workshops, and environmental education programs.

Further Reading

Csuti, Blair, Thomas A. O'Neil, Margaret M. Shaughnessy, Eleanor P. Gaines, and John C. Hak. *Atlas of Oregon Wildlife: Distribution, Habitat, and Natural History.* Corvallis: Oregon State University Press, 2001.

TOM MCCALL PRESERVE

The Tom McCall Preserve serves as both a tribute to the visionary work of one of Oregon's most famous governors as well as a safe haven for an incredibly diverse array of plants. More than 345 plant species can be found within the 271-acre preserve. April and May are dominated by vivid wildflowers, including desert shooting star, small-flowered blue-eyed Mary, glacier lily, cammon camas, Carey's balsamroot, pearly everlasting, red columbine, western spring beauty, and wild geranium. Hackberry, woods strawberry, common snowberry, blue elderberry, and chokecherry are a few of the berry-producing plants that sustain a variety of birds and small rodents. Although the preserve is dominated by herbaceous perennials, native bunchgrasses and other forbs, a number of large trees also provide cover for area wildlife. These tree species include Oregon white oak, quaking aspen, ponderosa pine, Pacific willow, black hawthorn, and hazelnut. The preserve is also home to Thompson's broadleaf lupine, Columbia desert parsley, Thompson's waterleaf, and Hood River milkvetch, all four of which are unique to the greater Columbia River Gorge. Birds thrive amid such diverse vegetation, with meadowlarks, canyon wrens, bluebirds, turkey, California quail, and red-winged blackbirds being commonly sighted by visitors.

Such biodiversity is due in large part to its location in a transitional zone between the drier eastern half of Oregon and its damp western counterpart. The climate of the preserve is further tempered by its close proximity to the Columbia River, which runs through the aptly named Columbia River Gorge. The preserve sits atop a broad, flat plateau overlooking the steep-sided gorge that was cut somewhere between 15,000 and 13,000 years ago by the catastrophic Missoula Floods. Even the plateau, which sits between 450 and 1,722 feet above the Columbia, was inundated with rushing water and consequently stripped of its topsoil. Over the next several thousand years, the remaining basalt would be covered in more than three feet of volcanic ash from Mount St. Helen's.

The flora and fauna of the Tom McCall Preserve benefit from thorough protection and management by the Nature Conservancy in collaboration with state and federal agencies, which manage the neighboring national forest lands and Mayer State Park. Similar to many of Oregon's protected lands, invasive plant species pose a constant threat to the flora and fauna of the Tom McCall Preserve because they rob nutrients, water, and space from native species, thus altering entire habitats. Many of these nonnative plants have traveled from nearby farms and gardens and include common sunflower, orchard grass, pale alyssum, alfalfa, dandelion, and timothy grass. Of the dozens of nonnative plant species growing in the preserve, most are kept in check by hungry herbivores in addition to numerous volunteers who routinely hunt for and hand-pull such weeds. Diffuse knapweed is the exception. The plant's woody stems and prickly seed heads grow in dense tangles on which no herbivores will graze. Furthermore, the plant is allelopathic, meaning that it secretes chemicals into the soil that prevent the growth of nearby vegetation. The tenacious weed, which was thought to have been introduced in a batch of alfalfa seed, first appeared in the United States in 1907 and has now infested 19 states, including all states west of the Rocky Mountains along with large portions of the Mc-Call Preserve. In response, a small army of volunteers worked from 1989 to 1994, logging over 300 person-hours per year hand-pulling and digging out the stubborn knapweed. By 2000, only a couple dozen plants were discovered and subsequently removed. The removal technique used to eradicate knapweed at McCall is extremely labor intensive and difficult to duplicate in areas that are more remote or haphazardly managed. For the extra effort, the flora and fauna of the preserve thrive in an herbicide-free environment that not only maintains its natural biodiversity but also increases what the late governor Tom McCall called Oregon's "livability."

While presiding as Oregon's governor from 1967 to 1975, Tom McCall sponsored several key pieces of legislation aimed at preserving Oregon's natural resources and improving the quality of people's lives. The Oregon Bottle Bill was the first law in the United States requiring that the aluminum and glass containers used to package beer, malt, soft drinks, and mineral water be returnable for a monetary refund. As a result, Oregon's citizens now recycle about 84 percent of all such beverage containers compared to a national average of 28 percent. The law has recently been expanded to include plastic water bottles and is expected to undergo several more updates in the future. The forward-thinking governor also put in place legislation that directed state land use and introduced urban growth boundaries, all in an effort to restrict urban sprawl and preserve Oregon's natural places.

Further Reading

Hilbruner, Roberta. *Columbia River Gorge: The Story Behind the Scenery*. Las Vegas, NV: KC Publications, 1995.

United States Department of Agriculture. *Plant Profiles: Diffuse Knapweed*. http://www. invasivespeciesinfo.gov/plants/diffknapweed.shtml.

Walth, Brent. *Fire at Eden's Gate: Tom McCall and the Oregon Story*. Seattle: University of Washington Press, 2000.

WASHINGTON

Washington is a diverse state comprised of temperate rainforest, arid grasslands, wetlands, deep fjords, channeled scabland, and shrub steppe communities. Like Oregon, Washington is divided by the Cascade Range and subject to the rain shadow effect, which leaves western Washington lush and green, while eastern Washington is subject to a vastly drier climate marked by hot summers and harsh snowy winters.

The state has also been heavily marked by geological forces, including glacial advances and retreats, volcanic eruptions (of which the most recent was the 1980 eruption of Mount St. Helens), and the prehistoric Missoula Floods, which carved out much of the topography of eastern Washington. The state is also crisscrossed by more than 20 rivers that drain both slopes of the Cascades. Rivers of the western slope drain directly into the Puget Sound, thus providing critical estuary habitat for the state's birds and salmon populations. The rivers that originate on the eastern slope of the Cascades drain into one of Washington's most renowned natural resources, the Columbia River. It was the damming of the Columbia that forever changed the natural history and economic base of the state. The 1933 construction of Grand Coulee Dam enabled the Columbia River Basin Irrigation Project to bring water to the fertile soils of the Columbia River Plateau, thus converting native shrub steppe vegetation into productive agricultural fields. The dam has also prevented and consequently eliminated a number of salmon species that can no longer migrate to their natal waters to spawn.

The Columbia River is also part of the world's largest and most costly environmental cleanup project. From 1944 to 1987, the Hanford Nuclear Facility relied on water from the adjacent Columbia River to cool its nine reactors. (This water was eventually returned to the river but was more often than not laced with radioactive waste.) The main role of the Hanford site was to produce elements of plutonium and uranium, which were then used to make nuclear weapons; however, the process also produced more than 53 million gallons of radioactive waste, which is now buried in and around the facility. Scientists estimate that many of these containers have already begun to leak and that their radioactive contents will enter the Columbia in 12 to 50 years if cleanup is not kept on schedule.

Although Washington faces some of the nation's most daunting ecological messes, the state continues to work toward implementing progressive environmental law that protects both the environment and its citizens. For example, in 2007, Washington became the first state to work toward eliminating all forms of toxic flame retardants from household products. In an effort to maintain the health of Washington's waterways and fisheries, the state has also passed legislation that limits phosphorus content in dishwashing detergents. While government leadership plays a substantial role in Washington's conservation practices, a number of private and nonprofit entities are working to keep Washington's biodiversity intact. Washington has approximately 29 land trust organizations working to preserve both privately held property, including working farms, as well as lands that are open to the public. The Nature Conservancy, American Farmland Trust, Washington Environmental Council, Quinault Indian Nation, and Audubon Society are also very much a part of Washington's conservation efforts.

DESERT WILDLIFE AREA

At one time, the Desert Wildlife Area of central Washington was a typical arid desert complete with shifting black sand dunes. This historically dry landscape sat atop the Columbia River Plateau and was just out of reach of massive quantities of water that rushed by via the Columbia River. So, in an effort to aid development of this area and the rest of the western United States, the U.S. government created the Bureau of Reclamation in 1902. The bureau then initiated the Columbia Irrigation Project, which led to the construction of Grand Coulee Dam. Construction of the dam began in 1933 and, upon its completion in 1942, held the record of the world's largest dam. The reservoir (also known as Lake Roosevelt) was created as water backed up behind the dam. It is from this reservoir that the water is pumped through about 2,000 miles of pipe and canals before reaching the farms of the Columbia Plateau. Irrigation began in 1952 and set in motion a series of phenomenal economical and ecological changes. The Bureau of Reclamation estimates that the Columbia River Project now diverts 2.3 million to 2.7 million acre-feet of water per year from Lake Roosevelt to water an estimated 670,000 acres of cropland, which in turn produce irrigated crops with a value of $630 million.

Once used for irrigation, this water eventually runs off and drains into a number of low-lying areas, including the Desert Wildlife Area. Within the Desert Wildlife Area there are two natural basins—the Winchester and Frenchman Hills Wasteways—that serve as gathering points for much of the agricultural runoff. Although a few black dunes still exist, they no longer shift and have, for the most part, been replaced by cattails, reeds, and bulrush. This wetland vegetation follows the water as it meanders through naturally cut channels and fills shallow ponds. A number of fish including perch, bass, sunfish, carp, crappie, and rainbow trout live in the wasteways. Millions of migratory

Grand Coulee Dam in the Desert Wildlife Area. (Courtesy of Rob Frechette)

birds also utilize the wetlands during their fall and spring migrations. Ample cover is available for nesting waterfowl; in fact, the area is considered among the most important waterfowl breeding and nesting habitats in the state. Ringnecks, gadwalls, blue- and green-wing teals, northern shovelers, northern pintails, goldeneyes, and wood ducks are some of the duck species that rely on the wildlife area for reproductive and feeding purposes. Canada geese, pelicans, Caspian terns, red-winged and yellow-headed blackbirds, killdeer, western meadowlarks, ring-neck pheasant, and chukar may all be heard before being seen in the thick vegetation. Also lurking about are sage grouse and sharp-tailed grouse, although their populations are in severe decline. Mammals abound and range in size from mule deer to coyotes to jackrabbits and a variety of small mice and shrews.

The largest threat to the Desert Wildlife Area comes from the very land by which it was created. The water that turned black sand dunes to wetland is also replete with pesticides, herbicides, fungicides, and other chemicals. A 2002–2004 study by the U.S. Geological Survey found 42 different pesticides in four drainage systems of the Columbia Basin Project. Current management practices in the Desert Wildlife Area only add to the mixture as aerial applications of herbicides are used to combat invasive Russian olive and purple loosestrife and mosquitoes (which are carriers of West Nile disease) are fought off with applications of methoprene.

In an attempt to improve state revenue, Washington's Department of Fish and Wildlife periodically treats the area's lakes with rotenone, a chemical that kills both fish and invertebrates. The fish kills are conducted to rid the selected waters of sunfish, large-mouth bass, and bluegill. The lakes and ponds will then be stocked with trout. Although visitors are deterred from entering the Desert Wildlife Area while rotenone treatments are taking place, the region is usually open to the public. The perimeter of the area is most easily accessible and conducive to wildlife viewing, photography, fishing, and hunting, while the interior is a maze of narrow waterways bordered by tulies well over eight feet high and therefore difficult navigate. The Desert Wildlife Area measures 35,100 acres and is managed by the Washington Department of Fish and Wildlife.

Further Reading

Harden, Blaine. *A River Lost: The Life and Death of the Columbia.* New York: W. W. Norton & Company, 1997.

Washington Department of Fish and Wildlife. "Columbia Basin Wildlife Area Management Plan." http://wdfw.wa.gov/lands/wildlife_areas/management_plans/pdfs/columbia_basin_plan-final.pdf.

ELLSWORTH CREEK PRESERVE

Ellsworth Creek Preserve is a place of striking contrast, where colossal old trees create an environment teeming with small life forms. Located in the far southeastern corner of the state, the preserve covers 7,600 acres and adjoins the Willapa National Wildlife Refuge, thus forming a continuous wildlife corridor of over 15,000 acres. The Nature Conservancy began acquiring the property in 2001 and now manages the preserve but does so via a tight working partnership with the Willapa National Wildlife Refuge. The history of the region (before it became a protected natural place) is anything but pristine. Decades of logging removed about 93 percent of the original old-growth forest, and careless road building cut off streams and diverted others. This type of habitat fragmentation has, however, given way to opportunity, and Ellsworth Creek is a living laboratory where scientists study and streamline forest restoration practices. For example, some areas of the forest are being selectively thinned of their young second-growth timber; researchers anticipated that young timber left in place will take on the characteristics of old-growth trees more quickly than if they had been left to compete with other trees for nutrients, space, and sunlight. Other parts of the preserve are undergoing road removal to see if their exclusion has any effect on forest recovery. Furthermore, some of these old logging roads are relatively unstable and are at risk for failing or washing out and would inevitably dump large amounts of sediment in sensitive areas such as creeks and streams. Still other parts of the Ellsworth Creek Preserve are being left as is, so that changes in experimental areas can be compared to an area that has been left to regrow at its own pace and with no human intervention.

Extensive biological assessments have been foundational to the work at Ellsworth and have included population surveys of forest birds, amphibians, macroinvertebrates, coho salmon spawns, and the distribution of other fish species. Even the forest canopy of

Ellsworth Creek. (Courtesy of Mark Faherty)

red cedar, western hemlock, and Sitka spruce has been measured for its shape, size, and spatial distribution. The canopy is home to lichens, mosses, and fungi as well as a number of birds and insects. Six new species of insects were discovered during a recent survey of the forest's insect biodiversity. Area streams and creeks provide habitat to many more species of invertebrates and amphibians, including the Pacific giant salamander, Cope's giant salamander, the tailed frog, and Van Dyke's salamander. Larger mammals such as black bear and Roosevelt elk roam the forest floor, while river otter, chum salmon, brook lamprey, and coastal cutthroat trout inhabit the streams.

Although numerous species benefit from the work at Ellsworth Creek, much of the restoration effort is aimed at providing nesting habitat for the marbled murrelet—a small seabird that spends most of its life bobbing around the coastal bays and protected inlets of the Pacific Northwest catching small fish and crustaceans. The bird's nesting behavior was a mystery until 1974, when it was discovered that, unlike other seabirds, which tend to nest on rocky seaside cliffs, the marbled murrelet moves several miles inland to nest amid the broad branches of coastal old-growth trees. Logging of old-growth timber is not the only activity that has contributed to declines in marbled murrelet populations. Oil spills, entanglement in fishing gear, and an increased presence of predators such as crows and Steller's jays, have all contributed to the murrelet's decline and its subsequent listing as threatened on the endangered species list. Such circumstances highlight the importance of the Nature Conservancy's work and research at the Ellsworth Creek Preserve, because the lessons learned in this forest will be applied to management and restoration practices in other coastal forestlands as well.

Further Reading

Dietrich, William. *The Final Forest: The Battle for the Last Great Trees of the Pacific Northwest*. New York: Penguin Books, 1993.

Mudd-Ruth, Maria. *Rare Bird: Pursuing the Mystery of the Marbled Murrelet*. New York: Rodale, 2005.

Washington Conservation and Science Planning. "The Nature Conservancy: Ellsworth Creek." http://waconservation.org/ellsworthIntro.shtml.

HALLIDAY FEN

Halliday Fen is a unique natural area that has been set aside for research purposes and is one of several hundred such areas in the United States. Research natural areas (RNAs) preserve a specialized region or ecosystem and enable scientists to gather baseline data by which to compare and contrast other natural systems. For example, Halliday Fen typifies an intact, undisturbed mountain wetland. Data gathered from studies at Halliday Fen can be compared to data gathered in similar mountain wetlands that have been altered in some manner. RNAs thereby serve as a sort of measuring stick by which other environments can be evaluated. In Washington, most RNAs are managed by the U.S. Forest Service; however, a number of other agencies including the Bureau of Land Management, Fish and Wildlife Service, Department of Energy, Washington Department of Natural Resources, the Nature Conservancy, and several branches of the U.S. military are also involved.

Similar to its lowland counterparts, Halliday Fen is a lush, moisture-laden wetland. By appearance alone, a fen like Halliday might be confused as a bog, but several underlying differences set the two ecosystems apart. By definition fens derive their moisture from groundwater in the form of seeps or springs, while bogs rely mainly on precipitation. In a fen, as water moves up through the earthen substrate, it takes with it a number of minerals that give the fen a characteristically basic (or alkaline) pH. (Bogs, on the other hand, lean toward having an acidic pH.) Halliday Fen garners its alkalinity from earthen deposits of limestone and marl, which are rich in calcium bicarbonate. These unique chemical features give rise to distinct plant communities. Sedges (water-loving grasslike plants) such as bladder sedge and Cusick's sedge are common in Halliday and are often mixed with other wetland grasses and forbs. Shrubs like willow, blackberry, and mountain alder thrive here, as do more prominent tree species including western red cedar, Engelmann spruce, seral water birch, Douglas fir, western hemlock, and grand fir. Halliday Fen is also home to 13 rare plant species, including crested shield fern, yellow sedge, and purple avens.

Several high-profile animals such as the mountain caribou, grizzly bear, and gray wolf live in the surrounding wilderness. Gray wolves once roamed the entire state of Washington but were locally extirpated (extinct) by the 1930s due to hunting and persecution by farmers. The gray wolf was listed as an endangered species in 1974, and subsequent programs to reintroduce wolves in their historic range have been successful but highly controversial. Proponents claim that the presence of wolves restores the natural balance and diversity of their native ecosystems by reducing the number of elk, which tend to overgraze sensitive areas like wetlands and meadows if their herd numbers grow unchecked. Wolves also compete with coyotes for similar resources and thus also keep coyote population down. Reductions in coyote numbers mean more rodents, which translates into more food for raptors and fox. Opponents cite concerns for livestock and pets and the economic hardships tied to such losses. In February 2002, the U.S. Fish and Wildlife Service de-listed the gray wolf and turned control over to the states. The de-listing move was quickly countered by a dozen conservation agencies that filed a lawsuit citing unlawful de-listing of a species whose populations were still too small and fragmented to remain viable without continued protection. In July 2008, the U.S. Federal District Court in Missoula, Montana, ruled to immediately reinstate the Endangered Species Act protection for the gray wolf. Although Halliday Fen has not yet been settled by a permanent pack of wolves, it is assumed that individuals have crossed through the area en route to other destinations in Washington, Canada, and Idaho. Halliday Fen is also within the recovery plan territory for the grizzly bear, which is listed as endangered under Washington state law and threatened under federal law. Attempts to reintroduce the bear back into its historic range were met with widespread opposition and abandoned in lieu of focusing on the recovery of existing populations. Despite multiple casualties due to poaching, hunting, and other human activities, the Selkirk grizzly population appears stable if not slightly increasing. A wide variety of less-domineering wildlife can be viewed at Halliday Fen and along the trail leading up to the wetlands. The area is rich with songbirds and raptors but is most frequently visited on account of the various plant species.

Further Reading

Burgess, Bonnie B. *Fate of the Wild: The Endangered Species ACT and the Future of Biodiversity.* Athens: University of Georgia Press, 2003.

U.S. Fish and Wildlife Service. "Mountain–Prairie Region Endangered Species Program: Grizzly Bear Recovery." http://www.fws.gov/mountain-prairie/species/mammals/grizzly/.

JULIA BUTLER HANSEN REFUGE

Although the Julia Butler Hansen Refuge straddles the Columbia River with half of its property in Washington State and the other half in Oregon, it is largely considered a Washington entity because the refuge's mainland parcel is in Washington and because it is part of Washington's greater Willapa National Wildlife Refuge. First established as the Columbian White-tailed Deer National Wildlife Refuge in 1971 under

Executive Order 11636, it was later renamed in honor of the first Democratic women elected to Congress from Washington State.

Providing habitat for the endangered Columbian white-tailed deer is the main concern of the U.S. Fish and Wildlife Service, which manages the 6,000-acre preserve. The deer is one of 30 subspecies of white-tailed deer but the only one found on the western side of the Cascade Range. Prior to the 1800s, the deer's population was steady and they could be found roaming from the Umpqua River in Oregon northward through the Willamette Valley, as well as through the Puget Sound and lower Columbia River. The 1800s marked a period of habitat loss and overhunting, and, by the 1930s, they were assumed to be extinct. Isolated populations were first found in and around the area that is now the Julia Butler Hansen Refuge and were subsequently federally listed as endangered in 1968. In 1978, a second population fragment was discovered living in southwest Oregon and it too was listed as endangered. Since being listed, the Oregon population has recovered substantially and was de-listed in 2003, with an estimated 5,000 or more individuals roaming the area. The Julia Butler herds have not been as robust and are still listed as endangered, with an estimated 300 deer within the refuge and another 300 to 400 living outside the refuge on private lands.

Cormorant drying his wings on one of the waterways at the Julia Butler Hansen National Wildlife Refuge. (Courtesy of Duane & Shirleen Hymas. http://www.flickr.com/photos/hymasimages/)

Several different plant communities provide various resources to the deer. Pasturelands of grasses, forbs, and herbs provide ample food, as do brushy woodlands of snowberry, wild rose, hazelnut, and dogwood. These woodlands also provide shelter, as do the forests of Sitka spruce, black cottonwood, willow, red alder, and western red cedar. Freshwater marshes, swamps, and wetlands are also plentiful as the Columbia River bisects the refuge into its Washington and Oregon halves. With such a wide range of habitats within its borders, it is no surprise that the refuge is home to a large number of other animals. Two hundred species of birds ranging from tundra swans to northern pygmy owls are here to either spend the winter or nest. More than 50,000 ducks like the American wigeon, cinnamon teal, and wood duck will winter here. Spring migrations will bring in another 50,000 shorebirds, including dunlins, western sandpipers, dowitchers, and killdeer. The bird life is joined by another long list of mammals—50 species, including beaver, bobcat, muskrat, nutria, bats, mink, river otter, California sea lions, black bear, and Roosevelt elk, to name a few. Last, over a dozen species of amphibians and reptiles including long-toed salamanders, rough-skinned newts, red-legged frogs, and northern alligator lizards round out the menagerie of the Julia Butler Hansen Refuge. For all this biodiversity, there are an additional 19 threatened, endangered, or candidate species ranging from Chinook and chum salmon to marbled murrelets and purple martins.

Comprehensive management plans are in place for the refuge and all its flora and fauna. Fire control and prevention are top concerns, as are public usage and education. Public access is restricted to an area of the refuge called Steamboat Slough Dike Road. From this roadway, the public may view wildlife, fish, bike, or walk or request further information at the office reception area. Depending on the season, other portions of the refuge may also be open; however, much of the refuge remains closed to the public due do sensitive vegetation, nesting birds, and imperiled species.

Further Reading

Askins, Robert. *Restoring North America's Birds: Lessons from Landscape Ecology*. New Haven CT: Yale University Press, 2002.

U.S. Fish and Wildlife Service. "Oregon Fish and Wildlife Office: Species Fact Sheet." http://www.fws.gov/oregonfwo/Species/Data/ColumbianWhiteTailedDeer/.

MIMA MOUNDS NATURAL AREA PRESERVE

No one really knows what formed the large soil mounds of this natural place, but theories range from glacial activity and earthquakes to giant prehistoric gophers. Regardless, similar, closely spaced mounds (called mima mounds) ranging in height from a few feet to over eight feet have also been found in China, Australia, California, and Alaska. In Washington State, these rare land formations are designated as a National Natural Landmark and receive special protection via inclusion in the Mima Mounds

Natural Area Preserve. The preserve covers 624 acres and is located in the southern portions of the Puget Sound in western Washington. Although the mima mounds are the primary attraction, the preserve also protects a rare and rapidly disappearing plant community.

The prairie lands of the United States have historically been prime locales for raising livestock, growing crops, and building developments, and the prairies of the south Puget Sound are no exception. In fact, the Nature Conservancy estimates that less than 3 percent of the United States' original prairie land still exists. The Mima Mounds and south Puget Sound prairies provide a lasting foothold for the flora and fauna that depend on the region's fertile soil and wide open spaces. Mima Mounds and the surrounding prairie are dominated by grasses such as fescue and other herbaceous perennials including violets, camas, buttercups, and yarrow, all of which tend to offer spectacular wildflower viewing in spring. Several rare plant species including golden Indian paintbrush, white-topped aster, Torrey's peavine, small-flowered trillium, and rose checker-mallow are closely monitored by the preserve's staff. Numerous efforts are being made to protect a long list of the area's rare animals, many of which are listed as threatened or endangered by either the state or federal government. This list includes the western gray squirrel, western fence lizard, streaked horned lark, mazama pocket gopher, sharp-tailed snake, and the Oregon vesper sparrow. The Pacific gopher snake, racer snake, Taylor's checkerspot butterfly, and mardon skipper butterfly are among the species to have already been locally extirpated—meaning they are considered locally extinct.

In an effort to save the last remnants of flora and fauna, the Nature Conservancy, Washington Department of Fish and Wildlife, Bureau of Land Management, Department of Natural Resources, and several private entities in addition to hundreds of volunteers work to preserve and restore several of the area's prairies, including Mima Mounds. Maintenance of the prairie entails several strategies, one of which is to control the spread of Scotch broom. This tall, nonnative, woody stemmed plant grows in dense patches and regularly outcompetes most native species and thus decreases plant diversity. Controlled burns, hand-pulling, mowing, and herbicide applications are used to control the spread of Scotch broom; however, efforts must be nearly constant since its seeds can lay dormant in the soil for over 50 years. While some agencies work on invasive weeds, others coordinate research, monitor vegetation and soil composition, propagate native prairie plants, and educate the public. Captive breeding programs for rare butterfly species have also forged partnerships with area zoos. Neighboring private landowners are also doing their part by conserving their lands and controlling Scotch broom. The Mima Mounds Natural Area Preserve is open to the pubic every day and encourages individuals to volunteer for various restoration projects.

Further Reading

Kruckeberg, Arthur R. *The Natural History of the Puget Sound Country*. Seattle: University of Washington Press, 1995.
South Puget Sound Prairie Landscape Working Group. http://www.southsoundprairies. org/basics.htm.

Moccasin Lake Ranch

The Moccasin Lake Ranch exemplifies the coexistence of conservation and agriculture and marries the traditions of rural America with progressive planning for the future. Set in the Methow Valley along the eastern foothills of the Cascade Range, this expanse of north-central Washington serves as a major watershed by which annual snowmelts fill the region's rivers and streams. The valley also marks the junction between the sagebrush-studded Columbia River Plateau and the pine forests of the Cascade Mountains and is therefore home to a vast number of plant and animal communities.

The ranch land has been in a constant state of evolution dating back to the late 1800s, when the original 120 acres were purchased. Since then, a long succession of landowners have acquired adjacent parcels and merged them into the original purchase. The sum of these purchases expanded the ranch to its current size of 2,327 acres. The ranch's most recent land transaction included a 1,400-acre easement that was established by the Pigott and Beatty families in conjunction with the Methow Conservancy. The easement protects a significant portion of the ranch's land from development and preserves its aspen groves, meadowlands, lodgepole and ponderosa pine forests, wetlands, and shrub steppe plant communities. Such diverse vegetation supports a variety of animal species ranging from cougar and black bear to songbirds and rodents. Raptors, snakes, bobcat, coyotes, rainbow trout, and mule deer also inhabit the ranch, as do plenty of cattle and horses.

Despite being set aside for conservation purposes, the remaining ranchland is still an active cattle ranch complete with pastures, alfalfa fields, and barns. Daily management of the family business has been tailored to meet the needs of the surrounding wilderness. For example, specialized fencing keeps cattle from grazing and congregating in sensitive areas such as the shoreline surrounding Moccasin Lake and the upland aspen groves. Water resources are also carefully managed and distributed between the working agricultural property and the conservation land. The farm's business strategy includes plans to go organic and thus eliminate the use of pesticides and other chemicals from its daily operations. Such efforts further protect water resources by reducing the potential of chemical runoff and seepage into the area's groundwater, ponds, wetlands, and lake.

Maintaining a profitable bottom line in a sustainable environment is not the only accomplishment of the Moccasin Lake Ranch. The ranch is also home to a nonprofit organization called Methow Valley Riding Unlimited (MVRU), which specializes in therapeutic horseback riding. MVRU offers persons with physical and mental impairments the opportunity to connect with both the horses and the natural landscape of the ranch. In fact, because Moccasin Lake Ranch is not open to the public, one of the best ways for visitors of all ages and abilities to view the ranch is via an organized educational field trip offered by MVRU. The only other location that is open to visitation is Moccasin Lake. Visitors are required to pay a fee and fishing is allowed—but it is restricted to fly-fishing, catch and release only, with a barbless hook. Furthermore, fishing access is limited to no more than six people at any one time.

The 1,400-acre conservation easement, which is part of the greater Moccasin Lake Ranch, is managed by the Methow Conservancy. The conservancy was formed in 1996 following the merger of the Methow Valley Environmental Center and the Methow Valley Land Trust. As a private land trust, the conservancy aims to conserve both the natural landscape of the Methow Valley and the rural lifestyle for which the valley is famous. The conservancy also supports environmental and conservation education through the establishment of an electronic library containing regional stream flow data, fire management and prevention plans, and habitat restoration handbooks.

Further Reading

Anella, Anthony, and John B. Wright. *Saving the Ranch: Conservation Easement Design in the American West*. Washington, DC: Island Press, 2004.

Duram, Leslie A. *Good Growing: Why Organic Farming Works*. Lincoln: University of Nebraska Press, 2005.

Methow Conservancy. http://www.methowconservancy.org/.

Moses Coulee–Beezley Hills

The Moses Coulee–Beezley Hills Preserve is a landscape of historic proportions. While time-honored wind, rain, and freeze-thaw cycles have done their part to shape the topography of the region, it was the cataclysmic bursting of an ice dam several hundred miles away that gave this land its dramatic features. The flooding events, known as the Missoula Floods, are thought to have occurred on several occasions near the end of the last ice age. Massive quantities of water ripped through eastern Washington, carving near vertical cliffs, coulees, potholes, and channeled scablands that are symbolic of the eastern half of this state. Fast forward a few thousand years and these geological features are now framed amid unique plant communities and home to numerous birds, mammals, reptiles, and invertebrates.

The Moses Coulee–Beezley Hills Preserve is owned by the Nature Conservancy and encompasses more than 30,000 acres of what otherwise might be called sagebrush. More formally called shrub steppe, this plant community is a dynamic mix of several species of sagebrush, including stiff sagebrush, big sagebrush, spiny hopsage, and rabbit brush. Grasses and other herbaceous perennials such as giant rye grass, northern buckwheat, daggerpod, silky lupine, Indian ricegrass, spiny phlox, and meadow death camas along with dozens of others live tucked amid the sagebrush. The shrub steppe community is critical habitat for many species but three in particular: the sage grouse, the Columbian sharp-tailed grouse, and the Columbia Basin pygmy rabbit are of primary concern. All three species have suffered from habitat losses to agriculture and urbanization and therefore face an uncertain future. While state and federal agencies are charged with monitoring and rehabilitating these populations, the Nature Conservancy works to keep the preserve's habitat favorable for their growth and reproduction. This includes not only maintaining the shrub steppe plant community but also preserving the area's unusual soil characteristics. The soils of many deserts, including the Great Basin, Columbia Plateau, and, by extension, the Moses Coulee–Beezley Hills preserve are covered in a biological crust. This crust is a slow-growing conglomerate of living microscopic organisms including algae, bacteria, moss, and fungi that help prevent soil erosion and act as a sponge by which water is absorbed and retained. (Biological crusts are extremely fragile and frequently killed by hikers, off-road vehicles, and grazing livestock.)

Despite appearances, water is at hand in several forms; intermittent and perennial streams, seeps, wetlands, springs, and lakes serve as a gathering point for thirsty wildlife and water-loving plants species. Riparian habitat complete with willows, black cottonwood, and red-osier dogwood are an oasis for songbirds, insects, and amphibians. In contrast, seemingly inhospitable features of cliffs and rock piles known as talus are inhabited by 14 species of bats as well as snakes, rodents, and lizards. The preserve's diverse landscape and vegetative life is also utilized by roaming herds of mule deer, badger, porcupine, western rattlesnakes, Washington ground squirrels, golden eagles, loggerhead shrikes, and bluebirds.

In an effort to sustain the region's biodiversity, the Nature Conservancy operates the preserve under a Conservation Action Plan (CAP). The CAP for the Moses Coulee–Beezley Hills area has identified nine threats that are poised to alter this ecosystem in some way: residential and recreational development; invasive species; chance events such as fire, flood, and disease; and excessive groundwater withdrawal are the top four threats. Another threat listed in the CAP is a lack of information regarding many of the preserve's biological communities and species. For example, there are no baseline data on any of the area's 14 bat species, making it impossible to know with any certainty whether their populations are fluctuating or precisely what resources they are using over the course of their life cycle. The conservancy and its many partners and volunteers are actively working to fill in such informational gaps in addition to addressing a long list of other pressures.

Further Reading

Nisbet, Jack. *Singing Grass, Burning Sage: Discovering Washington's Shrub-Steppe*. Portland, OR: Graphic Arts Center, 1999.

Soennichsen, John. *Bretz's Flood: The Remarkable Story of a Rebel Geologist and the World's Greatest Flood*. Seattle, WA: Sasquatch Books, 2008.

PORT SUSAN BAY

Port Susan Bay is located in western Washington along the coast of the northern Puget Sound region. The bay is sheltered from the greater Puget Sound—and, by extension, the open waters of the Pacific Ocean—by Whidbey Island and Camano Island, which run nearly parallel to the shore. Since the bay is protected from pounding surf and rushing currents, the sediments brought into the bay via the Stillaguamish River are allowed to drift and settle, thereby creating a vast delta of mudflats, marshes, and sloughs. The meeting of the freshwater river and the saltwater sound are also significant in that it defines Port Susan Bay as an estuary. As an ecosystem, estuaries are renowned for their high levels of productivity and biodiversity. Estuaries such as Port Susan Bay are extremely complex environments because of the dynamic mixing of fresh and salt water. Seasonal snowmelts, summer droughts, and daily tidal fluctuations keep estuarine environments in constant motion.

As is true of most estuaries, Port Susan Bay supports a myriad of migratory birds and serves as a nursery for large numbers of juvenile fish. The bottom of the food chain here is supported by microscopic photosynthetic plankton called phytoplankton, which are living organisms that are able to capture energy from sunlight. Phytoplankton and regular plankton—which consists of the larvae of other sea-dwelling animals such as sea urchins, clams, mussels, and sea stars—are then fed upon by numerous invertebrates as well as newly hatched fish. Invertebrates and young fish are then preyed upon by larger fish and birds. Birds are one of the preserve's most prominent features, numbering well over 50,000 individuals during spring and fall migrations and representing flocks of all sizes, shapes, and colors. Spindly legged shorebirds, including great blue herons, greater yellowlegs, western sandpipers, and dunlins, are often seen near the water's edge.

Port Susan Bay. (Courtesy of Greg Johnston)

Blue-winged teals, green-winged teals, northern pintails, and northern shovelers are among the preserve's other water-loving birds. Peregrine falcons, gyrfalcons, short-eared owls, American kestrels, and a number of other raptors patrol the area, as do coyotes and long-tailed weasels. An equally diverse set of plants such as algae, seaweed, cattails, maritime bulrush, seashore salt grass, pickleweed, hawthorn, crabapples, alders, and cottonwoods are distributed according to water salinities and offer shelter for life of all sizes.

The Nature Conservancy is charged with protecting and managing the 4,122-acre preserve but does so with cooperation and collaboration with a number of public and private agencies and volunteers. Efforts are focused on controlling invasive cord grass and common reeds, both of which overtake and crowd out native vegetation. Neighboring farmlands, which were long ago diked to reduce flooding, have also been restored and are now the site of newly established wetlands. The dramatic transformation of the farmland in Port Susan Bay inspired the Farming for Wildlife program, which partners the conservancy with farmers of the Skagit Delta in hopes of benefiting both the business of farming and the environment. Rehabilitation of fish habitat is another a major focus since four species of salmon, steelhead, coastal cutthroat trout, bull trout, surf smelt, and several other species of fish all utilize the bay. Port Susan Bay is open to the public, but requests for access must be made in advance. The conservancy periodically offers free guided bird-watching trips and tours of the bay.

Further Reading

Knox, George A. *The Ecology of Seashores*. Boca Raton, FL: CRC Press, 2000.

Ricketts, Edward F., Jack Calvin, and Joel Walker Hedgpeth. *Between Pacific Tides*. Stanford, CA: Stanford University Press, 1992.

ROSE CREEK

Rose Creek is located in southwest Washington within a larger area known as the Palouse. The softly undulating hills of the Palouse span great distances of eastern Washington and north-central Idaho and were once part of a vast prairie. Due to fertile and soft, silty soils, the area quickly became recognized as prime agricultural land, and, by the 1890s, nearly the entire Palouse prairie had been converted to wheat. Not much has changed in the decades since, and the production of wheat, lentils, and other grains remains a defining characteristic of the Palouse. The grasslands that once dominated now cover less than 1 percent of their native soils. Furthermore, the prairie that remains exists in relatively small parcels that are extremely fragmented; many miles of land may lie between one intact parcel and its closest neighbor. Such an arrangement essentially creates isolated islands of prairie habitat, thus making it difficult for some species to disperse from one habitat island to another.

Rose Creek is among the remnants of the original Palouse prairie, encompassing 12 acres of grassland, riparian woodland, and rare cow parsnip plant communities. The grassland portions of the preserve are dominated by bluebunch wheatgrass, Idaho fescue, and bluegrass and are sprinkled with a variety of herbaceous perennials including yarrow, Palouse thistle, camas, wild blue flax, and balsam root. These open grasslands are patrolled overhead by a number of raptors, including long-eared owls, barn owls, red-tailed hawks, and American kestrels that feed on voles, moles, mice, and the occasional small bird or cottontail rabbit. While the grasslands tend to be somewhat arid, the riparian plant community depends on water. Rose Creek brings water to the quaking aspen, lilies, wild iris, willow, and Fendler's waterleaf that thrive in the cool, moist environment. The rare cow parsnip community also thrives in a moist environment and can be found growing under a canopy of black hawthorn. The parsnip is an herb of huge proportions, measuring up to 6 feet high with large compound blooms over 10 inches across. The plant totes a long list of medicinal and practical uses from healing sores to making yellow dye.

Collectively, these three vegetative habitats are home to an equally distinctive set of animals. Western tanagers, red-naped sapsuckers, orange-crowned warblers, lazuli buntings, rufous hummingbirds, and white-crowned sparrows are just a few of the colorful songbirds that frequent the preserve. One hundred species of birds have been observed at Rose Creek in addition to 16 mammal species; among them are elk, yellow-pine chipmunks, badger, long-tailed weasel, and white-tailed deer. Of all the flora and fauna in Rose Creek, perhaps the most notable and most sought after is the giant Palouse earthworm. Very little is known about this behemoth albino worm, but it is believed to grow up to three feet in length and is nearly an inch in width. The worm's burrows are up to 45 feet deep, making the animal extremely difficult to find. It is assumed that their populations have sharply declined because of intensive agricultural practices; they were even thought to be extinct at one time. Infrequent run-ins with the worm have proven otherwise, the latest of which occurred in 2005 near Rose Creek.

The Rose Creek property is managed by the Palouse-Clearwater Environmental Institute (PCEI) and is owned by the Nature Conservancy, which received the land as a donation from the Hudson family in 1966. Management practices are centered on improving and protecting the flora and fauna of Rose Creek as well as educating the public about its value. Being as fragmented as it is, Rose Creek and other similar patches of prairie are especially susceptible to invasion by surrounding crops, herbicide drift, and introduced species. To prevent and remedy these issues, the PCEI operates various volunteer and educational programs that help to maintain and monitor the preserve and connect the public with this rare ecosystem. Rose Creek is located seven and a half miles northwest of Pullman, Washington, and is open to the public; however, reservations are required for groups.

Further Reading

Duffin, Andrew P. *Plowed Under: Agriculture & Environment in the Palouse*. Seattle: University of Washington Press, 2007.

Palouse-Clearwater Environmental Institute. http://www.pcei.org/.

Wenas Wildlife Area

The Wenas Wildlife Area is located in eastern Washington between the cities of Ellensburg to the north and Yakima to the south. The locale is notable for being nestled against the foothills of the Cascade Range as well as for its position on the western fringe of an ancient basaltic lava flow that once oozed over the lower half of the state, dribbled into Idaho in the east and Oregon to the south, and came to rest against the Cascade Range in the west. This geological formation is now referred to as the Columbia River Plateau. The area's unique physical geography hosts a variety of habitats including riparian forests, ravines, grasslands, shrublands, evergreen forests, and wetlands in addition to old agricultural fields. A steady history of agriculture, timber harvest, and unrestricted vehicle use has impacted the Wenas Wildlife Area in several ways. Agricultural endeavors left behind miles of old broken and snarled fence line, which deters the free roaming habits of wildlife and can ensnare animals. Abandoned agricultural fields and areas heavily grazed by livestock were frequently taken over by invasive and nonnative plant species, which subsequently spread from one place to another via motorized vehicles. Unrestricted vehicle use and timber harvests both contributed to soil erosion and often caused sedimentation in neighboring streams and creeks. Such soil disturbances provided further opportunity for the spread of invasive plant species such as knapweed, thistle, and cheatgrass.

Major ongoing efforts are attempting to restore the native vegetation in virtually all of these habitats. Agricultural fields have been reseeded with a mix of native grasses such as bluebunch wheatgrass, needle-and-thread grass, and Idaho fescue. Herbaceous perennials including arrowleaf balsam root, lupine, heartleaf arnica, and other grasslike forbs and shrubs have also been reestablished. Seedings of native sagebrush and bunchgrasses have restored the shrubland plant communities, while the riparian forests have been renewed via a regime of thinning, pruning, and felling of dead or dying trees. New growth of young cottonwood and willow saplings are protected within fenced enclosures in an effort to guard them from browsing herds of mule deer and elk.

Although most management practices and financial expenditures are focused on restoring and renewing plant communities, animal populations are far from ignored. Within the Wenas Wildlife Area are several species of concern that are regularly monitored: the Rocky Mountain elk, mule deer, jackrabbit, sage grouse, prairie falcon, burrowing owl, goshawk, mourning dove, golden eagle, and California bighorn sheep. The plight of the bighorn sheep is especially noteworthy as it was once extirpated from the Wenas Wildlife Area. A small herd of 8 bighorn sheep were reintroduced in 1972 and have since grown to number about 200 animals and now constitute the largest herd in the state of Washington. In fact, animals from this herd are used to reestablish bighorn populations in other parts of the state. In addition to the previously mentioned species, all neotropical birds (those that winter in South or Central America and breed in the northern latitudes) are also closely monitored.

The Wenas Wildlife Area was formed in 1997 by consolidating the Oak Creek Wildlife Area, L. T. Murray Wildlife Area, and both the Wenas and Cleman Mountain Units into a single property that spans 105,221 acres and is managed by three governmental agencies. The Bureau of Land Management, the Washington Department of Fish and Wildlife, and the Department of Natural Resources oversee various aspects of management, including fire control, vegetative restoration, wildlife monitoring, public access, and irradiation of invasive weeds. Although the area is open to the public, much of the terrain is quite rugged and difficult to navigate; moreover, a vehicle permit must be applied for in order to take a motorized vehicle into the wildlife area. Most visitors utilize the Wenas Campground, which can be used free of charge but also lacks facilities.

Further Reading

Apostol, Dean, and Marcia Sinclair, eds. *Restoring the Pacific Northwest: The Art and Science of Ecological Restoration in Cascadia*. Washington, DC: Island Press, 2006.

Elton, Charles S. *The Ecology of Invasion by Animals and Plants*. Chicago: University of Chicago Press, 2000.

Washington Department of Fish and Wildlife. "Wenas Wildlife Area." http://wdfw.wa.gov/lands/wildlife_areas/wenas/.

GLOSSARY

AIRSHED An area of the atmosphere that behaves in a consistent manner so that emissions or pollutants are concentrated within a given region or the region may be marked by remarkably clean air.

ARROYO A wash or draw that temporarily fills with water following heavy rainfall. The term is most often applied to washes within desert ecosystems.

AVIAN BOTULISM An often lethal disease affecting birds that have ingested toxins produced by the bacterium *Clostridium botulinum*. The bacterium occurs naturally in the soil but may proliferate under certain environmental conditions.

BADLANDS An area characterized by very irregular topography and rock formations that have been shaped by the forces of water, wind, and erosion. Such areas are typically dry and devoid of human settlement.

BASALT One of the most common types of solidified lava that forms fine-grained dark gray rocks.

BIODIVERSITY The measure of the abundance and variety of species, including plants, animals, and microorganisms, that inhabit a particular ecosystem, biome, or the entire earth.

BIOLOGICAL CRUST A semifirm but fragile layer of lichens, mosses, and bacteria that grows atop various soils, particularly those in the Great Basin and arid deserts of the American West.

BIOMASS The total mass of all living things within a specific area. Such measurements are indicative of energy available for growth and development of other life forms.

BIOME   A major ecological community characterized by the dominant form of vegetation and climate.

BRACKISH   Water that is slightly more saline than fresh water but less salty than seawater.

CENTRAL FLYWAY   Occasionally referred to as the flyway of the Great Plains, this corridor is utilized by migratory birds traveling to and from the northern coast of the Arctic Ocean to Patagonia.

CHAPARRAL   One of the world's smallest biomes characterized by a plant community of dense shrubs and small trees that are characteristically adapted to fire and long, dry summers.

EASEMENT   A legal transaction that grants an individual or organization the right to use land that belongs to someone else.

ECOLOGICAL SUCCESSION   A set of predictable steps by which an unoccupied habitat is settled by various communities of microorganisms, plants, and animals.

ENDEMIC   A species whose natural habitat and occurrence is restricted to a limited and specific region.

EXTIRPATION   The localized or regional extinction of a species, compared to global extinction.

FJORD   A narrow, steep-sided inlet carved by glacial gouging and filled with seawater.

FOSSIL WATER   Groundwater that has remained sealed within bedrock for anywhere between 1,000 and 40,000 years. Such water is considered to be a nonrenewable resource, because the bedrock is impermeable to surface water and thus the aquifer does not recharge.

HARDPAN   A hardened layer of soil that is often impervious to both water and plant roots and may also contain high levels of salts and minerals. This soil condition may occur naturally or be induced by human endeavors.

HOODOOS   Irregularly shaped spires or columns of soft stone topped by slabs of harder stone. Such formations are often found in badlands and desert landscapes.

INDICATOR SPECIES   A living organism whose presence and abundance or absence is used to gauge the overall health and stability of the community or ecosystem upon which the species in question is most dependent.

INVERTEBRATE   An animal lacking a spinal column or backbone.

MESA   A flat area of elevated land surrounded by steep cliffs. These tablelands are typically less extensive than plateaus.

MIGRATION CORRIDOR   A strip of terrestrial or aquatic habitat through which wildlife may travel.

MONOCULTURE   The practice of growing only one crop in a given area, thus resulting in a decrease in biodiversity.

Pacific Flyway A major north-south migration route used by migratory birds and extending from Alaska to Patagonia.

Parthenogenesis The production of offspring by female animals from an unfertilized egg. Common in insects yet also occurring in some reptiles.

Phytoplankton Free-floating microscopic aquatic plants consisting mainly of algae and found in both marine and freshwater ecosystems. Similar to land-based plants, phytoplankton form the foundations of marine food chains.

Plankton A generic term for any free-floating aquatic organism. The term often refers to microscopic animal life that plays a critical role in both marine and freshwater ecosystems.

Playa A dried lake bed that is characteristically flat and lined with fine sediments that often have an alkaline pH. Heavy rainfall may temporarily refill the lake.

Rain Shadow Refers to the leeward side of a mountain range that receives significantly less rainfall than the windward side of the same mountain range.

Riparian An ecosystem or area of land close to a body of fresh water and containing distinct vegetation such as cottonwood and willow.

Scree The loose piles of rock that form at the base of an eroding cliff. Also called talus.

Sedimentation The process by which soil particles settle out of water.

Shrub Steppe An arid ecosystem of grasslands dotted with shrubs.

Subsistence The self-sustaining way in which a native culture obtains the food and shelter needed for survival.

Symbiotic The relation between two or more organisms that live together in close association.

Vernal Pool A temporary and often seasonal pool of water formed by the collection of rainwater or runoff in a depression. Also called ephemeral pools, they are devoid of fish and therefore critical breeding areas for amphibians.

Watershed A geographical drainage area or basin that captures and drains all water into a single source such as a stream, river, or lake.

BIBLIOGRAPHY

Alaska Bird Observatory. http://www.alaskabird.org/.

    This site is replete with information regarding Alaska's bird populations; where and when to see what species, and in what habitats. The Alaska Bird Observatory also publishes online various newsletters, journal articles, annual reports, teaching materials, and research reports. Cursory information regarding avian influenza is also available along with an extensive list of Web links for further reading about the disease.

Alaska Department of Fish and Game. http://www.adfg.state.ak.us/.

    This is one of the state's leading sources of information regarding the rules and regulations of hunting, fishing, and trapping in Alaska. The site also provides detailed maps of the region, statewide news releases, species information, and publications regarding subsistence living and wildlife conservation. Additional emphasis is placed on informing the public about the state and health of and rules and regulations governing the state's famous fisheries.

Alaska Wilderness League. http://www.alaskawild.org/.

    This site serves as a platform for those engaged in Alaska's most pressing conservation issues and incentives with an emphasis on protecting the Arctic National Wildlife Refuge, Tongass National Forest, National Petroleum Reserve, and the Beaufort and Chukchi Seas. Although not particularly extensive, the site offers a brief overview and history of each area along with reference to the region's flora and fauna. The league has also published an insightful look at climate change in Alaska in addition to news updates, newsletters, fact sheets, and printable brochures that offer broad range of supplementary information.

American Rivers. http://www.americanrivers.org.

> American Rivers is the only national organization that focuses its efforts on protecting America's rivers. The Web site serves as a point of public education and community advocacy promoting the restoration of natural free-flowing rivers, protection of water quality, and ensuring sustainable use of existing water resources.

Arizona Department of Water Resources. http://www.azwater.gov/dwr/.

> The Department of Water Resources site is almost exclusively devoted to water rules and regulations. Although highly technical and vast, the site provides firsthand information regarding issues of compliance, enforcement, surface water rights, flood mitigation, and conservation.

Arizona Land and Water Trust. http://www.aolt.org.

> This land trust organization and its accompanying Web site are focused on the conservation of three main habitats in southeast Arizona: grasslands, desert mountains, and riparian habitat. Water is also pivotal to the organization's conservation efforts as exemplified in its Desert Rivers Initiative, which highlights the need for water to preserve the state's disappearing riparian habitat.

Bishop Museum. http://www.bishopmuseum.org/.

> This site serves as a gateway to the largest museum in the state of Hawaii. The Bishop Museum contains a wealth of historical and cultural artifacts and houses one of the world's largest natural history specimen collections. Visitors to the site may explore portions of the collection and read about the plants and animals (many of which are extinct) and their role in Hawaiian history and culture.

Bureau of Land Management. http://www.blm.gov/wo/st/en.html.

> A vast amount of public land in the western United States is presided over by the Bureau of Land Management (BLM). The Web site provides detailed information regarding a variety of programs implemented by the BLM in an effort to manage and conserve these public lands. Extensive and often lengthy management plans are also available via the site's numerous links. These management policies often go into great detail in their description of the region's climate, geology, topography, water resources, flora, and fauna as well as the threats posed by invasive species, fire, erosion, and misuse by the general public.

Butcher, Gregory S., and Daniel K. Niven. *Combining Data from the Christmas Bird Count and the Breeding Bird Survey to Determine the Continental Status and Trends of North American Birds*. Ivyland, PA: National Audubon Society, 2007.

> This study examines the methodologies of combining data from two prominent long-term bird surveys. Several decades of data derived from work done by the U.S. Geological Survey (USGS) and the Audubon Society have been merged and analyzed in order to access population trends among 550 avian species. The work is somewhat heavy in statistical analysis, but many sections of the study are easy to follow and

elucidate some of the pros and cons of each study's sampling methodology. This is especially important when considering the role of citizen scientists who have contributed the majority of data for the Audubon study compared to that of the USGS study, which has been conducted by trained personnel. A lengthy list of references including Web links serves as a supplementary research guide.

California Chaparral Institute. http://www.californiachaparral.com/.

One of the most detailed online resources devoted to the world's smallest terrestrial biome. The site starts at the beginning with a thorough explanation about the vegetation that makes up the chaparral ecosystem and then continues with an in-depth account of the geology, role of fire, and animal life that is dependent on these scrublands. A large portion of the site is devoted to conservation issues and efforts.

California Department of Fish and Game. http://www.dfg.ca.gov/.

This site provides information regarding the rules and regulations in place to protect California's natural resources. Clearly labeled icons guide readers to literature regarding climate change, salmon fisheries, California bird species of special concern, hatchery information, as well as detailed profiles of the state's most threatening invasive species. Considerable space is reserved for educating the public about California's Marine Life Protection Act. Data regarding both commercial and sport fishing are readily available, as are many other documents.

California State Parks. http://www.parks.ca.gov/.

This site serves as a gateway to more than 270 park units managed by the state of California. These land parcels encompass vast tracts of land, including nearly one-third of California's coastline, more than 600 miles of lake and river frontage, and over 1.4 million terrestrial acres. Given both the quantity and diversity of habitat under the state's charge, this site offers an in-depth look at how the state manages its natural resources.

Catalina Island Conservancy. http://www.catalinaconservancy.org/.

The conservancy's Web site is designed as much for travelers and visitors to the islands as it is for nature enthusiasts, offering an extensive history of the island and its inhabitants, both human and otherwise. Numerous photographs support the site as do various links. Most notable is the Catalina section of Isla Earth Radio Station, which offers a radio program designed to showcase the natural wonders of the island.

Coalition for Otero Mesa. http://www.oteromesa.org/.

The Coalition for Otero Mesa manages this Web site with the dual purpose of educating the public about the natural wonders of the mesa as well as the threats that stand to degrade this habitat. One of the more notable sections of the site is devoted to the topic of gas and oil exploration, covering the policy, politics, geology, logistics, and environmental consequences of such endeavors.

Cosumnes River Preserve. http://www.cosumnes.org/.

> Despite appearing a bit outdated, this site covers nearly every aspect of life on the Cosumnes River, including extensive species lists, a virtual herbarium, and a long list of recreational and volunteer opportunities. However, the site's capstone document is the Cosumnes River Preserve Management Plan and Watershed Assessment, which consists of seven chapters detailing the history, hydrology, and biota of the river habitat along with the methodologies by which the river is being restored.

Earth Discovery Institute. http://www.earthdiscovery.org/.

> As the primary body in charge of the Crestridge Ecological Reserve, the Earth Discovery Institute operates a Web site that is relatively simple and brief, except for the 300-plus-page PDF document that outlines in detail the management and monitoring plan for the Crestridge Reserve. The reserve's soil composition, fire history, budget, invertebrate data, bird surveys, and seed collections are a few of the headings in this comprehensive document.

Earth Justice. http://www.earthjustice.org/.

> This site is home to a nonprofit law firm that works on behalf of the public interest to protect America's natural landscapes while defending citizens' rights to live and work in a healthy environment. An extensive list of legal cases is accompanied with a short synopsis highlighting the pertinent points of each lawsuit.

Greenbelt Land Trust. http://www.greenbeltlandtrust.org.

> The literature and supporting documents contained on this site are specific to the conservation of land in and around Corvallis, Oregon. However, both the Web site and organization exemplify the role of land trusts within local communities and offer a thorough explanation along with examples of how conservation easements, land donation, bargain sale of land, and trade land programs work. A large portion of the site is also committed to educating the general public about the land trust's various projects and conservation successes.

Kachemak Heritage Land Trust. http://www.kachemaklandtrust.org.

> As Alaska's oldest land trust organization, the Kachemak Heritage Land Trust Web site provides a preliminary tutorial regarding the ins and outs of conservation easements, property evaluation, costs, land trade, bargain sales, tax benefits, and gifts of land. While outlining the general principles of land trust acquisitions, the site also provides regionally specific information regarding conservation projects within the Kenai Peninsula.

Kahoolawe Island Reserve Commission. http://kahoolawe.hawaii.gov/plan-strategic.shtml.

> The commission has established this site, which is both interactive and rich with visual and audio support. The reserve's history, cultural significance, restoration, and ocean-based resources are all addressed in a straightforward manner that lends itself

to an easy and interesting read. Several more extensive documents that govern land use and restoration of the island are also available for further research.

Kaua'i Watershed Alliance. http://www.kauaiwatershed.org/.

This site is aimed at educating the public about the importance of a plentiful, sustainable, and clean source of water. Ungulate management, control of invasive weeds, and watershed monitoring are all discussed as part of the alliance's strategies for conservation of this watershed. The site also contains numerous maps, extensive photo galleries, and additional links to other related Web sites.

Kaufman, Kenn. *Lives of North American Birds*. New York: Houghton Mifflin, 1996.

This comprehensive book is much more than a field guide, providing iconic photographs of hundreds of North American birds species followed by descriptions of habitat, diet, breeding and nesting habits, migration, and conservation status. A color-coded map of North America accompanies each specie's entry and provides a visual about where each bird spends its summers and winters. It has been written and organized for the layperson and is free of heavy scientific jargon; however, the author has included several bibliographic references that allow readers to pursue a more complex set of works regarding avian biology, behavior, and conservation.

McCloud Watershed Council. http://www.mccloudwatershedcouncil.org.

This private nonprofit organization operates a site devoted to keeping the citizens and businesses of northern California abreast of issues affecting the McCloud Watershed. Technical documents, including economic impact reports, are also available. The site is an important source of information regarding contractual details and potential impacts of the Nestlé corporation's deal to purchase water from the Mc-Cloud Watershed.

Methow Conservancy. http://www.methowconservancy.org.

The Methow Conservancy is focused on promoting conservation and stewardship of the lands within the Methow Valley of eastern Washington. The Web site describes several of the land trust's major conservation easements and educational projects, which include several courses on environmental topics ranging from bird ecology and conservation to water ecology.

Napa Land Trust. http://napalandtrust.org/.

This private nonprofit land trust operates a simple site, and only select conservation projects have been given extensive treatment. The handful of properties that are fully represented contain historical, cultural, and some biological information. One of the most interesting features of the site is the account of the Connolly Ranch and its role as a place for connecting children to nature.

National Audubon Society. http://www.audubon.org/.

One of America's leading birding organizations is also on the forefront of avian conservation and scientific study. This site serves as the organization's national home base and presents the links to more than 500 regional chapters. It is, however, within the national site that readers may access the 2007 Common Birds in Decline report, along with additional studies and documents. Other portions of the site are devoted to exploring the issues that most greatly affect bird conservation efforts, including global warming, population, agriculture, the Endangered Species Act, clean water, and wind power.

National Oceanic and Atmospheric Administration. http://www.noaa.gov/.

This site contains a number of links to the National Oceanic and Atmospheric Administration's numerous offices, including the National Marine Fisheries Service; National Ocean Service; Office of Oceanic and Atmospheric Research; and the National Environmental Satellite, Data, and Information Service. A wide range of environmental data bases, e-journals, e-books, subject guides, and maps are also available.

National Park Service. http://www.nps.gov/.

A well-organized, easy-to-navigate government Web site that aims to introduce the general public to the landscapes of the U.S. national park system. In addition to providing thorough information regarding a park's native plants and animals, special attention is also granted to regional history and culture, particularly Native American history, geology, and management activities. Additional links allow readers to plan a visit, view multimedia presentations, browse through photo galleries, and review the rules and regulations that govern the country's national parks.

Native Plant Society of New Mexico. http://npsnm.unm.edu/.

This seemingly limitless site holds a wealth of information regarding New Mexico's native flora, including plant checklists, photographs, and field identification tips. The topics of conservation, education, climate change, and invasive species are also addressed on the site.

Nature Conservancy, United States. http://www.nature.org/wherewework/northamerica/states/.

As one of the country's largest private conservation organizations, the Nature Conservancy maintains a Web site that is rich in both the quality and quantity of information provided. Visual images in the form of maps, photographs, and illustrations are plentiful and engaging. Internal links frequently lead to extensive and detailed lists of flora and fauna for many of the areas under the conservancy's management and care. The site is especially useful for those interested in volunteer opportunities, and contact information for conservancy personnel is easy to access.

New Mexico Wilderness Alliance. http://www.nmwild.org.

This well-organized, visually engaging Web site provides a broad base of knowledge regarding the wildlife, ecosystems, and general landscape of New Mexico. Several of the alliance's conservation campaigns, including the Otero Mesa, are discussed in great detail and are accompanied by color photographs, additional links, maps, and fact sheets.

North Slope Science Initiative. http://www.northslope.org.

This site is home to the collaborative works of 13 agencies engaged in promoting a scientific basis for understanding and regulating the northernmost reaches of Alaska. The site caters to users with an advanced understanding of these agencies and the scientific research they carry out. Links to current research, real-time data stations, climate information, interactive maps, and Geographic Information System data offer a wealth of firsthand scientific information.

Oregon Natural Desert Association. http://www.onda.org/.

The Oregon Natural Desert Association works to protect the high desert of eastern Oregon. The up-to-date site contains descriptions of recent conservation efforts, imperiled species, and issues surrounding protection of eastern Oregon's wild and scenic rivers. Special attention is paid to legal actions and cases pertaining to conservation efforts along with numerous links to public comments regarding some of eastern Oregon's most hotly contested conservation measures.

Palouse-Clearwater Environmental Institute. http://www.pcei.org/.

The mission of this organization and its accompanying Web site is to connect the people of Idaho and eastern Washington to the region's natural landscape and promote sustainable living. In-depth descriptions of the institute's wetlands and streamside restoration projects are available along with information pertaining to community gardening, local food systems, transportation options, environmental education, and alternative energy.

Pima County. "Sonoran Desert Conservation Plan." http://www.pima.gov/CMO/SDCP/index.html.

The Sonoran Desert Conservation Plan is both an official set of documents outlining Pima County's conservation strategies and a Web site. The site contains a tremendous amount of information in addition to conservation plans. Also easily accessible are scores of reports detailing habitat restoration, environmental impact statements, species monitoring plans, ranch conservation efforts, and urban growth plans.

Pyramid Lake Paiute Tribe. http://www.plpt.nsn.us/index.html.

This site provides an introductory look into the cultural and biological history of the Pyramid Lakes and their role in Paiute culture. The geology, wildlife, and oral legend of the lake is clearly depicted and supported with a number of color photographs and additional links.

Sierra Club. http://www.sierraclub.org/.

As the oldest and largest environmental organization in the United States, the Sierra Club maintains a dynamic Web site whose content aims to inform the public about current environmental issues, including clean energy, climate change, transportation, and safeguarding communities. The site also stays abreast of current political sentiment and environmental policy.

Sierra Vista's Water Resources Center. "All about Water." http://www.sierravistawater. com.

An unusual site on water conservation in that it goes well beyond advising readers to fix dripping faucets and reduce lawn watering, the city's Web site approaches water conservation on a large scale with various water reclamation projects that aim to reclaim both used municipal wastewater as well as storm water. Information regarding the city's water rebate program and water conservation codes is also available.

Southeast Alaska Conservation Council. http://www.seacc.org/.

As a nonprofit organization, the Southeast Alaska Conservation Council's Web site provides a platform for the communities of Southeast Alaska to publicize the environmental issues that affect their region. The site provides a regionally specific view of the concerns surrounding management of the Tongass National Forest and timber production. Other issues pertaining to the region and specifically addressed on the site include mining, land entitlements, pesticide use, transportation, and land exchanges.

Trout Unlimited. http://www.tu.org.

As a national organization, Trout Unlimited works in a widespread field of communities and aquatic habitats to preserve trout fisheries, particularly those native to various areas of the United States. Trout Unlimited has developed a well-organized site with a notable online library containing documents on dam removal, watershed restoration, acid rain, salmon recovery, and a particularly notable section entitled Western Water Project. This project section highlights a number of issues and supplies documents and reports that are key to understanding the role and value of water in the western United States.

Truckee Donner Land Trust. http://www.tdlandtrust.org/.

This private nonprofit organization operates a site devoted to several conservation projects, including the Donner Memorial State Park Expansion, Truckee Open Space and Trails Campaign, Truckee River Corridor Project, Sierra Nevada Checkerboard, Conservation Easements, and Donner Lake Rim Trail Project.

United States Department of Agriculture, Natural Resources Conservation Service."http:// www.nrcs.usda.gov/.

An extensive government Web site that addresses the needs of communities, farmers, ranchers, homeowners, policymakers, educators, students, and volunteers as they pertain to conservation of natural resources. The site is an excellent source for information on the union of agriculture and conservation under the 2008 Farm Bill.

United States Department of the Interior. http://www.doi.gov/.

As a major branch of the federal government, the Department of the Interior's Web site is a complex network of initiatives and programs designed to protect the nation's publicly owned lands. The site is also a gateway to many of the agencies overseen by the department, including the U.S. Geological Survey, Bureau of Reclamation, Mineral Management Service, and the Office of Surface Mining.

United States Environmental Protection Agency. http://www.epa.gov/.

A wealth of information regarding environmental law and policy is available on this extensive yet navigable site. This is the firsthand source for detailed information regarding the Clean Air Act, Clean Water Act, and Nuclear Waste Policy Act, among many others. The site also includes a breakdown of regulatory information by business sector as well as state-specific regulations.

United States Fish and Wildlife Service. "Conserving the Nature of America." http://www.fws.gov/.

This site contains detailed information regarding the 93 million acres of land that make up the National Wildlife Refuge System in the United States. The flora, fauna, history, and management efforts of more than 520 national refuges are cataloged here along with recent updates regarding the Endangered Species Act and other pertinent environmental rules and regulations.

United States Forest Service. http://www.fs.fed.us/.

As a major branch of the U.S. Department of Agriculture, the Forest Service operates a content-heavy Web site that aims to educate the public about the department's role in managing national forests and grasslands. The site is comprised of maps, brochures, research publications, regulations, and permit instructions in addition to links to the sites of all of the forest and grasslands managed by the forest service.

Washington Biodiversity Project. http://www.biodiversity.wa.gov.

This site is a comprehensive introduction to Washington State's natural history via the paradigm of the past, present, and future. The site's maps are useful for depicting the state's ecoregions: Northwest Coast; Puget Trough; North, East, and West Cascades; Okanogan; Columbia Plateau; Blue Mountains; and Canadian Rocky Mountains.

Washington Department of Fish and Game. http://wdfw.wa.gov/.

This site introduces the natural landscapes of Washington State and provides ample detail regarding the state's plants, animals, and ecosystems. The site also provide information regarding water access sites, wildlife areas, and Washington State species of concern, along with extensive management plans for the each of the wildlife areas under state management.

Washington State Department of Natural Resources. http://www.dnr.wa.gov.

Washington's Department of Natural Resources manages more than 5.6 million acres of forest, rangeland, aquatic habitats, and agricultural lands. Management of these lands generates over $200 million for public schools and other state institutions and preserves the state's fisheries, forests, rivers, and other natural resources. The site contains a mass of information regarding the department's administration of these resources via its numerous divisions, including geology and earth resources, asset management and protection, aquatic resources, and resource protection.

INDEX

About the Author

Methea Kathleen Sapp teaches environmental biology, marine biology, and human anatomy and physiology at Spokane Community College. She earned a BS in natural science with a minor in English from Loyola Marymount University in 2000, followed by a master's degree in zoology from Oregon State University. Sapp is an alumna of the National Oceanographic and Atmospheric Administration's Teacher at Sea program.